The Truth about the Mutiny on HMAV *Bounty*

THE TRUTH ABOUT THE MUTINY ON HMAV *BOUNTY*

Glynn Christian's painstaking research into his notorious ancestor has resulted in a fascinating new insight into the mutiny on Her Majesty's Armed Vessel *Bounty* on 28 April 1789, and in particular events thereafter. He describes in a detail that I have never come across before all the characters involved, which makes the account truly compelling. His book gives a real flavour of what life was like in ships during that period and in particular the extended deployments amongst the Pacific islands on the other side of the world.

He wrestles with the psychological drivers of the key protagonists raising some fascinating views.

But what I found most intriguing was the depth of research into the women who played such a key role in events and particularly the settlement on Pitcairn and its subsequent development. His anthropological research about the Pacific islanders and their lives is riveting and I had not realised how key their traditions and women were to the drama. The book is a must for anyone interested in gaining a balanced view of the mutiny and its aftermath. **Admiral Lord West GCB DSC Former First Sea Lord and Chief of the Naval Staff**

. . . an insightful book on the beginnings of Pitcairn's history and on his ancestor Fletcher Christian.

It's a first class read, historically accurate, highly recommended. **Councillor Leslie Jaques OBE | Government of Pitcairn Islands**

. . . explores the remarkable link between Milntown, the Christian family's ancient Isle of Man seat, and the political revolution on Pitcairn that gave the first votes to women and education to girls. **Charles Guard, Chairman, The Milntown Trust, Isle of Man**

We should not celebrate mutiny but learn from it. Glynn's scholarly research reveals Fletcher Christian as a courageous leader and social pioneer, clearly looking for better, fairer and more inclusive community life. **Commodore Gerry Christian AM Royal Australian Navy**

A unique and definitive history of *Bounty* and her passengers' fates on mysterious Pitcairn. **Major-General Peter Williams CMG OBE**

. . . a compulsive and fascinating read. Written by a direct descendant of Fletcher Christian, it shines new light on both the mutiny and what came after, including votes for women. **Robin Hanbury-Tenison OBE FRGS Gold Medallist Royal Geographical Society**

Praise for Mrs Christian *BOUNTY* Mutineer

Sensationally exciting . . . I had no idea Pitcairn's women were first to have the vote. **Joanna Lumley OBE FRGS**

. . . sheds tremendous light on the Pitcairn story. **Distinguished Professor Dame Anne Salmond, South Pacific Anthropologist**

. . . not only a thoughtful but also a gripping and moving story with wide implications. **Rolf DuRietz, Bounty scholar**

The Truth about the Mutiny on HMAV *Bounty*

And the Fate of Fletcher Christian

Glynn Christian

PEN & SWORD
HISTORY

AN IMPRINT OF PEN & SWORD BOOKS LTD.
YORKSHIRE - PHILADELPHIA

First published in Great Britain in 2021 by
Pen & Sword History
An imprint of
Pen & Sword Books Ltd
Yorkshire - Philadelphia

ISBN 978 1 39901 418 2

Printed and bound in England
By CPI Group (UK) Ltd, Croydon, CR0 4YY

Pen & Sword Books Ltd. incorporates the Imprints of Pen & Sword Archaeology,
Atlas, Aviation, Battleground, Discovery, Family History, History, Maritime,
Military, Naval, Politics, Railways, Select, Transport, True Crime, Fiction,
Frontline Books, Leo Cooper, Praetorian Press, Seaforth Publishing,
Wharncliffe and White Owl.

For a complete list of Pen & Sword titles please contact

PEN & SWORD BOOKS LIMITED
47 Church Street, Barnsley, South Yorkshire, S70 2AS, England
E-mail: enquiries@pen-and-sword.co.uk
Website: www.pen-and-sword.co.uk

or

PEN AND SWORD BOOKS
1950 Lawrence Rd, Havertown, PA 19083, USA
E-mail: uspen-and-sword@casematepublishers.com
Website: www.penandswordbooks.com

Contents

Introduction   vii

An HMAV *Bounty* Chronology   ix

The Mission   1

The Ship   2

The Men   7

HMAV *Bounty*'s Muster 1787   8

Fletcher Christian   11

William Bligh   17

Voyage to Tahiti: 1787-88   22

Tahiti: October 1788-April 1789   33

The Mutiny: 28 April 1789   41

Mad to do it – or Mad?   62

Bligh's Open-Boat Voyage   71

Democracy at Sea   78

Fort George, Tubuai   86

Oblivion   99

The Second Breadfruit Expedition   108

Pitcairn Pioneers   117

20 September 1793: Massacre Day   125

HMS *Pandora*'s Box   141

Courts Martial and Defences   145

A Brother's Defence   156

Pitcairn as Establishment Pawn   163

Fletcher Christian's Fate - I   168

Fletcher Christian's Fate - II   178

My Pitcairn Descent   194

Sources and Bibliographical Notes   195

About the Author   201

Index   202

Introduction

It is now more than 230 years since Fletcher Christian's 1789 mutiny aboard HMAV *Bounty* that took the ship from William Bligh, yet the amount of misinformation and twisting of facts still published is astonishing.

Here are the facts collected by me during more than forty years research and writing, including a sailing expedition from Tahiti to Tubuai and Pitcairn Island. Where something is an interpretation or my opinion, I make this clear.

There is much more about Fletcher Christian than William Bligh because there are many books about Bligh, and what young Christian did as a social revolutionary on Tubuai and Pitcairn Island after the mutiny is remarkable, but little known or appreciated.

Bounty's epic search for a home included building a massive fortress on Tubuai Island before the mutineers made remote Pitcairn Island the first permanent British settlement in the South Pacific. As eighteenth-century Europeans they had no idea how to settle and thrive there, so finding that hideaway was no guarantee of survival.

The story of the mutiny on HMAV *Bounty* is that of men; the subsequent history of Pitcairn Island is about women, revolutionary women who reinvented themselves to create a better future for their sons and daughters than ever was possible on Tahiti.

Because history has usually been written by men about men, the Polynesian women who made life possible for the refugees are little known. Yet Pitcairn's Foremothers became the first women in the world permanently to have the vote and to make education compulsory for girls, direct results of the revolutionary social thinking of Fletcher Christian.

You'll discover, as I did, that the story of the 1789 mutiny aboard HMAV *Bounty*, and what happened afterwards, proves fact is stranger than fiction.

Glynn Christian
London, 2021

Author's note:
When they were discovered in 1808, Pitcairners called Polynesian men 'blacks'. Few of the children had seen one, because the six Ma'ohi men who arrived on *Bounty* were long dead. Pitcairn›s foremothers never referred to themselves as black, so it's likely the term was copied from the white men, further to differentiate their Pitcairn identities from those they escaped on Tahiti, Tubuai and Huahine. When used in this book, I feel the pejorative sense it gives paints an accurate picture of how Europeans thought all 'coloured' races inferior at the time, and by no means reflects my own opinion or that of the twenty-first century.

An HMAV *Bounty* Chronology

1754
9 September   William Bligh born; baptised Plymouth, 4 October.

1764
25 September   Fletcher Christian born at Moorland Close,
Cumberland: baptised at St Mungo's, Brigham

1768
13 March   Charles Christian, father of Fletcher, dies
Exact date   Jane Bligh, mother of William, dies
unknown

1774
2 September   Bligh signs on to HMS *Ranger* based in Douglas,
Isle of Man. Based there until March 1776

1776
12 July   Bligh sails for South Pacific as Sailing Master
aboard Captain Cook's HMS *Resolution*. Returns
1780

1779/80
Uncertain dates   Fletcher's mother Ann Dixon Christian
loses Moorland Close, moves to Isle of Man.
Whereabouts and activity of Fletcher unknown

1781
4 February   Bligh weds Elizabeth Betham on the Isle of Man

1783
25 April   Christian signs on as Midshipman aboard HMS
Eurydice, sails for India
24 May   In Madras, Fletcher Christian is promoted to
Acting Lieutenant and Watch Master, aged 19

June	Fletcher returns to UK. Applies to sail with Bligh to West Indies but has to wait almost two years
1785–87	Bligh commands merchant ships to the West Indies; Fletcher Christian sails with him for nine months aboard the *Britannia's* last two voyages
1787	
15 May	George III gives orders for an expedition to Tahiti to collect breadfruit plants and deliver them to the West Indies
23 May	Coastal collier *Bethia* bought by Navy Board
8 June	*Bethia* commissioned as HMAV *Bounty*
31 July	Bligh and Christian return from West Indies aboard the *Britannia;* Bligh told he was to lead an expedition to Tahiti to collect breadfruit
16 August	Lt Bligh appointed Commander of *Bounty* with courtesy rank of Captain
7 September	Fletcher Christian signs on to *Bounty* as Master's Mate
25 September (post)	The East India Company's *Middlesex* returns from India: Fletcher discovers his brother Charles, who was surgeon aboard, participated in a mutiny against the captain
27 December	After Admiralty delays and bad weather, *Bounty* sails from Spithead, Portsmouth
1788	
6 January	*Bounty* at Tenerife: Christian represents Bligh
2 March	Fletcher Christian promoted to Acting-Lieutenant for second time
23 March	*Bounty* hits heavy weather off Cape Horn
22 April	*Bounty* turns and heads for Cape of Good Hope
23 May	*Bounty* anchors at Simonstown, False Bay. FC tells Bligh 'a day of reckoning would arrive'
1 July	*Bounty* sails from False Bay
20 August	*Bounty* anchors in Adventure Bay, Bruny Island

4 September	*Bounty* sails from Adventure Bay
9 October	James Valentine dies
26 October	*Bounty* anchors in Matavai Bay, Tahiti
	Fletcher Christian officer in charge of breadfruit camp on shore
15 November	Breadfruit collection completed
9 December	Thomas Huggan dies

1789

4 April	*Bounty* sails from Tahiti
23 April	At Annamooka: Bligh insults Christian publicly
27 April	Bligh accuses Christian of stealing coconuts
28 April	Fletcher Christian mutinies, takes command
	Bligh begins open-boat voyage with 18 other men
29 April (approx.)	Christian introduces voting aboard *Bounty*
30 April	Christian orders sails to be cut up to make uniforms for all men aboard; repeats this days later
24 May	*Bounty* arrives at Tubuai
31 May	*Bounty* sails for Tahiti
6 June	*Bounty* back in Matavai Bay
14 June	Bligh arrives at Coupang
16 June	*Bounty* sails for Tubuai again
23 June	*Bounty* arrives at Tubuai; construction of Fort George starts
20 August	Bligh sails in *Resource* from Coupang
17 September	Christian abandons Tubuai: asks for *Bounty;* eight others agree to sail with him
22 September	*Bounty* in Matavai Bay
23 September	*Bounty* sails early in the morning with nine European men, twelve Polynesian women, six Polynesian men and a baby girl. None is kidnapped
23 September onwards	*Bounty* searches for a home as far west as the southern Fijian Islands before turning to find Pitcairn 4,000 miles/6,400 kms to the east
1 October	*Resource* arrives in Batavia

16 October	Bligh sails for Europe in *Vlydte*
1790	
15 January	Christian sights Pitcairn Island after discovering it has been mischarted by over 200 miles/325 kms. Notably, no Polynesian woman is pregnant
23 January	*Bounty* burns and sinks
14 March	Bligh arrives in Portsmouth, via Isle of Wight
October (date uncertain)	Thursday October born to Fletcher and Mauatua, first Pitcairn child nine months after arrival
22 October	Bligh court-martialled for loss of *Bounty* and acquitted
7 November	HMS *Pandora*, Captain Edward Edwards, sails in pursuit of Fletcher Christian
1791	
23 March	*Pandora* anchors in Matavai Bay, Tahiti. All ex-*Bounty* men are treated as mutineers and arrested. Edwards constructs an inhuman Pandora's Box on the open deck, keeping the men shackled inside
8 May	*Pandora* sails with prisoners still in the box
3 August	Bligh sails on second breadfruit expedition aboard HMS *Providence*
28 August	*Pandora* strikes Great Barrier Reef and sinks. Prisoners except for Hillbrant freed at last minute. He, Richard Skinner and George Stewart drown
1792	
Date unknown	Charles Christian, second child of Fletcher and Mauatua, is born with a club foot but allowed to live, a revolutionary rejection of Tahitian tradition
10 April	*Providence* arrives in Tahiti
19 June	Survivors of *Pandora* wreck arrive at Spithead, including *Bounty* crew
19 July	Bligh sails in *Providence* from Tahiti
12 September	Trial of *Bounty* prisoners begins aboard HMS *Duke*

17 September   Captain Edwards court-martialled for loss of
                    Pandora and acquitted
18 September   *Bounty* trial verdicts given
29 October   Mutineers Burkett, Ellison and Muspratt hanged
                    aboard HMS *Brunswick*

1793
23 January   *Providence* delivers breadfruit to St Vincent
7 August   Bligh returns to Deptford
20 September   Massacre Day on Pitcairn Island; Fletcher
                    Christian shot; daughter Mary born

1794
Mid-year   Publication of Stephen Barney's *Minutes of the
                    Proceedings of the Court-Martial . . . with an
                    APPENDIX containing a full Account of the real
                    Causes and Circumstances . . . the most material
                    of which have hitherto been withheld from the
                    Public.* The Appendix summarises the research
                    of Edward Christian
                    Bligh's Answer published

1795
                    Edward Christian publishes *A Short Reply to
                    Capt. William Bligh's Answer*

1808
6 February   American sealer *Topaz*, Captain Mayhew Folger
                    of Nantucket, finds Pitcairn Island, solving the
                    mystery of what happened to *Bounty*. Mauatua/
                    Mrs Christian gives Folger the Kendall K2 chro-
                    nometer and Fletcher's Chinese porcelain bowl

1830
30 March   Ann Dixon Christian dies aged ninety. She does
                    not know if her son Fletcher is dead or alive and
                    has never seen her only grandchildren, half-
                    Tahitian and on the other side of the world

1831

7 March   *Comet* and *Lucy Ann* take the 87 Pitcairners to
                   Tahiti, where they are essentially abandoned and
                   then begin to die from an influenza-like epidemic
                   that kills 16 of them

2 September   Surviving Pitcairners arrive home on US whaler
                   Charles Doggett

1832

28 October   Joshua Hill arrives on Pitcairn, falsely claiming he
                   represented the British Government and creates
                   deep divisions through authoritarian and cruel rule

1837

9 December   Joshua Hill removed aboard HMS *Imogene*

1838

29 November   The next ship to arrive is HMS *Fly*, Captain
                   Russell Eliott. He accepts Pitcairn as a Crown
                   Colony and authorises Pitcairn's unique laws.
                   Pitcairn's women become first in the world
                   permanently to have the vote, certainly a reaction
                   to Hill's regime but also a direct continuity of
                   Fletcher Christian's revolutionary social ideals.
                   Education for girls is made compulsory, another
                   first for female emancipation

The Mission

The 1786 Declaration of Independence by the American states created a problem for the British owners of sugar plantations in the Caribbean. Bacon, flour and other supplies from the new country to feed their slaves became scarce and more expensive. The Standing Committee of the West India Planters and Merchants, all slave owners on Caribbean islands, decided the solution was the recently discovered breadfruit of Tahiti.

It must have seemed unfair that the British, unquestionably the most civilised of Christian nations, had to labour and pay for their daily bread, whereas indolent pagans of the South Pacific were given it *gratis*, just as the Lord's Prayer suggested it should. Breadfruit for their slaves would be more reliable, infinitely cheaper and make the Standing Committee members much richer.

Breadfruit trees are one of the world's most productive, but a hardworking man, woman or child slave could not live on breadfruit alone. Although a good source of Vitamin C, breadfruit is 70 per cent water. About 25 per cent is carbohydrate (energy) and only 1 per cent is protein, so it would give slaves energy yet little to build or keep muscle strength, but this would not then have been understood.

In March 1787 Sir Joseph Banks Bt. presented George III with a plan on behalf of the Standing Committee for a breadfruit-tree gathering expedition by a special ship: the king signed agreement on 15 May 1787.

The Navy Board chose *Bethia*, a two-and-a-half years old, snub-nosed coastal trader built in Hull, then lying at Wapping Old Stairs on the Thames in London. The price, including extra for anchors was £1,950, about £150,000 today. By 6 June, she had been sailed the short distance down the Thames to the Royal Naval Dockyard at Deptford and had been rechristened *Bounty*.

The Ship

It is incorrect to say 'the *Bounty*'. The ship of this story is HMAV *Bounty* or *Bounty* and properly it is the mutiny on *Bounty*. No Royal Naval vessel should be prefixed by 'the', with or without such abbreviations as HMS. Adding 'the' means you are saying 'the His/Her Majesty's Ship', which would never be done. Considered too small to be an HMS, she was dubbed HMAV, for His Majesty's Armed Vessel and she was to be commanded by Lt William Bligh, recently returned from Jamaica in the merchant service aboard the *Britannia* and with whom Fletcher Christian had sailed.

Bounty was the Royal Navy's first ship bent neither on scientific exploration nor on colonial conquest but was simply to bear the fruits of such endeavours from one part of the world to another. Before this, she had to become a floating greenhouse.

An eighteenth-century sailing ship's worst enemy was the shipworm *teredo navalis*, a voracious beast that could eat up a hull in a very short time. The simplest solution was to sheathe the hull in more wood that could be replaced as it was eaten. *Bounty* had an outer hull of planks 1¼ inches/about 32mm thick, secured by iron nails. Even this was not suitable for a voyage to the South Pacific and back. Her hull was sheathed again with English copper and her fastenings were replaced with copper or bronze to avoid galvanic interaction with iron and subsequent corrosion. The enormous expense probably equalled *Bounty's* purchase price.

She was to have four short-carriage 4-pound/1.8kg cannons and ten half-pound/225gram swivel guns. Her complement was to be twenty officers (none commissioned other than Bligh) and twenty-five able seamen, forty-five crew in all.

At just 91 feet/ 27.75 metres long, *Bounty* was hardly bigger than many a diesel-powered pleasure craft that today carefully hugs a coast. Her maximum width of 24 feet 4 inches/7.5 metres makes her squat, an impression confirmed by an almost flat bow and upright stern. This shape gave great internal volume, her particular advantage.

Bounty had no superstructure of day cabins, not even a galley cookhouse. Everything but steering and sail handling went on below the flush main deck, meaning cooking, eating, sleeping and the storage of supplies. *Bounty* would be a microcosm of self-sufficient life carried on in virtual darkness and impossible cramp. There were no portholes in the lower deck. Fresh air and light came only through the 3-foot/.9 metre hatches to the ladderways, open only if conditions were suitable or when men changed watch, every four hours.

Officers and gentlemen amidships had headroom of 7 feet/ 2.15 metres and for a few of them the doubtful advantage of tiny airless cabins, ventilated only by slits in the doors.

Undivided from this mid-ship area except by occasional canvas sheets, the able seamen forward had 6 feet 3 inches/1.9 metres and directly abutted the galley and the pens in which goats, pigs and sheep were often kept. In a single dark area, everyone ate and most slept. The ship had been built like this because she was to have been a collier, operated by just thirteen men; coal doesn't need light and air.

The average space a man could call his own was the 30 in/76 cms width he had to sleep on his canvas hammock, which was only 6 in/15 cms wider when opened flat.

Bounty's Great Cabin stretched across the whole of the stern and was the only part of the lower deck well-lit and ventilated. There were five tall, small-paned windows across the stern and a large lantern window on both the port and starboard sides. That comfortable space should have been Bligh's headquarters, but Banks' instructions said this was to be a greenhouse for the breadfruit. A new bulkhead was built, trebling the room's length forwards from the stern to 30 feet/9.2 metres, one-third of the lower deck. Its width stretched from port to starboard, just to the rear of the aft hatchway.

Bligh was reduced to a small unventilated cabin on the starboard side and it's not surprising he was said always to have his cabin door open, not conducive to the sexual relationships he was suspected in the twentieth century of having with Fletcher Christian.

A few other cabins were down companionways in even smaller, darker, smellier cells on newly built platform decks, called cockpits, where headroom was only 5 feet, just over 1.5 metres. The fore cockpit accommodated the boatswain and the carpenter as well as the sail room and the storeroom of the boatswain, gunner and carpenters. The aft platform had cabins for the botanist, the surgeon, the captain's clerk and the gunner, as well as a steward room, captain's storeroom and a slop room for spare clothing. The added usefulness of the aft cockpit was that by boring holes through the floor of the greenhouse directly above, water which drained from the pots could be collected in barrels below. More deck space had been added than that taken by the new greenhouse, but living was no less cramped, lighter, airier or more gracious.

The greenhouse's deck was lined with lead, and then the room was furnished with three tiers of raised platforms that ran fore to aft with narrow gangways between them. The planks on the platforms were pierced to hold earthenware pots. On the outer walls were suspended a line of similar potholders that were five and six deep across the stern windows so that, instead of the original plan for 500 pots, there were '629 pots in all' each carefully drawn and counted on the plans dated 20 November 1787. New gratings on the decks and scoops in the sides provided added fresh air but not to the rest of the lower deck or cockpits. A stove was installed to keep the plants warm on the homeward voyage.

Bligh's sailing experience with Captain James Cook meant he was up to date with modern thought about health at sea. To enhance the usual diet of salted meat, ship's biscuits and low-alcohol beer, The

Commissioner of Victualling was directed to supply 'Sour Krout, malt [dried], wheat and Barley [instead of oatmeal], sugar [instead of oil], juice of wort [condensed brewing malt], and salt for salting fresh meat and fish'. Sauerkraut was an excellent and good-keeping source of vital Vitamin C; without that and the lime juice added to the daily rum allowance, scurvy raged and killed men. A week later there was approval for five hundredweight/254kgs of portable soup, something normally supplied in small quantities only for the sick.

Blind fiddler Michael Bryne was signed on to play for compulsory daily dancing aboard, continued in the Royal Navy into the twentieth century.

With fortuitous foresight, Bligh asked that the three boats be exchanged for bigger ones. The launch was biggest and became 23 feet/7 metres instead of 20 feet/6 metres and thus able to carry another four men. There was also a 20-foot/6 metre cutter and a 16-foot/ 4.9 metre jolly-boat.

By August Bligh was hiring crew and on 7 September, a few days after the ship came out of Deptford dry dock, Fletcher Christian signed on as Master's Mate. This was an important role and very unusual to be given to such a young man, but his worth had been proven and rewarded aboard HMS *Eurydice* to India, and then when sailing with Bligh to and from the Caribbean. They were old shipmates and friends, too.

The importance of the breadfruit expedition and recognition of Bligh's navigational skill were underlined by the Board of Longitude choosing to give him use of Kendall's K2 chronometer, one of the first that kept perfect time and thus could be used to calculate longitude by knowing how far east or west of Greenwich a ship was. The invention increased a ship's safety almost beyond calculation. Bligh had used this on his voyage to the South Pacific with Cook and the instrument was valued at £200, over £17,000 today, more than 10 per cent of *Bounty's* purchase price. K2 was to have many adventures and is now in the Royal Observatory, Greenwich, London.

On 15 September 1787, Bligh wrote to Banks regretting progress was slower than expected, 'owing to a great struggle to get the masts and yard shortened a circumstance I am happy I persisted in'. He was subsequently proven wrong, as in the South Pacific he had to raise royals, small sails that fly high above the normal square rigging.

The Men

Because *Bounty* was so small and Bligh was a Lieutenant (Captain was a courtesy rank because he was in command), the ship did not qualify to have Marines aboard to ensure discipline or to have other commissioned officers to support him; his were Warrant Officers, superior tradesmen. He did have more young Midshipmen or those acting as them aboard than might be expected, but this was not at the expense of berths for Marines or Officers; there were never to be any.

Bounty's South Seas destination was supposedly secret until at sea, yet her crew had all volunteered, thought to be another Royal Navy first; there had been press-ganged crew, but they all 'ran'. This created a unique new dynamic aboard a Royal Navy ship because no-one felt trapped or victimised and few had wives or partners for whom they might pine. It must have felt more like an adventure than being in the Royal Navy.

HMAV *Bounty*'s Muster 1787

20 August 1787

Lt William Bligh	33: Commander with courtesy title of Captain
John Huggan	Surgeon
John Fryer	35: Master
Thomas Hayward	20: AB to 1 Dec. 1787 then Midshipman
David Nelson	Botanist
William Brown	About 25: Assistant Botanist

27 August

William Cole	Boatswain
William Purcell	Carpenter
William Peckover	Gunner
Lawrence Lebogue	40: Sailmaker
Henry Hillbrant	24: Able-seaman; Cooper
John Samuel	26: Clerk
George Stewart	21: Able-seaman serving as Midshipman to 30 Nov. 1787, then Acting- Master's Mate to 2 March 1788
Peter Heywood	15: AB to 23 Oct. 1790 then Midshipman

29 August

William Elphinstone	36: Master's Mate
Peter Linkletter	30: Quartermaster

31 August

Isaac Martin	30: Able-seaman
Joseph Coleman	36: Armourer

September 7

Charles Churchill	28: Master-at-arms
Alexander Smith	20: Able-seaman; his real name was John Adams
Fletcher Christian	21: Master's Mate to 2 March 1788 then Acting-Lieutenant
Thomas Burkitt	25: Able-seaman
John Millward	21: Able-seaman
Thomas McIntosh	25: Carpenter's Mate to 31 Dec. 1787 then Carpenter's Crew
John Mills	29: Gunner's Mate
James Morrison	27: Boatswain's Mate; responsible for floggings
John Williams	26: Able-seaman
John Sumner	22: Able-seaman
John Hallet	15: Midshipman
Robert Tinkler	17: Able-seaman

7 October

James Valentine	28: Able-seaman

8 October

George Simpson	27: Able-seaman to 14 Oct. then Quartermaster's Mate
Robert Lamb	21: Able-seaman; Butcher
Thomas Ellison	19: Able-seaman
Thomas Hall	36: Able-seaman; ship's Cook

13 October

John Norton	34: Quartermaster

16 October

John Smith	36: Able-seaman: Bligh's servant

23 October

William Muspratt	27: Able-seaman: cook's assistant, tailor

Matthew Thompson   37: Able-seaman

Edward Young   21: hired as Able-Seaman but sailed as
                      Midshipman

16 November

Michael Byrne   Able-seaman, blind, ship's fiddler

21 November

Charles Norman   Carpenter's Crew to 1 Jan. 1788 then
                      Carpenter's Mate

28 November

William McCoy   Able-seaman: also known as McKoy

Matthew Quintal   Able-seaman

6 December   Thomas Ledward AB to 11 Dec. 1788:
                      Surgeon's Assistant then Acting-Surgeon

Fletcher Christian

Born 25 September 1764, Fletcher was the seventh child of Charles and Ann Christian who lived in the stone-built farmstead of the substantial landholding of Moorland Close in Eaglesfield, Cumberland. It sits on the brow of a long hill that slopes 2½ miles/4 kms to the market town of Cockermouth, on the edge of the Lake District. He was baptised in St Mungo's Church, Brigham, the same day.

Once, the Close's house and outbuildings had been clustered inside tall and ancient red-brick fortifications. In the east range of the wall was the main entrance, guarded by a high, square watchtower with a pointed roof. To enter you had to dismount and walk through a succession of low narrow doors under the tower, a lesser version of the defences of a medieval castle. Ancient buildings were still inside the walls when Fletcher was a boy and it's hard to think of a more romantic backyard for an adventurous child.

Fletcher's father Charles was the fifth son of John Christian, the fourteenth documented head of the Christians of Milntown on the Isle of Man, where the heads of the family had been First Deemster for generations. Milntown and its mill and milling rights was bought 1511, rebuilt 1750, enlarged and Gothicised in the 1830s; it is now open to the public. Since the 1660 Restoration of King Charles II, the family was more settled at Ewanrigg Hall, in Dearham above Maryport, Cumberland, which had been rebuilt in 1640, extended in the 1680s and added to in the 1770s and '80s; it is now demolished.

Charles worked in the legal profession but claims he was a Coroner of Cumberland are not proven by the records of Cockermouth Castle, where Lord Egremont had the right of appointment.

Fletcher's paternal grandmother was Bridget Senhouse of the enormous family seat Netherhall, now derelict. Bridget had direct descent from the Plantagenet king Edward I and Queen Eleanor of Castile through their daughter, Princess Joan of Acre, later Countess of Hertford, meaning every descendant of Fletcher Christian has a spot of both royal Plantagenet and royal Castilian blood.

Fletcher's mother Ann Dixon was co-heiress of Moorland Close with her widower father, Jacob. Ann's mother Mary was a Fletcher and, though not as rich as the Christians, they had been in Cumberland far longer.

Fletcher went to Eller Cottage Dame School in Brigham and then daily rode a pony to Cockermouth Free Grammar School, where navigation was part of the curriculum. According to the St Bees School Archivist, he did not go to this ancient school on the Cumberland coast, as claimed by his brother Edward, who was an Old St Beghian.

Fletcher's father died in 1768, when his son was 3½ years old. Fletcher's living siblings were:

John: 1752–1791	Charles: 1762–1822
Mary: 1760–1786/7	Humphrey: 1768–1790
Edward: 1758–1823	

In 1780 Ann was in debt for the staggering amount of £6,490 0s 11d, well over £500,000 in today's values according to National Archives. Much of this was debts of John. Ann owed money everywhere. As well as Moorland Close, everything else had to go.

The head of the family now was John Christian XVII of Ewanrigg, Ann's nephew and Fletcher's first cousin. He sorted out the mess, using the family's fortune based on agriculture, mining and shipping. Ann Dixon Christian went to live in Douglas, Isle of Man, probably in 1779. She took her daughter Mary and her two youngest sons, Fletcher and Humphrey. Charles joined the West Riding of Yorkshire Militia in

Liverpool and by 2 May 1780, he was marching to Leeds but planning to be a surgeon.

Fletcher Christian's privileged landed-gentry background should have guaranteed him a university education, a probable legal career and a future in society, perhaps even in Society. Banished to the Isle of Man when only 14 or 15, Fletcher Christian was assured of nothing, unless he re-created it himself or married well.

In *The Life of Vice-Admiral William Bligh* by George Mackaness, Fletcher Christian is said to have been aboard HMS *Cambridge* in 1782-83, during which Bligh was the vessel's 6th Lieutenant. Assiduous searching and diligent cross-checking do not reveal Fletcher's name on the muster sheet of *Cambridge* and so we currently do not know what he did between 1779 and going to sea in 1783; perhaps he was continuing his education on the Isle of Man, but there is no evidence.

In October 1782, Fletcher's exceptionally rich cousin Isabella Curwen (aged 17), of Workington Hall and Belle Isle on Lake Windemere, eloped with his first cousin John Christian XVII (27) as his second wife. Had Fletcher hoped to recover financial security by marrying her himself? This is surmise, but Isabella was the English name he gave his Tahitian consort Mauatua.

On 25 April 1783, 18-year-old Fletcher signed on as a Midshipman, the entry-level rank of officer, aboard HMS *Eurydice*, Captain George Courtenay. Courtenay was just 19 and a first cousin to the Earl of Bute. He had been posted captain at 18, considered the youngest man ever to be so promoted.

The Royal Navy was Britain's greatest defence, its fabled Wooden Wall against all comers. Here, ability was noted and rewarded with promotion unlike the Army, where you could buy yourself in, up, down or out if you had the money and connections; the Duke of Wellington said at least three-quarters of army commissions were so filled.

Other than by marrying an heiress, joining the Royal Navy was the finest way Fletcher could acceptably and independently recover and improve his social position and expected future in Georgian society. Eighteenth century Naval officers were highly trained specialists with enormous responsibility for the king's ships and all who served on them. Unlike the Army, a Naval officer of any background could be dismissed for incompetence but even a publican's son could rise to become an admiral and be accepted socially.

On 11 October 1783 *Eurydice* sailed with 100 men aboard for India via Madeira and Cape Town, to help mop up a battle with France. *Eurydice*, was a 6th-rater, the last of the Royal Navy ships that could also be propelled by oars, which must have been useful for getting in and out of difficult harbours and moorings. The ship called at the spice-trading port of Tellicherry on India's western Malabar coast and by June was in Madras, now Chennai. Captain Courtenay noted the arrival of a big East Indiaman called *Middlesex*. Fletcher's brother Charles was later to serve as surgeon in this ship and what happened when he did so could gravely have affected Fletcher's attitude to the behaviour of captains.

On 24 May 1784, after just seven months' experience at sea and four months before his 20th birthday, Fletcher was promoted to Acting-Lieutenant and entrusted with a Watch for the return voyage, a remarkable achievement. It seems the exceptional young Captain Courtenay recognised Fletcher as equally talented.

Eurydice was back in June 1785. Fletcher's brother Edward gave a quote from Fletcher, apparently said to a relative when the ship was in Woolwich:

> It was very easy to make one's self beloved and respected aboard a ship; one had only to be always ready to obey one's superior officers, and to be kind to the common men, unless there was occasion for severity, and if you are when there is a just occasion they will not like you the worse for it.

Fletcher now lived in London, hoping to use the Season and such influential family friends as the Duke of Norfolk to be appointed mate on a West Indian trader. He was brown skinned, brown eyed and dark haired and 5 feet 9 inches/1.78 metres tall. His body was notably muscular, marred only by a slight outward bending of his knees, which in breeches would look bowlegged.

In mid-1786 Captain Taubman arrived in London from the Isle of Man and Fletcher asked his advice. Taubman's late wife Dorothy was sister of John XVII and thus Fletcher's first cousin. He wrote to William Bligh, a man whom he knew well and who owed him favours. Taubman thought it very desirable for Fletcher to serve under so experienced a navigator as Bligh, who was currently commanding merchant ships to and from the Caribbean.

Bligh replied, saying he had his full complement of officers. Edward Christian said Fletcher answered prophetically:

> Wages were no object, he only wished to learn his profession and if Captain Bligh would permit him to mess with the gentlemen, he would readily enter the ship as a fore-mast man until there was a vacancy amongst the officers. . . we Midshipmen are gentlemen, we never pull at a rope; I should even be glad to go one voyage in that situation, for there may be occasions when officers are called upon to do the duties of a common man.

Under the terms he suggested, Fletcher did sail with Bligh, but it was fifteen months before he voyaged twice with him in the merchant ship *Britannia*. Fletcher signed on for the first voyage as an ordinary seaman but ate with the midshipmen and officers. This was the spirit Bligh appreciated and for a man with his lesser background it was no bad thing to have a member of the influential Christian family in his debt.

Also aboard was Lawrence Lebogue, an illiterate sailmaker, possibly from Annapolis, USA, and at 40 one of the oldest men who later signed on in *Bounty*. When Edward Christian and William Bligh were sniping at each other in pamphlets in 1794, Lebogue said, 'I knew Captain

Bligh was always a friend to Christian when he sailed with him to the West Indies as well as afterwards . . . Captain Bligh was the best friend Christian ever had.'

The difference between the Merchant Service and the Royal Navy was that men were not serving under strict disciplinary rules and, often, armed guards. Perhaps Bligh behaved differently when working for Campbell and possibly Christian did too.

Edward Lamb served aboard the *Britannia* on the same voyages. He said about Bligh's relationship with Christian:

> When we got to sea and I saw your partiality I gave him every advice and information in my power though he went about every point of duty with a degree of indifference that to me was truly unpleasant; but you were blind to his faults, and had to dine and to sup very other day in the cabin, and treated him like a brother in giving him every information.

He also said about Fletcher and women that he was 'then one of the most foolish men I ever new [sic] in regard to the sex.'

Only one thing is certain about the *Britannia* voyages. Bligh and Christian were firm friends and well pleased with one another. In my view, because Bligh had sired only daughters and Fletcher's father died when he was less than four, it seems like an ideal mentor/student rapport, perhaps even a substitute father/son relationship.

They returned to England in late July 1787 and soon afterwards, when still anchored in the Downs off Deal, Bligh was told he had been given command of an expedition to the South Seas, to Tahiti to collect breadfruit, which were to be delivered to the Caribbean.

In September, Bligh invited 22-year-old Fletcher Christian to join him in the important post of Master's Mate, a startling appointment for one so young. John Fryer the Master was 34 and newly married and William Elphinstone, the other Master's Mate was 38 years old.

William Bligh

In the Bligh family Bible, William was born 9 September 1754 and baptised at the church of St Andrew in Plymouth on 4 October. He was ten years older than Fletcher Christian, except for two weeks.

William's father Francis, a Collector of Customs, married a series of widows. The first was Jane Pearce, who was William's mother. She died before he was 16 and he was the single child of this marriage.

The power of the movies is such that it is constantly necessary to reiterate that the picture of Bligh as an upstart redneck who rose to position from before the mast is wrong. Even so, many of the charges still brought against Bligh are difficult to disprove, for if his father attracted widows, William Bligh attracted dispute and his future was marked by accusations, courts martial, trials and involvement in three mutinies.

William Bligh first appears in the Admiralty records on 1 July 1762, aged seven years and nine months, as servant to the captain of HMS *Montrose*. Being registered at such an early age was a ploy to ensure rapid promotion later in life. A man had to serve at least six years at sea before he could qualify as a lieutenant. It was much more unusual for Fletcher Christian to have waited until he was 18 to go to sea than for Bligh to begin putative service aged seven.

Promotion at the other end of a Royal Navy career was equally illogical. Once a man had been promoted to Post Captain, exertion or appearance at sea became academic. Progression up the charts through Commodore and the degrees of Admiral was automatic, as those at the top died one after the other. Bligh's eventual rank of Vice-Admiral was not a reward for skill at sea but because he had lived longer.

Bligh's supposed service aboard *Montrose* lasted six months. In 1770 he was 15 and aboard *HMS Hunter*, a 10-gun sloop, rated as Able

Seaman but almost certainly serving as a Midshipman, which was formalised on 5 February 1771. In September he was transferred to 36-gun HMS *Crescent*, serving aboard her until 23 August 1774.

On 2 September 1774, William Bligh signed on as an AB in HMS *Ranger*, there being no place for a 'middy'. *Ranger* was based at Douglas, Isle of Man, her duty to hunt and apprehend smugglers in the Irish Sea, under the eye of Richard Betham, who was HM Collector of Customs. The ship spent most time being repaired, so Bligh sensibly capitalised on inactive service by improving his connections ashore, equally important for naval advancement. This probably included his first meeting with the Christians and the Heywoods. Peter Heywood Senior represented the Duke of Atholl's interest there. The duke was the previous owner of the Isle of Man but had sold it to the British Crown, hence the presence of HM Customs there

As he approached 21, William Bligh presented a striking appearance with a skin of marble-whiteness plus the startling combination of piercing blue eyes and raven hair. His face was broad, but in proportion to the length of his head and he had a nose as noble and fine as his skin demanded. The firm set of his chin was shadowed by a dark beard and contrasted strangely with lips that had never grown out of their childish cupid's bow.

In September 1775 Bligh was re-entered on the books of *Ranger* as a Midshipman, a post he held until March 1776.

His father had probably been able to give an introduction to Richard Betham, being a Customs man himself, and Betham's daughter Elizabeth seems to have been a willing and enjoyable social partner. Their relationship was interrupted because Bligh was to sail to the South Seas with James Cook, his idol and touchstone, as Master of HMS *Resolution*. Being appointed Master of the flagship of James Cook's third voyage to the South Pacific when aged 22 is a clear signal of Bligh's professional superiority. The position of Master aboard a ship was senior and responsible, requiring a man of great seamanship with above average ability in administration and navigation.

Cook is likely to have seen journals or charts prepared by Bligh for his lieutenancy exams and chose him from this evidence of ability. His certificate is dated 1 July 1776, and states:

> He produces Journals kept by himself kept in the Crescent and Ranger, and Certificates from Captains Henshaw, Morgan, Thompson and Lieut. Samber of his Diligence, Sobriety and obedience to command. He can splice, Knott, Reef a Sail, work a Ship in Sailing, Shift his Tides, keep a reckoning of a Ship's way by plain sailing and Mercator, observe by Sun or Star, find the variation of the Compass, and is qualified to do the duty of an Able Seaman and midshipman.

From Bligh's many charts, journals and letters that survive, we know that he was gifted both in powers of observation and the ability to set what he saw on paper in words or pictures. The journals he kept as a Midshipman, part of the training in observation required of all young gentlemen, were bound to have been exemplary.

Bligh's voyage with Cook, during which the Hawaiian Islands were visited and Cook was murdered, was both the final ingredient and the crystallisation of Bligh's complexity. He venerated Cook and was one of the few who followed his revolutionary ideas about diet and exercise at sea. There was an ugly side of Cook that Bligh also copied, his vile temper and extraordinary cruelty. He flogged men more often and for less than Bligh ever did yet inspired a devotion that bordered on veneration. Bligh was equally famed for his outbursts of invective, but his personal abuse was wounding in a way Cook's foul language never was. Sailors respected tough discipline because it kept them safe; this was a lesson Bligh seemed not to learn.

As Master, Bligh led the expedition home after Cook's death, helped immeasurably by having Kendall's K2 chronometer aboard, making it possible to be certain of longitude. Once back in the UK, Bligh said Cook's death might have been averted if men on the beach of Kealakekua had been of the calibre expected of Royal Navy officers. He said cover-ups smudged the facts of Cook's murder and he was bitter because charts he made were attributed to other hands. Being the only officer to air such different opinions meant that in 1780 he was mortified to be the only man excluded from the general promotion of officers from the voyage. It was a clear insult and comment on his manner that came from the highest ranks of the Royal Navy.

Bligh thus returned from his first South Pacific voyage demonstrating the basis of his many future downfalls. Confident always of a faultless personal morality, he thundered at the weakness of others. The weapon he invariably mounted was an acerbic and wounding tongue and he was then surprised and hurt when he was not rewarded for his views.

Experienced, travelled, confident but snubbed, he returned to life on land, first in the West Country and then in the Orkneys, where a family called Stewart had welcomed him when *Resolution* had called. Eventually he returned to the Isle of Man, at home again with the Taubmans, Christians, Heywoods and Bethams, and soon with a wife. Both aged 27, William Bligh and Elizabeth Betham were married on 4 February 1781, at Kirk Onchan, just outside Douglas.

Ten days afterwards, Bligh was Master of *Belle Poule*, a captured French ship that had been returned to service against her former proprietors. After a battle at Dogger Bank early in August he was finally promoted to Lieutenant, was transferred briefly to *Berwick*, then as 5th Lieutenant aboard *Princess Amelia*. In March 1782, he went to *Cambridge* as 6th Lieutenant, taking part in the relief of Gibraltar, and was paid off in January 1783.

Bligh returned to Betsy and the Isle of Man on half pay. By May they were expecting their first child and Bligh was writing everywhere for an appointment, hoping his wife's family might help. Elizabeth's mother was a Campbell, and her uncle Duncan Campbell was an influential and a rich man, a merchant trader and a plantation owner in the West Indies as well as the proprietor of convict hulks.

Campbell advised Bligh that to hedge his bets he should obtain official permission from the Lords of the Admiralty for leave to quit the kingdom. That way he might be able to join the merchant service, for Duncan Campbell, ever the opportunist, saw in this nephew-in-law someone to whom he might entrust his ships and his business in the West Indies. Offered £500 a year, about £43,000 today and a great deal more than he was paid in the Royal Navy, William Bligh was happy to comply and moved his family to 100 Lambeth Road in London, close enough to the Admiralty so he could show his face as often as he wished.

Bligh successively commanded the *Lynx*, *Cambria* and then the *Britannia* for Campbell. Apart from his duties aboard, he was responsible for finding cargoes to be carried home, in competition with others. On the *Britannia* he eventually employed Fletcher Christian and at the end of their second return voyage together he was told he was to command an expedition to the South Seas and soon afterwards invited Fletcher Christian to sail with him as Master's Mate.

Life in the Merchant Service was much easier than in the Royal Navy. Discipline was important for everyone's safety but flogging and food were all less severe than in the king's service. Edward Christian tells us that, when Fletcher Christian returned from his first voyage to the West Indies with Bligh, he had shared the labour of the common men but had also been helped by Bligh, who had shown him the use of charts and instruments, furthering Fletcher's knowledge of navigation.

Fletcher added that although Bligh was very passionate, which presumably means temperamental, he prided himself on knowing how to humour him. So far, so good.

Lawrence Lebogue, who sailed with the men both to the West Indies and to the South Pacific, was later asked if Bligh's treatment of Christian aboard *Bounty* had been the same as on the *Britannia*. He answered, 'No, it would not long have been borne in the merchant service,' suggesting Bligh's favouritism aboard *Britannia* swung in the other direction on *Bounty*.

Voyage to Tahiti: 1787-88

Admiralty incompetence and bad weather meant *Bounty's* proposed departure was severely delayed by months, which contributed to almost everything bad that subsequently happened.

An unexpected bonus for Fletcher Christian is that while *Bounty* waited, the East Indiaman *Middlesex* arrived from Madras with his surgeon brother Charles aboard and Fletcher went to meet him. Although I have written this was in Spithead in November, this is impossible.

On 19 September 1787 the *Middlesex* arrived at the Downs, off Deal, an assembly point for merchant ships before heading in to the Thames. At the time *Bounty* was still at the Royal Navy Dockyards, Deptford, on the south bank of the Thames, opposite the point of the peninsula known as the Isle of Dogs. When I went back to Charles's unpublished autobiography, as I should have done earlier, I found this: 'When the Middlesex returned from India Bounty lay close to where she moored. Fletcher came on Board, coming up the river . . .'

The river can only have been the Thames in London. Before the building of the West and East India Docks, the bank of the Isle of Dogs was closely lined with wharves and warehouses. Thus, the meeting that is so important to the story happened upriver from Deptford, probably in East London somewhere on Limehouse Reach, and not far from today's soaring Canary Wharf business development.

Fletcher, soon to be 23 and his brother Charles, 25, spent the evening together with an officer from the *Middlesex* who had previously been in the Royal Navy and Fletcher 'remained till next day'. That night, Charles revealed to his brother that two weeks earlier there was a mutiny aboard the *Middlesex* and he had been a co-conspirator. The last conversation Fletcher had in England with a family member was about mutiny against a mean and cruel captain.

The *Middlesex* was not a naval ship, so Charles was not threatened with execution but punished by suspension from working for the East India Company for two years.

Writing in his autobiography 25 years later, Charles remembered his brother as being:

> ... full of professional Ambition and of Hope. He bared his Arm, and I was amazed at its Brawniness. 'This,' says he, 'has been acquired by hard labour.' He said, 'I delight to set the Men an Example, I not only can do every part of a common Sailor's Duty, but am upon a par with a principal part of the Officers.

> I [Charles] met with a Surgeon [Thomas William] in East India who had gone out with him in the *Eurydice* Frigate, commanded by the Honble Captain Courtney, [n.b. an incorrect title and spelling] and also with an Officer on my Return to London who had sailed in the same ship with Fletcher. They corroborated to me his Assertions Captain Courtney had appointed him to act as Lieutenant [by giving him charge of a watch]. They said he was strict, yet as it were, played while he wrought with the Men he made a Toil a pleasure and ruled over them in a superior, pleasant Manner to any young Officer they had seen.

Charles' later life, detailed in his unpublished biography now in the Manx National Archives, included serving on a slaving ship, and being captured at sea by a Spanish Privateer. He died on the Isle of Man in 1822.

Bounty finally sailed on 23 December 1787, with new orders agreeing Bligh could sail via the Cape of Good Hope if the many delays meant he could not breach Cape Horn.

If Bligh had no Marines or other commissioned officers aboard to share his command, Fletcher Christian had no-one of his peer group, and would never again have the companionship or support of someone of his intellect, education or landed-gentry background. There was no-one of his social class aboard *Bounty* who could share glittering stories of London Society, no-one else who had sat in salons to discuss views arising from the Age of Enlightenment about a new world order, revolution even, with such as brother Edward's university friend William Wilberforce, or to rehash parties with his brothers or 1st-cousins Jane and Bridget in grand town houses and country seats. There was peer group with Captain Courtenay and the officers in *Eurydice* but not in *Bounty*.

I think extended isolation from intellectually stimulating companionship with those who shared his background contributed to Fletcher's later distress; it marked him immediately as different aboard *Bounty*, a gilded loner by default. It could be borne for short journeys, but this expedition was to last for years.

After a calm Christmas Day, the Atlantic erupted and began to crash over the ship. On the 27th *Bounty's* stern windows collapsed under the weight of gale-driven salt water and an icy flood raced through the ship. Bligh lost an azimuth compass and rescued the Kendall chronometer only with great difficulty. The tormented crew was chilled, wet and frightened and had no hot food, for the stove could not be lit. Instead, rations of grog were added to their beer and they had to fill up with ship's hard biscuit.

When the storm abated, extra spars had been washed away and the ship's three boats had been damaged. Their repair took priority in case there was another such storm, or worse. Seven full hogsheads of beer had washed overboard, and two casks of rum had split, their contents dribbling into the bilge. Most seriously, sea water had drained through the greenhouse floor and contaminated *Bounty's* vital supply of biscuit, which had laboriously to be unpacked, checked and repacked. Bligh's thoughtful innovation was then to store ship's biscuits in casks, protecting them also from vermin.

Bligh concentrated on drying the men's gear, their bedding and the ship's interior. When the stove was finally lit, two men from each watch were detailed to wash and dry clothes. The hatches were opened to air the ship and the lower decks were rinsed with vinegar to prevent mildew.

On New Year's Eve men were still sorting and repacking the spoiled ship's biscuit and hoisting planks from the hold to repair the boats. When they opened some barrels of meat, four 4 lb/1.8 kg pieces were missing from the pork and three 8 lb/3.6 kg pieces from the beef, but this was expected by men in the King's Navy. On New Year's Day 1788, the sorting of the biscuits was finished but a whole cask of cheese was found already to be rotten.

On 6 January 1788 *Bounty* called at Tenerife. Fletcher Christian was sent to pay respects to the Governor, the Marques de Branchforte, who insulted Bligh by saying he would return an equal number of gun salutes only to someone of the same rank. Bligh bought almost 4,000 litres of wine thinking this better for the crew's heath than spirits and five days later headed for Cape Horn.

Only after leaving Tenerife could Bligh officially reveal the ship's destination. He also announced he had purchased a drop-stone filter to improve the men's water but that he had reduced the ship's biscuit allowance by one-third to ensure there was enough for the future; at the time it was being supplemented with fresh provisions.

Captain Bligh then improved life and safety on board considerably by introducing a three-watch system, rather than two of four hours on, four hours off. This meant men not standing watch had eight hours free rather than just four, helping ensure they might get uninterrupted sleep, could join the compulsory dancing and were in better shape in case of emergency. The man in charge of the third watch was to be Fletcher Christian, well experienced in this during his return voyage from India.

All of the above shows that as a captain at sea, Bligh was exceptionally capable and humane, especially when there were problems to solve.

On Sunday 2 March 1787, after inspecting the cleanliness of everyone aboard (he cut their grog rations if they were dirty), Bligh conducted Divine Service, at which the Articles of War were always read, and announced he had given Fletcher Christian a written order to act as a Lieutenant and thus as second-in-command. George Stewart, from the family who had hosted Bligh in the Orkneys, was promoted to Acting-Master's Mate.

It is not true that Fletcher's promotion was an insult to the Master Fryer. Fryer would not have expected the promotion and never once said he did, as it was against Royal Navy precedent to promote a Master at sea. The Master was chosen with more care than any other officer and had the status of a Lieutenant, although ranked below any of those who would also be on board. On shore, the Master was in charge of ensuring the sailing supplies for the voyage and then for stowing the hold to safeguard the ship's balance and to protect it against overloading. At sea, the Master checked the ship's position at least daily and then set the sails according to the ship's projected passage and the weather. The Master supervised the lowering and hoisting of the anchor off-shore and for docking and undocking where there was a quay. He was the man to whom any issues with a ship's chandlery, sails, armaments or supplies were reported and, as well as other navigation-based Log entries, he noted all financial expenditure and was in charge of such parts of the official log as weather, position, and expenditures. If a Master was promoted to other duties, who would have the skills to take over? The Master's Mates were certainly accomplished but they were assistants, not replacements.

Soon, the weather had turned to its most furious because it was far too late in the year to attempt the Horn from the East.

I discovered a previously unknown eye-witness account of *Bounty's* challenges in the Cumberland Pacquet of 26 November 1788, almost certainly by Manx teenager Peter Heywood:

'During the 29 days we were beating off the Cape, we had to encounter the most violent storms that I suppose were ever experienced; and I can safely say the wind was not 12 hours easterly during that time, and we never had more canvas spread than close reefed top sails; but most chiefly, when not lying to, reefed courses. . . After beating above three weeks, to no purpose, and the ship at last beginning to be leaky, so as to oblige us to pump every hour; and many of the people being ill, by the severity of the weather, and want of rest, (there being seldom a night but all hands were called three or four times) the captain, on the 18th of April, in the forenoon, thinking it dangerous, and very improper to lose so much time, bore down for the Cape of Good Hope, to the great joy of everyone on board.'

Bligh says this happened on the 22nd.

Peter Heywood's description of Bligh's attempt to round the Horn suggests only a small part of the terrifying ordeal the ship of wood endured. Bligh wrote on 2 April that 'the storm exceeded what I had ever met before' and there were another three weeks to go. On 3 April, the snow was no longer lying on the decks but came in large flakes, the hail was sharp and severe, and the entire ship was battened down. The only access to the lower deck was through the aft hatchway and Bligh's own mess place.

By the 12th Bligh had given up his cabin at night, so those with no dry hammock due to leaks could sleep in comfort. He did everything he could to keep the ship warm and dry and saw that no man went on watch in wet clothes. When at last he knew his men could take no more and as the danger of their position increased, with more and more men injured or ill with rheumatics and other complaints, Bligh ordered the ship to bear away toward the Cape of Good Hope, for which he was loudly cheered.

It is Bligh's combination of determination and sailing skill at treacherous Cape Horn that first led me to call him Foul-Weather Bligh. When the sea and weather was at its worst, Bligh was at his best and I'd want him to be in command if I were in peril on the sea. For the moment, Bligh was magnificent because he was utterly in charge in ways few other captains could be.

Fresh hog meat was roasted from the few animals that survived, the aroma of which would have made a cheering comfort. Bligh exerted himself to improve his men's 'jaded' physical and mental health. He made each man have a breakfast of boiled wheat with sugar and a pint of sweet wort (a malt extract) each day, plus fine old rum, sauerkraut, mustard and vinegar. At first some of the men were worse after abandoning the Horn, reaction to the horrific mental and physical challenges and dangers that affirmed *Bounty* had turned away just in time.

The month-long voyage across the Atlantic to the Cape of Good Hope was not pleasant. Headwinds meant the lower deck was constantly blighted with smoke from the galley. When *Bounty* arrived on 23 May, Bligh's superior care meant he had not lost one man to disease, injury or scurvy, whereas ships sailing direct from Europe had disease, death and scurvy aboard.

Bounty docked in Simonstown, east of Cape Town. It took 38 days before she was recaulked, refitted and provisioned and *Bounty* sailed at four o'clock on the afternoon on Tuesday 1 July. It was the last time Fletcher Christian was to see a European settlement and, if one of his shipmates can be believed, he had not enjoyed it.

It has long been said that disagreements over money while in Simonstown began the animosity between Christian and Bligh. Many years later John Adams, who had signed on as Alexander Smith and was the last of the mutineers alive on Pitcairn Island, said:

> Mr Christian . . . was under some obligations to him [Bligh] of
> a pecuniary nature, of which Bligh frequently reminded him
> when any difference arose. Christian, excessively annoyed at
> the share of blame which repeatedly fell his lot, in common
> with the rest of the officers, could ill endure the additional

taunt of private obligations: and in a moment of excitation told his commander that sooner or later a day of reckoning would arrive.

I discovered previously unrecognised proof of the 'obligation' in a draft letter from Bligh to Joseph Banks in the NSW State Library in Sydney, saying: '... and Mr [Edward] Christian knows from his Brother's Note of Hand [which he received] that he was supplied by him with what money he wanted.' It is well within Bligh's known character to hold any debt over Fletcher, using this to niggle at and demean him in circumstances where repayment was impossible for years.

The ship's next passage took 51 days across the immense, uncharted, landless ocean from the Cape of Good Hope to Adventure Bay on Bruny Island off Tasmania's south-east coast. It was the longest stretch of the voyage and there must have been great relief aboard to drop anchor on 20 August.

Peter Heywood said that Fletcher Christian had enjoyed demonstrating his strength and could make a standing jump from inside one barrel directly into another. He would hold a heavy musket at arm's length and ask that it be measured as absolutely straight. At other times he helped Heywood complete the education that had been interrupted, with lessons in mathematics and classical languages.

On 26 August, still at Adventure Bay, the carpenter William Purcell refused to assist with such general duties as hoisting water into the hold. This was probably a sulk, for Purcell had already earlier felt Bligh's disapprobation of his conduct with a wooding party ashore, when Purcell had answered back 'in a most insolent and reprehensible manner'. Bligh should have confined him until he was court-martialled, but that could not be until the ship returned to England. Loath to lose the assistance of an able-bodied man, he sentenced him instead to labourer's duties aboard the ship. Purcell was given a 'chance by his future conduct to make up in some degree for his behaviour . . .' but he would not labour on board, somehow convincing Fryer, that he was exempt because he was a warrant officer, or because he had carpentering to do.

Refusing orders was mutiny, or near enough, and if *Bounty* had not been so far from civilisation Purcell would have been in the deepest trouble. Bligh could not ignore the event. He gathered useful evidence for a future trial and ordered that, until Purcell worked as commanded, he should have no provisions. Severe punishment was promised to any man who dared assist him. Purcell was 'immediately brought . . . to his senses' but he had not been punished as he should have been.

Captain Bligh's Log says:

> It was for the good of the voyage that I should not make him or any man a prisoner. The few I have even in the good State of health I keep them are but barely sufficient to carry the duty of the ship, it could answer no good purpose to lose the use of a healthy strong Young Man in my situation. I therefore laid aside my power in the particular for the good of the Service I am on, altho' it continued in force with equal effect.

Bligh's reasoning can be understood if it was the only time he punished with less severity than he could. By not confining Purcell, Bligh had side-stepped a personal crisis but laid a firm foundation for a bigger one. It is understandable but was a course of avoidance he took again and again. That slowly eroded confidence in his command.

Boatswain's mate James Morrison, who wrote two accounts of the voyage, said events in Adventure Bay had sown 'seeds of eternal discord' because Bligh made officers and able seamen alike collect wood and water. When Bligh joined them 'only to criticise', according to Purcell, he left the ship in the hands of seamen rather than officers and came on shore with a guard of armed able seamen. Duties and ranks were blurred, consciously breaking the rules a ship lives by, undermining both officers and seamen, presumably to bolster himself rather than the crew.

Morrison wrote that Bligh '. . . produced continual disputes everyone endeavouring to thwart the others in their duty and in this way they found their account and rejoiced in private at their good success.' It seems a remarkable situation, with no man doing his duty except to win points off one another.

Bounty sailed on 4 September, heading south of New Zealand and then into the Pacific at last, discovering a group of thirteen uninhabited granite isles and outcrops 670 km/416 miles east-south-east of the South Island, which Bligh named the Bounty Islands.

On 9 October Bligh was to sign the expense books of the boatswain and carpenter. The Master Fryer also had to sign but refused unless Bligh first signed a certificate saying that his behaviour had been blameless throughout the voyage. It was more gross impertinence and Bligh had to be authoritative. Fryer's bluff was called and 'this troublesome man saw his error and before the ship's company signed the Books'. Fryer had capitulated but like Purcell he had not been punished.

Bligh might have thought himself a humanitarian by not punishing Fryer or Purcell but, in reality, he had shown weakness and was ripe for exploitation, especially by those to whom he had been most unpleasant. On the same day Bligh was astounded to learn Able-Seaman James Valentine from Montrose had died of sepsis because of infection after bloodletting by Surgeon Huggan. Bligh thought it monstrous he had not been told he was ill, let alone dying, and under normal circumstances Huggan, his assistant Ledward, or another officer should have alerted him. Yet remember, Morrison wrote that every man was simply trying to do his job while avoiding Bligh and thus causing as little trouble as possible.

Huggan was an alcoholic and his continued inebriety and incapacity was just as insolent as the actions of Purcell and Fryer. On 21 October Bligh asked Huggan to stop drinking 'in a most friendly manner' but Huggan was insensible to the suggestion. In his private Log, Bligh bears out my belief that he shrank from punishing anybody, hoping that problems would disappear simply because of his superior caring. He wrote:

> The Surgeon kept his Bed all this day and always drunk without eating an ounce of food. If it is ever necessary this should be publickly known, I may be blamed for not Searching his Cabbin and taking all liquor from him; but my motive is that . . . hoping every day will produce a change in him, I forbear making a public matter of my disapprobation of his conduct, in expectation as he has done many times this voyage, he may turn sober again.

Can a captain consider himself responsible if, once he has identified a problem and knows the solution to it, he sits back and hopes the man comes to his senses? It is inviting every other man aboard to behave as he will. As *Bounty* was sailing closer to Tahiti, discipline aboard seems only to have been what the crew wished.

On Sunday 19 October, Bligh describes the muster of all hands thus: 'I think I never saw a more healthy set of Men and so decent looking in my life.' Anyone who has sailed at sea for many months would find that hard to believe. Even if the crew's appearance was healthy and decent, what they thought was less encouraging.

The superb Foul-Weather seamanship shown by Bligh in saving both *Bounty* and her crew at Cape Horn was not enough to boost confidence in himself or to win the respect of his officers and crew.

Tahiti: October 1788–April 1789

*B*ounty anchored within the reef of Matavai Bay on the north coast of Tahiti on Sunday 26 October 1788 after logging 27,086 miles (about 44,000 kms) over almost ten months; the ship had sailed further than circumnavigating Earth.

Tahitian has fewer consonants than English and just as Cook had become *Toote,* Bligh became *Parai* and Christian became *Titreano.* Tahitians preceded proper nouns with 'O', so referring to Tahiti as Otaheite was saying 'it is Taheite', something Europeans took a very long time to understand; the famed painting of Omai by Reynolds is of a man called Mai. Greeks do the same today; ask Panos his name and he will say 'Opanos'.

There was no overall king of Tahiti in 1788. The highest chief of the Matavai district was a boy called Tu or Otoo but he was too sacred to be met and was represented by his parents. Tu's father Teina was 6ft 3in/1.9 metres tall and described as a fat, lethargic, whiner. His mother Itia was as tall but iron-willed, acquisitive and competitive, scorning gifts of beads and mirrors, instead wanting nails and iron. Bligh's gifts were kept on board *Bounty* in a specially constructed chest. Then, in case Bligh stopped giving, Itia daily transferred some of the contents, so the chest always had room for more. Teina and Itia even supervised Bligh's munificence to chiefs and nobles from other districts, and he noted they were not as generous as he would have been.

Acting-Lieutenant Fletcher Christian was appointed in charge of a camp ashore on Point Venus. The shore party included Peter Heywood and gunner William Peckover. He had been here on all Cook's voyages, spoke excellent Tahitian and had a perfect understanding of the Tahitian mind. The botanists Nelson and Brown were essential members of the permanent shore party and up to another four crew may have been rotated as guards.

Otherwise, Bligh allowed only two men shore leave each day. The majority lived on the ship, hotter and more airless than ever, so most living, including love making, was done on deck, and constant visitors gave *Bounty*'s men ample opportunity to make girlfriends of the *vahine* and *taio* of the men, blood brothers who were welcomed into their families. Willing and compliant women went out to the ship and stayed overnight, commonly on deck because being below and having people above their heads was considered an invitation to evil spirits.

The camp was *Bounty* ashore, Royal Navy discipline ruled, and Bligh inspected regularly. At night, life was freer but none of the men could set up home with a woman. There is no evidence Fletcher Christian did this here or anywhere else, and his future consort Mauatua is never mentioned.

In contrast to *Bounty*'s hairy European men with unwashed bodies and sweat-staled clothes, their foreskins and rotten mouths, Tahitian women bathed daily, depilated all body hair and had perfect teeth; they had short haircuts because Tahitians were infested with nits, which they regularly harvested and crushed in those teeth. Men had their foreskins supercised, that is slit on top, and were allowed long hair but also bathed daily, depilated and had good teeth.

Why were there any sexual relationships between dirty, hairy white men and fragrant Tahitian women? Because Europeans had white/pink skin and came in huge ships with sails but no outriggers, had metal including nails, scissors, guns and cannons, vinegar that killed nits and alcohol that had different effects from Tahitian *'ava*. Their arrival had been foretold by priests and in *Bounty*'s time most Tahitians still believed they were gods, or close to being so, even though venereal diseases also accompanied them.

Sexual freedom in Tahiti was controlled by severe punishment, including death, for those who crossed social boundaries and thus threatened bloodlines. There were three social classes on Tahiti, which matched the ranks on visiting ships. The darker-skinned *manahune* were the workers and the lowest class; their women were permitted sexual relations with ordinary sailors. Next were the *ra'atira*, who were landowners and nobles and would consort only with officers. *Ari'i* were the chiefly class and not only superior in height (often over 6ft/1.82m) but quite pale-skinned and corpulent, both something admired. Only captains were thought suitable partners for them but neither Cook nor Bligh seem to have accepted the offers.

In spite of untrammelled sexual freedom aboard the ship and during crew members' rare freedom ashore, *Bounty*'s long stay did not create and leave a new generation of mixed-blood children. The failure of historians to note this dearth of births demonstrates how limited their interest in Tahitian women or the reality of their lives. Bligh's investigations knew how birth control worked for Tahitians but the information was never applied to his crew's activities.

Tahitian girls were expected to learn everything practical also taught to boys, from making fishhooks and fishing lines to thatching and gardening. Once they had menstruated and been tattooed to prove this, everything changed. As women, they were forbidden to eat most things enjoyable, including pork and shark meat. Food touched by them was considered unclean by men, who did most gardening and alone prepared the pit ovens. Women danced lasciviously while pork was roasted over embers but then could never share it.

Tahitian women were not permitted motherhood except under men's rules. Most girl babies, and any girl or boy in any way deformed, too small, the wrong colour, or who crossed class lines, would be killed before they took their first breath. Girls who survived enslaved their mothers, because they could only eat food gathered and prepared by their mothers until they were married. Surviving boys had to achieve warrior height on maturity but could then be clubbed to death by priests as a sacrifice. Bligh recorded women who had lost six and eight babies to the strictures of men and it is possible that most babies conceived did not live. As well as all women having to isolate during menstruation, new mothers were considered so unclean they could not use the same doors as men and anyway could be divorced at whim. Although bound by the strictures of priests, women were not allowed to share any religious ceremonies on the sacred maraes, equivalent to our churches.

These imprisoning and profoundly demeaning facts must all be remembered when the idea of reluctant Polynesian women having to be kidnapped by Fletcher Christian arises later.

Within two weeks, between 7 and 15 November, 774 breadfruit plants were collected for Fletcher's Point Venus camp, more than the pots available. As the island had no ceramics, it's probable new ones were made of wood from *Bounty*. After another month for repairs and to ensure the shoots were successful, *Bounty* could have sailed six weeks after arrival. Instead, she stayed another twenty weeks, waiting for the winds to change so Bligh could follow orders and sail westwards via the Endeavour (Torres) Straits, south of India and perhaps calling again at South Africa before delivering his cargo to the Caribbean.

Bligh spent the months profitably recording Tahitian life for a journal he later published for personal gain. He noted long-board surfing (before it was recorded in Hawaii) archery, javelin throwing, boxing and wrestling, a game we would recognise as hockey and another like soccer, infanticide, effeminate *mahu*, his disgust at penis acrobats and the extravagant carnivals of the *arioi*, a cross-class society that combined preparation for battle with orgies during which different classes could copulate, as long as any pregnancy was terminated or killed at birth.

Upper-class Tahitian men and women dressed like classical Greeks, swathed in white cloth called *tapa*, beaten and felted from bark. Women's essential dress was a sleeveless shift and for men a breech clout, with or without a *tiputa* or poncho. The higher your rank, the more drapes of tapa you added, so the *ari'i* wrapped exorbitant amounts around themselves.

Fletcher Christian and his compatriots were among the first Englishmen to submit to the agony of traditional, hammered tattooing.

The word tattoo is an anglicisation of the Tahitian *ta'tau* and *Bounty* men who returned to England, including Peter Heywood, introduced the custom to sailors at large. Tattooing on Tahiti was then a painful and dangerous process, infection from which could be fatal. English and French missionaries destroyed Tahiti's culture more than any other South Pacific island and so there is little known about traditional Tahitian tattoo design. Fletcher Christian had a Garter star tattooed on his breast and was tattooed on the backside, perhaps the entire blackening of his buttocks, the sign of a mature Tahitian man and indicative of the time he had to himself at night and the closeness he felt to Tahiti and Tahitians.

Tahiti had no metal but used bamboo shards, sharks' teeth and sharpened shells for cutting. They did not know the wheel. The nails *Bounty* carried for barter were soon prized by women as payment for sex, commonly at the instigation of male family members, husbands even. Scissors were planted, hoping their seeming magical properties would multiply as easily as everything else planted on Tahiti.

Early in December storms made the waters of Matavai Bay's lagoon as violent as the open sea and the breadfruit camp was threatened with floods. Bligh had the breadfruit pots loaded on to the ship, which then sailed just a mile inside the reef around One-Tree Hill to Toaroah, a journey that almost wrecked the ship and its expedition, when she went aground on a coral shoal. Bungled efforts to free the ship meant the operation took a whole day and demonstrated that discipline and seamanship had dissolved. It was a rot Bligh never stopped.

On 9 December surgeon Huggan was found helpless in his dark, fetid cockpit-cabin, from which he had not moved for days. Soon after he was brought into the air he died, and Tahitians dug him a grave on Point Venus. Ledward was appointed surgeon.

At 4am on 5 January 1789 the new Watch discovered three men had deserted, taking the launch, the ship's biggest boat. Duty officer Midshipman Hayward was asleep on duty, even though the penalty was death, but he was only put into irons. As a Midshipman he could have been bent over a cannon and beaten with up to twelve strokes of a rattan cane, said to be painful for up to two weeks and even this was often a precursor to more serious punishment. Yet again, Bligh was too lenient.

The missing men were Able-Seaman John Millward, Bligh's personal cook William Muspratt, and Charles Churchill, Master-at-Arms with overall responsibility for discipline in lieu of Marines; Muspratt and Churchill are surprising because both worked closely with Bligh and would be thought to be especially loyal, an indication of how far from normal life had become. Bligh blamed the desertions on his entire officer complement, calling them neglectful and worthless. The missing men had managed to escape with eight muskets, probably for use as barter goods to ensure the secrecy of their hideout. Fryer should have kept the keys to the arms chest, but it was more convenient to give them to Coleman, the Armourer. What their part was in how the escapees were armed has never been explained.

The stolen launch was sailed from Toaroah around One-Tree Hill into Matavai Bay and then abandoned. The runaways took a local sail-canoe and headed for the atoll of Tetiaroa, some 30 miles/38 kms north. Ariipaea, Teina's braver and more trustworthy brother, wanted to lead a search party but was delayed a week by bad weather. Eventually Bligh himself found and heroically arrested the runaways, but again treated them more leniently than he should. He said he found in their possession a list of men who planned to mutiny and stay in Tahiti by damaging the ship in some way. Bligh later wrote to his step-nephew Lieutenant Francis Bond that Christian's name was on the list. Christian laughed when challenged and Bligh believed his rebuttal, although he came back to it when defending himself in later years. Those who could write or read aboard the ship would know that a list of would-be mutineers was not the thing to make. If there were one, it was probably of those thought ripe because of ill-treatment rather than of certainties.

One of the ship's lines was cut. Was it the result of coral friction or a plot to hole *Bounty* so the stay would be extended? Maybe it was a Tahitian trying to revenge his *taio* Hayward, still in irons? Meanwhile, Bligh discovered some of the stowed unused sails were rotten and neglect of a ship's sails was probably more serious than desertion. Rotting sails may have been the particular fault of the Master Fryer and the Boatswain William Cole but were ultimately Bligh's responsibility. The situation was an affront to Bligh's vanity, a piercing reminder that he had perhaps been paying too much attention to his noble guests and to writing his journal and not enough to the well-being of his ship and crew. Tools and equipment also went missing and Bligh ordered a Tahitian to be flogged far more severely than he had punished any of his own miscreants, an inconsistency agreed by both English and Tahitians. Bligh did have to flog some of his men in Tahiti, but these incidents further illustrate his leniency of punishment, tempting admirers of Bligh to cite this as proof of his humanity when it was actually a show of his fear of imposing discipline.

I agree with Bligh biographer Gavin Kennedy who suggests it is likely that harsher punishment, more correct punishment according to Royal Navy regulations, would have meant better discipline. Many of those who became hard-line mutineers had been flogged by Morrison on Bligh's orders, but this is grossly overplayed. Flogging was as much part of naval life as weevils in biscuits. The miscreants are unlikely to have wanted revenge but more simply were the most hot-headed aboard.

Foul weather and contrary winds delayed *Bounty's* departure until 4 April 1789. Over 1,000 flourishing breadfruit plants had been ferried aboard and pens were filled with 25 pigs and 17 goats. With masterly succinctness Bligh recorded:

> At five o'clock . . . we bade farewell to Otaheite, where for twenty-three weeks we were treated with the greatest kindness and fed with the best meat and finest fruit in the world.

The first few days at sea, even after as little as a week on shore, can be agony as men attempt to smother individuality. A sailing ship is safe only when all aboard think with a single mind but more than five months without working together at sea had dissolved that. Few crews were so ill-prepared as was *Bounty's* for the long, dangerous journey ahead.

The Mutiny: 28 April 1789

Bligh now needed urgently to get everything and everyone ship-shape and he seemed to think he could do this by overworking the ship's complement. After 12 April, when he punished John Sumner for neglect of duty, 'Cleaning down below' was ordered daily rather than every two to four days each week.

Fletcher Christian was expected to shoulder far more than his fair share of duties. Bligh's log shows that Christian was to oversee small-arms practice on a daily basis, something not mentioned once on the outward voyage. Cleaning and mending hammocks, normally ordered weekly, was expected daily and as second-in-command it was Christian who had to supervise this. It is right that Bligh should want his ship clean, tight and tidy, because he had neglected to keep up standards or discipline in Tahiti. The extra work he now ordered was well beyond that, seeming a spiteful punishment for everyone but himself and targeting his second in command.

Difficult winds meant it was 23 April before they anchored at Annamooka, now Nomuka, on the eastern limits of the Friendly Islands, today the Kingdom of Tonga. The stop was to collect fresh water but the Nomukans were fractious and had no fear of guns. It was the first time anybody aboard *Bounty* had been threatened by unwelcoming armed warriors. Fletcher Christian was in command of the watering party and told Bligh the martial islanders meant he and his men could not do the task. Bligh publicly damned him for a cowardly rascal, asking if he were afraid of a 'set of Naked Savages while he had Arms'. Fletcher Christian replied, 'The Arms are no use while your orders prevent them from being used.'

This inconsistency by Bligh and the cross words were not the first since they left Tahiti. Fryer said that Mr Bligh and Mr Christian:

> ... had some words when Mr Christian told Mr Bligh: 'Sir your abuse is so bad that I cannot do my duty with any pleasure. I have been in hell for weeks with you. . . several other disagreeable words passed which had been frequently the case in the course of the voyage.'

'Hell for weeks' suggests the renewed antagonism began before the ship left Tahiti.

On 26 April, the day after being called a cowardly rascal in front of others, Christian was again collecting water with a party of men. Bligh ordered Fryer to go and hurry the party along. The watering hole, previously used by Cook, was a quarter of a mile/about 400 metres inland from the beach, which was crowded with islanders throwing stones. Fryer told Christian to get the casks down to the boats empty or full and using bribes of nails, employed some of the troublemakers to help. On the beach they found even more aggravation. The sailors in Fryer's boat had ignored his orders and, instead of standing off with oars, had anchored with a grapnel and gone ashore. While they were playing tricks with local boys and girls, someone had stolen the grapnel.

Bligh 'was very warm about the loss of the grapnel' and said he would detain some of the chiefs until it was returned. Fryer said they had plenty of grapnels on board and plenty of iron to make another, so he did not feel the loss was great, and by reasonable standards it was not. Bligh was not being reasonable. 'The loss not very great Sir, by God! Sir if it is not great to you it is great to me.'

Bligh had the boats hauled in and the anchor raised, even though there were Nomukans aboard. As Fryer was supervising the unfurling of sails, Bligh ordered the ship's crew to arms. Fryer dashed from his duty to Bligh, to learn his commander had taken prisoner the chiefs aboard. Keeping custody of four, Bligh sent a relieved fifth back to shore, who made signs to *Bounty* the anchor had been carried off to another island.

Bligh, conscious that many of his men were awkward and uncommitted about bearing arms in such an unnecessary circumstance, threatened them, calling them a 'Parcel of good for nothing Rascals', adding he would 'trim them all'. When the chiefs protested against their arrest, they were sent down to peel coconuts for Bligh's dinner, a terrible insult but Bligh was in an insulting mood.

He claimed that with just four other men and stout sticks he could easily disarm the ship's entire complement and aimed a pistol at William McCoy, threatening to shoot him for not paying attention.

At last Bligh freed the chiefs, gave them presents and ordered them into the canoe that had followed. The general opinion aboard *Bounty* was that if a weakly manned ship were subsequently to call at the island it would pay handsomely for Bligh's irrational treatment of the chiefs. Fryer had no doubt that if Bligh had gone ashore his fate would have been that of Cook and he would have been murdered.

The contradictory orders on Nomuka, where once again Christian and other officers were made to look publicly foolish, continued what Bligh began long before in Adventure Bay. There could be few men of dignity who could honestly feel respect for their captain. For Fletcher Christian, it must have been horrifying to see his erstwhile friend and mentor like this, and he was more than an observer. He was directly in Bligh's sights and must have wondered what wound would be next.

Bounty sailed overnight towards Tofua with difficulty, for the wind dropped almost to a calm. As they approached the island, they could see its volcano erupting, belching columns of smoke and flame. Bligh, smarting from his defeat at the hands of the Nomukans, continued his search for status at the expense of others.

There are anomalies of date in what happened next, explained by Royal Navy custom. At sea, the day began and ended at noon, so the afternoon, evening and night of a certain date preceded its morning. When remembering what happened on *Bounty* while becalmed within sight of erupting Tofua, some men used naval time and some civil.

Perhaps the most telling example of Bligh's ability to blame everyone but himself for anything is that his published accounts do not mention the following 'coconuts' event, even though everyone else gave it great importance. The coconuts involved cost one nail for twenty.

Some time on the morning of 27 April Bligh said a pile of 'his' coconuts stacked between the guns had shrunk overnight, by which he meant stolen. Fryer agreed the store seemed smaller but thought men could have flattened it by walking over them during the night. Bligh ordered every coconut on board to be brought on deck and subjected each man who owned some to the most mortifying cross-examination: 'How many coconuts did you buy?' How many did you eat?' How could any man admit to theft under such circumstances, even if he were guilty?

When collecting evidence some years later, Edward Christian spoke to men who had been aboard *Bounty*, but who were not mutineers. They confirmed and extended the story with what must be considered primary evidence. Edward deduced a far more dramatic and wounding confrontation between his brother and Bligh.

He says that, as officer of the morning watch from 4 am to 8 am, his brother was in his hammock asleep when Bligh began his coconut tirade. Nonetheless, he was summoned, and Bligh accosted him with 'Damn your blood you have stolen my coconuts'.

Christian answered: 'I was dry, I thought it of no consequence. I took one only and I am sure no one touched another.'

'You lie, you scoundrel, you have stolen one half!' was Bligh's rejoinder.

Hurt and agitated Christian asked why he was treated thus. Bligh shook his hand in his face and said: 'No reply,' but he continued to call him a thief and other abusive names. This version amplifies those of Fryer and Morrison. It was injury of the deepest and most unforgivable kind for his second-in-command to be accused of petty theft in such arbitrary and public fashion, outrageous even if he were a mere able seaman.

Christian was allowed free access to Bligh's personal spirit supply simply by asking John Smith for the keys. If he were allowed alcohol, why not a coconut, which had been bought at the rate of 20 for an iron nail? It speaks badly of Bligh that he did not even hint at the coconut incident in his account of the events. He knew there was no way he could come out of it well so he ignored it, lied about it some might say.

The importance of the coconut incident is thought by Fletcher's brother Charles to be the final, irrevocable insult. In his autobiography, he writes with much emotion:

> What scurrilous abuse! What provoking insult to one of the chief officers on Board for having taken a coconut from a heap to quench his Thirst when on Watch base, mean-minded wretch!!

Bligh's behaviour, first over the grapnel at Nomuka and then over the coconuts cannot be considered normal, even if it was an everyday event. Officers and gentlemen required public respect, whatever they might have done. Without it they were unlikely to be heeded by the seamen. By humiliating his officers publicly, Bligh was encouraging the inefficiency he hated. Yet it seems that any inefficiency to which he could reduce his officers served to make him think himself the better sailor and more self-righteous man.

During the coconut incident Bligh threatened that only half his officers and young gentlemen would return home, saying they would be made to jump overboard before they got through Endeavour Straits, or they would be left behind at Jamaica. It's childish bullying and terribly cruel to men at sea, pushing for discipline rather than leading, and Bligh was later described as a 'pusher rather than a leader of men'. When Bligh added that his officers were to have their grog rations stopped and their allowances of yams reduced, he was still not finished. He confiscated some of his officers' coconuts to replace those he thought stolen because, whoever had taken them, he considered it the incontrovertible fault of all his officers, not just Fletcher Christian. Then he told his officers that if they stole from him tomorrow, he would reduce their yam rations even further. In other versions this threat was made to the entire company.

If the momentum of events was not so dramatic this extraordinary moment would be laughable. A Royal Navy officer and commander of a pioneering South Seas expedition was nursing feelings of persecution about coconuts that had cost one nail for twenty. His officers murmured in astonished groups, having been threatened with forced suicide or abandonment. Some scurried about secreting food like nervy squirrels. England and sanity were further away than when *Bounty* sailed from Tahiti, only weeks before. The day of reckoning Fletcher Christian had foreseen was almost here.

Later the same day Bligh once more abused his second-in-command. Fletcher ran forward with tears welling. Purcell stopped him, asking what had happened. Fletcher said, 'Can you ask me and hear the treatment I receive?'. Purcell suggested he had received the same treatment, but Christian pointed out a difference. As a Warrant Officer, Purcell could not be flogged, so had a degree of protection when he defended himself to Bligh. Christian reminded him that even though Acting-Lieutenant and second-in-command he was still officially Master's Mate, no more than a superior Midshipman, and could thus be beaten:

> ' . . . if I should speak to him as you do he would probably break me, turn me before the mast and perhaps flog me, and if he did it would be the death of us both, for I am sure I should take him in my arms and jump overboard with him.'

Purcell reminded Christian it was only for a short time longer but Bligh's threats about sending his gentlemen overboard in Endeavour

Straits bothered Christian. Going through them would be added Hell. He dared not defend himself the way Purcell might, and it was typical of Bligh to take advantage of Christian's vulnerability, driving him to the very limits of self-restraint with conscious and pernicious bullying. If Christian ever were to defy Bligh, he would lose his chance of promotion on their return, yet by not defying him, he would seem weaker and thus a softer target for further abuse. As young Fletcher wept, he protested:

> I would rather die ten thousand deaths than bear this treatment.
> I always do my duty as an officer and a man ought to do, yet
> I receive this scandalous usage.

Bligh was to say later that Christian did not do his duty and that he had put the ship in great danger just a couple of weeks after leaving Tahiti.

'Flesh and blood cannot bear this treatment,' Christian cried. It was the only time men on board had seen him in tears 'He was no milksop,' said one, something even his literary foes would concede. Through inflexible responsibility to duty but in defence of his dignity, Fletcher Christian was not prepared to descend to battle with Bligh. Instead, he decided to leave the ship. It was rash and it was desertion, but it was brave and it allowed him to keep his pride intact while making an unmistakable comment upon Bligh.

Fletcher Christian gave away his Tahitian curios. He tore up his letters and papers and threw them overboard. He clearly wanted no one to know the intimacies of his misery. There is no evidence that he was bent on revenge as malicious as his own torture had been. So far, his plan was to escape with maximum dignity and as little added ill-feeling as possible. He turned for help to the Carpenter Purcell, Boatswain William Cole, Acting-Master's Mate George Stewart and Midshipman Thomas Hayward. These men and others, who told Bligh and Courts of Justice they knew nothing of Fletcher Christian's initial plans to leave the ship, were lying to save their lives and future careers. Helping an officer desert his duty was a serious offence against the Lords of the Admiralty and no one would freely admit it. In the super-charged atmosphere of insult and injury in the small, almost becalmed ship, Christian went in and out of the fore cockpit with George Stewart, a part of the ship neither would normally visit. He was collecting nails and other barter items from Purcell.

He also collected wood and binding because now his plans were firm enough to let his confidantes know he was going to slip overboard and sail away on a raft. This seems impractical but perhaps Fletcher Christian was simply 'doing something'? Arranging a method of escape could have been a therapeutic exercise. This achieved, he might well have been content. Such gestures are common in tense situations.

As evening passed into night, Christian lashed two masts from the launch to a plank and hid some left-over pork and breadfruit. Fletcher used the flimsy excuse to stay on board that there were too many men on deck for him to leave in secrecy. Many were awake and watching sharks and the erupting volcano on Tofua. George Stewart risked everything to help his friend. He humoured Fletcher, supporting him when he most needed fellowship, so that nothing really dangerous or suicidal would happen. There was enough practicality in his scheme to work and Stewart could never be certain that Fletcher would not make the attempt. Christian was an excellent navigator and sailor and with his childhood life on a farm and his long stay on Tahiti, he was capable of self-sufficiency on any island.

There was never any evidence that either Tahiti or a woman was the reason for Fletcher's intended desertion. No man aboard the ship ever entertained that idea except Bligh, who was always the last person to know what another man thought. He can't have known what his second-in-command was planning because, with extraordinary insensitivity to the coconut incident earlier that day, Bligh sent his servant John Smith to invite Fletcher Christian to join him for supper. Bligh also expected him to dine with him the following day.

Bligh's officers took turns at his dinner table, attending once every three days, dinner being served at midday. Fletcher was regularly invited to supper in the evening as well. It was out of the question that Fletcher should accept, and he sent a message that politely saved Bligh's face, saying he was unwell. Bligh believed him, sensing nothing wrong. The officers agreed they would never again join Bligh at his table. Fryer and the late Dr Huggan had decided that on the outward voyage, more than a year earlier. Smith begged others to replace Fletcher at Bligh's table and when Hayward broke ranks to agree he was hissed.

At midnight, Peckover and his watch relieved Fryer's men. Those in the new watch included Edward Young and George Stewart. Fletcher Christian was awake and restless and went to his hammock only an hour before he was due on watch at 4am. Still on watch, George Stewart soothed Fletcher, pointing out the unlikelihood of any chance of survival if he left the ship. In any case, he added, if Christian left, *Bounty* would be in a worse state; the men were 'ripe for anything'.

Did George Stewart mean the men were ready for mutiny and that his friend should lead them? It is absolutely out of character and the only evidence that supports this is subsequent conjecture. Stewart had no motive to suggest mutiny. He was a strict disciplinarian, a stickler for duty, undoubtedly his reason for humouring Christian into staying at his post. Stewart did have a regular girlfriend on Tahiti to whom he was very much attached but a woman on a South Seas island was no reason for such a talented young man to abandon friends, family and career. Stewart would know that even to suggest such a thing was mutinous.

The simpler explanation is that he was cajoling, using any and every appeal to Christian's loyalty to his friends, telling him in return there was enormous sympathy for him on the ship. Christian was looked to for leadership and sympathy far more than Bligh and if he stayed the men would help put things right. There are always methods, and, apart from the sneaky Hayward, the officers had already quickly demonstrated united defiance by refusing to eat with Bligh, remarkable evidence of the widespread disrespect for his command that is rarely given the importance it should have.

It's a fact that no *Bounty* man ever blamed Christian for what he was about to do or felt personally injured by him. Plenty were willing to blame or to seek revenge upon Bligh but not one did the same to Christian, whatever their loss or distress, not even those subsequently tried and hanged.

Many men aboard *Bounty* later persuaded themselves – or were persuaded – that Stewart suggested mutiny but his friend Peter Heywood always firmly declared that Stewart did not mention the subject even obliquely. Heywood thought the imputation of Stewart's guilt distasteful, an insult to the memory of a fine sailor and an upright young man. Yet, if Stewart did not think of mutiny, Christian certainly did. His breaking point had been passed and all thought of duty dissipated.

As soon as he was on watch, on *Bounty's* almost empty, early morning deck, the resolution suddenly became simple and practical. At some fatal moment he must have thought, 'Why should I go? Why shouldn't Bligh go?'

Put like this, it didn't even sound like mutiny and hadn't his own brother been forced to act against another captain? Familiarity with any crime can make the human mind see it as less prohibited, more acceptable.

Hayward was already asleep on the empty arms chest on deck. Hallet had not appeared for duty. With not even a warrant officer about to gainsay him, *Bounty* was for the taking. The other men on Christian's watch were the gunner's mate John Mills, the carpenter's mate Charles Norman, plus Isaac Martin, Thomas Burkitt, Thomas Ellison and Matthew Quintal, all ABs.

Christian settled upon Cornishman Quintal as the first to approach. Quintal was 5 feet 5 inches/1.65 metres tall. Strong and muscular, he is said to have been the only AB who had a serious attachment in Tahiti. He was heavily tattooed on the backside and elsewhere. Quintal refused but the black-bearded American, Isaac Martin, thought it a capital idea. He assumed responsibility for raising a party and then Quintal quickly changed his mind.

Fletcher Christian could have considered taking Bligh back to face his superiors in England but now he wanted to be rid of him, together with Hayward, Hallet and Samuel. Hayward and Hallet were universally unpopular for their arrogance. Samuel was Bligh's clerk and connected in everyone's mind with the cutting of rations.

They needed arms and were helped by a small but significant breaking of the rules. Fryer, as Master, was supposed to keep the keys of the arms chest but against the rules they were in the care of Coleman, the Armourer. Christian woke Coleman and asked for the keys, saying he wanted to shoot a shark. Coleman handed over the keys and went back to sleep. Once they were crowded around the arms chest, Christian and his supporters quickly agreed the cutlasses, pistols, muskets and bayonets were only to be deterrents. There would be bloody threats but there was to be no bloodshed.

It would have been so easy for Christian to strike or murder Bligh that morning that accusations of his having little or no control of his temper cannot be supported. There was plenty of precedent. Insurrections, including mutiny, happened on naval and merchant ships all the time, but even the bloodiest of these, where a captain was slowly flayed while bound to a mast, are rarely remembered because they happened so often it was a banality of life at sea.

Although acting illegally and perhaps in the grip of a temporary mental breakdown (see Mad to do it – or Mad?), Fletcher Christian demonstrated great control. It was Bligh whom most of the ship thought was out of control, infecting others, including Christian, with ideas of abnormal action. A wide belief on *Bounty* that Bligh's mind was unbalanced is why plans to confine him or take some other unusual action were accepted without question by almost all those to whom they were put. The lack of protest or action by others after Fletcher Christian arrested him means they were unsurprised, even if unapproving.

As the insurrectionists mounted the fore ladderway, they were seen by Hayward, who asked why they were armed and then started aft, apparently to warn the sleeping Bligh. William McCoy, tattooed and scarred from knife fights, had been loading his musket on deck. He banged it heavily three times on the deck, warning them they were suspected. Christian quickly emerged carrying a musket with a fixed bayonet and a cartouche box in his left hand, a cutlass and pistol in his right. He ordered Burkitt to take the pistol. When the raw-boned heavily-tattooed man wavered, Christian yelled in fury, 'Damn your blood, lay hold of it.'

From this moment on, Christian kept his dark face stern, 'darker than thunder', and by constantly threatening death and injury, kept everyone in fear of him, including his own party. Hurriedly the group caught up with Hayward. 'Damn your blood Hayward, Mamoo!!' said Christian, using the Tahitian word to tell him to hold his tongue and threatening him with a drawn cutlass.

It hadn't taken long. At about 4.30am, Fletcher Christian descended the aft ladderway without disturbing Fryer, who slept directly opposite Bligh. Followed by Burkitt, Mills and Churchill, he burst through the habitually open door of Bligh's cabin, waking his victim with a flourish of naked steel and shouting, 'Bligh, you are my prisoner!'

Bligh shouted, 'What's the matter? What's the matter?' When he saw the cutlass blade at his throat he yelled: 'Murder!' Unable even to don 'trowsers' and with his hands bound tightly behind him Bligh was hustled on deck and demanded an explanation from Christian, 'What is the meaning of all this?'

'Can you ask, Captain Bligh?' Christian answered. 'Can you ask when you know you have treated us officers and all these poor fellows like Turks?'

Fletcher Christian made the cause of the mutiny perfectly clear to Bligh from the first moment he was asked to explain. Treating people like Turks meant working them like slaves and everyone on board would have understood this at once. Christian held Bligh just forward of the ship's wheel. In one hand he had the end of the rope binding his prisoner, in the other was a bayonet that he had exchanged for the cutlass and now pointed at Bligh's breast. To young Tom Ellison, just a few yards away at the wheel, Christian seemed like a madman. His long black hair hung loose, and his shirt collar was wide open, exposing his tanned and tattooed chest. His eyes seemed to flame with vengeance.

The rope that bound Bligh's wrists had also caught the tail of his night shirt. Burkitt did not like to see his captain stand exposed, the stark ivory-whiteness of his skin contrasting deeply with his black pubic hair. Putting down a musket, Burkitt went to adjust Bligh's shirt, hauling it out of the tight lashings. Disregarding Christian's orders to take up his arms again, Burkitt called down to Sumner for some clothes for the captain but as John Smith came past, he suggested he do this instead. Christian drew out a small pistol that Bligh had once carried and warned Burkitt to take care, that he was being watched. Burkitt retrieved his musket and moved away to a less conspicuous place.

Christian ordered the small cutter to be put out and told Hayward and Hallet they were to disembark and until they left, the two men kept up an incessant duet of tearful pleading, asking what they had done to deserve such treatment.

Ellison made up his own mind and joined Christian's party with a spirited offer to stand guard over Bligh. It must sorely have tried Bligh, for Ellison was a protege of his earlier employer, Duncan Campbell.

Fryer pleaded to be let out of his portside cabin so he could speak to Fletcher but was refused. When Christian relented and he was escorted up, Fryer said, 'Mr Christian, consider what you are about.'

'Hold your tongue', was the sharp reply. 'I have been in Hell for weeks passed, you know Mr Fryer. Captain Bligh has brought this upon himself.' Fryer persisted, telling him his disagreement with Bligh need not result in the ship being taken and then that something better than the leaky small cutter be employed and made a motion to speak to Bligh. Christian aimed his bayonet at Fryer's heart and told him if he advanced further, he would be run through. No officer or crew member supported Fryer on the only real appeal to Christian that came from anyone on board. Fryer was returned to his cabin and John Millward was added as a third sentinel to guard him.

The small cutter was so unseaworthy that the Carpenter's Mate Norman had to sit in it and constantly bail. Like the rotten sails, the condition of the boat could be blamed directly on Bligh, perhaps a reason he failed to mention this in his version of 28 April 1789. Then Christian found others wished to leave *Bounty*. All morning he listened to the requests and suggestions of both the mutineers and those who wished to leave the ship, further indication that he was as unprepared for mutiny as anyone. The large cutter was ordered out to replace the small one and Michael Byrne sat in it to keep it off the ship. Isolated by his poor eyesight and inability to hear what was happening on deck, he cried miserably, terrified he would be forgotten.

A considerable number thought they would join Bligh's party, being loyal to themselves and to the king as well as to Bligh. There was no suggestion then that Bligh would attempt crossing half the South Pacific to Timor and so the choice seemed simple. Should they renounce their duty and stay aboard or loyally sail to nearby Tofua with their captain? England was a long way off, perhaps never to be seen again, whichever course they took. The only men likely to have followed Bligh through true personal loyalty were his servants Smith and Samuel, although the latter had to be forced overboard.

Bligh wrote that Samuel was forbidden:

> ... on pain of death, to touch either map, ephemeris, book of astronomical observations, sextant, time-keeper or any of my surveys or drawings. [Mr. Samuel] attempted to save the time-keeper, and a box with my surveys, drawings, and remarks for fifteen years past, which were numerous; when he was hurried away, with 'Damn your eyes you are well off to get what you have.'

When told the large cutter was not big enough to hold those who wished to leave, Fletcher Christian must have been sorely exasperated.

What began as a small and simple act of personal revenge on Bligh and three others was getting out of hand. Only the launch remained, the most valuable part of the ship's furnishings and Fletcher Christian was adamant that Bligh should not have it. After much pleading, discussion and hesitation, he relented. For the third time the heavy task of hauling one cumbersome wooden boat back on board and then another lowering an even bigger one onto the South Pacific was undertaken. To encourage the men, Christian ordered Bligh's servant to give a dram to each man under arms. This does not mean the mutineers quickly became drunk, incapable of decent or reasonable behaviour.

A dram means a tipple, a mouthful. A dictionary defines it as only ⅛ fl oz, just over 3.5mls, but it is hardly likely there was exact measuring on *Bounty* that morning. Only one bottle was fetched, and John Smith was unlikely to bring glasses. In any case, to men who were drinking rum every day, a quick refresher of spirits would be only a psychological lift. If Fletcher Christian had ordered a serving of grog, suggestions of drunkenness would be hard to dismiss. The imprecations hurled at Bligh and others are likely to have been fuelled by exhilaration and the unfamiliar privilege of freedom of speech.

The launch slowly filled with men and their possessions. Only Bligh took most of his and his selfish gathering of unnecessary bits and pieces was a major contributory factor to delay and to the boat's overloading, discomfort and to the subsequent danger of his fellow passengers. When the time came for Fryer to be escorted to the ship's side, Bligh ordered him to stay aboard for the safety of the ship and in the hope that he might retake it. The Master, anxious to obey, implied to Christian that without his skills Christian could never be master of the ship.

Insulted, Christian once more brandished his bayonet at Fryer. 'Go into the boat or I will run you through.' Fryer now thought of his young brother-in-law, Tinkler, and begged he also be allowed to leave. Churchill, who as Master-at-arms should have been the first to defend Bligh, protested but Christian once more relented.

Fryer was amazed that so few armed men had been able to take the ship and turn so many out of her. He had forgotten that in Nomuka, Bligh boasted he could take the ship with four men armed with stout sticks.

Christian agreed to let Carpenter Purcell go but kept most of his tools and both his assistants. He also kept Armourer Coleman on board, and he was a most useful man in the days to come. Peter Heywood and George Stewart were kept on board as essential to the safe sailing of the ship, insurance against any future incapacity or loss of Fletcher Christian.

Bligh alternated fruitless appeals with attempts to humour and dissuade Christian. Losing the breadfruit and *Bounty* was serious and anything Bligh could do to avert this must have seemed fair. Fairness to others wasn't one of his virtues and his protestations were ignored. The day before, Bligh had pointedly refused to answer Christian when asked the reasons for his ill-treatment. Today, Christian clearly and repeatedly answered Bligh's same enquiry in a manner that left no doubt about his reason for the seizure. The only cause of the mutiny was Bligh and his behaviour towards Fletcher Christian. It was said so often in the evidence and reaffirmed so clearly by Rolf DuRietz in 1965 in *The cause of the Bounty mutiny;: Some comments on a book by Madge Darby (Studia* Bounty*ana)*, that I never fail to be amazed at writers who claim still to search for the mutiny's cause.

The biggest reactions raised by Bligh's shouts for assistance were abuse and bad language, something he was used to giving rather than getting. There was to be no reversal of the situation and the defiance that men had suppressed so long now poured forth. Christian was advised to 'shoot the bugger' at least. Bligh was taunted with his handling of the food rations and there was satisfaction that he would have to try to survive on reduced rations and 12 ounces/340 grams of yams a day. The show of solidarity must have pleased Christian. He was being unduly modest when he told men that something other than fear must have prevented anyone from acting against him. His determination and threats were enough and anyway there was enormous sympathy and understanding for him as well as widespread onboard unhappiness and resentment.

When Bligh wrote about the dramatic morning, he omitted to mention that all three boats had been put out, for only the immediate putting out of the launch would support his belief in the story he wanted the world to accept, that he was the victim of a conspiracy, a well-laid scheme to which more than half the ship was party. Edward Christian thought readers of Bligh's *Narrative* would have the perspicacity to realise that it was not possible for twenty-five people, more than half those on board, to have conspired in such a plot beforehand without being overheard. Bligh was convinced otherwise and published a memorable paragraph:

> Notwithstanding the roughness with which I was treated, the remembrance of past kindness produced some signs of remorse in Christian . . . I asked him if this treatment was a proper return for the many instances he had received of my friendship. He appeared disturbed at my questions and answered with much emotion, "That Captain Bligh that is the thing: I am in hell I am in hell."

As is always the case with Bligh's defensive published recollection of events that might have dishonoured him, there are other memories of that morning. Most of those that follow were collected from men who were not party to the ship's seizure. Purcell said of the confrontations between the two men, one so pale, one so swarthy:

> Captain Bligh attempted to speak to Christian, who said, "Hold your tongue and I'll not hurt you. It is too late to consider now. I have been in hell for weeks past with you.'

From others on deck at the time, Edward Christian collected accounts of a similar conversation and the details confirm Purcell's memories. Bligh said:

> 'Consider Mr Christian, I have a wife and four children in England and you have danced my children on your knee.'

> 'You should have thought of them sooner than yourself, Captain Bligh. It is too late to consider now, I have been in hell for weeks past with you.'

Thomas Burkitt, who was to be hanged for his part in the insurrection, gave an even more poignant account. While the second of the three boats was being hoisted out, he said he heard Bligh say the following (and like the rest of these reports it is more likely to be in the words of the storyteller than of Christian and Bligh):

> 'Consider what you are about, Mr Christian. For God's sake drop it and there shall be no more come of it,' said Bligh.

> 'Tis too late, Captain Bligh!'

> 'No, Mr Christian it is not too late yet. I'll forfeit my honour if I ever speak of it. I'll give you my bond that there shall never be any more come of it.'

For Bligh to speak of honour was dangerous. In defence of his duty to the king he could do whatever he thought fit. No sooner was he free than he could have pursued Christian with every means at his disposal and would not have had the slightest qualms about forfeiting his 'honour'. Christian was right not to trust his word. When Bligh was deposed as the Governor of New South Wales in Australia, he signed a solemn agreement to quit the colony but, as soon as he was aboard the ship to sail him to England, he commanded it to stay in the colony's waters for almost a year. A second appeal for Fletcher to change his mind came from Cole and Purcell, party to Christian's initial plan. Christian reminded them that they well knew how he had been used. When Cole answered, he settled once and for all the cause of the mutiny. 'I know it very well, Mr Christian,' [he said.] 'We all know it, but drop it for God's sake.' Cole identified that almost the entire ship's company knew and understood Fletcher Christian's personal situation, even if they did not agree with his solution.

To Bligh, Christian seemed to be 'meditating' destruction on himself and everyone else. Bligh played for time by asking for arms, a request greeted by laughter. Domineering Churchill forced the climax, when he told Christian that the heavily laden boat waited only for Bligh. 'Come, Captain Bligh,' said Fletcher Christian. 'Your officers and men are now in the boat and you must go with them. If you attempt to make the least resistance you will instantly be put to death.'

A group of armed mutineers untied his hands and forced him over the side and once Bligh was in the boat the jeering and ridicule increased. There was some bargaining for possessions. Christian gave Bligh his own compass; further food and clothing were thrown down plus four cutlasses.

There was a plan to tow them closer to Tofua but Bligh was terrified that the noisy men on board would shoot into the boat. After pitiless hours, the Captain Bligh and his loyalists were finally cast adrift on the open ocean.

Ellison climbed up to unfurl *Bounty's* main top-gallant sail and Bligh says he saw George Stewart come on deck and dance in the Otaheitian manner.

In Bligh's words *Bounty* was now in the hands of twenty-five men, 'the most able men of the ship's company'. He fancied he heard cries of 'Huzzah! for Otaheite' and may well have, for whatever side a man was on, in the strange, strained exhilaration of those first independent hours, the indolence and flesh of Tahiti would have been especially attractive, perhaps the only concrete idea of what might happen next. Bligh's immediate and consoling thought was that Tahiti's allures were the cause of the mutiny and that there had been a conspiracy by the majority to throw out a loyal minority. It never occurred to him that Fletcher Christian's mutiny was against him. Bligh had to include everyone, or it was too shameful for words.

The William Bligh who found himself sitting cramped and half-clad among his hastily packed possessions and with men for whom he had daily expressed contempt, had a great deal of work to do to patch up his pride. Almost immediately he cross-questioned the boatload to reinforce his suspicions. He was convinced of a conspiracy and that both George Stewart and Peter Heywood were hard-core plotters, relying for evidence on their friendship with Fletcher Christian.

He always overlooked that not a shot had been fired or a single person injured through the use of force, because that would look as though the entire ship wanted to be rid of him.

Professor J. C. Beaglehole, who was Emeritus Professor of British Commonwealth History at the Victoria University of Wellington, gave an enlightening lecture on 3 August 1967, 'Captain Cook and Captain Bligh', in which he contrasted the two. Cook punished more often, was crueller physically and had a smouldering irascibility that made both him and others jump up and down when he was in a rage but he was a 'character'. His men, whom he flogged until their ribs were exposed, loved him, calling him 'the old boy'.

Well over 6 feet/1.8 metres tall, this made him especially admired on Tahiti, where height was akin to godliness. Cook had charisma, presence and a natural ability to command respect, which recommended him to the men before the mast, where manliness was highly regarded. Bligh was short. With the unusual combination of blue eyes, delicate white skin and black hair he looked like a doll, so when Bligh went into a Cook-like rage he merely looked silly. His infamous bad language made it worse.

Bligh must have developed his legendary linguistic ability consciously, as a weapon against the attacks on his vanity he so feared. Every spirited coward attacks before he is threatened and Bligh so developed his arsenal of insult that the most hardened users of foul language were stunned by his inventiveness, which made him more, rather than less, ridiculous. He was later to be court-martialled and found guilty of using insulting language to a junior officer.

Bligh's conspiracy theory relied on his absolute belief that his constant aspersions on the abilities and reputations of his officers and men were justified. Professor Beaglehole points out:

> Bligh habitually talked to his officers, and wrote about them afterwards, as if it had been the special purpose of the Divine Power, for some unrevealed reason, to inflict upon him for every voyage a unique collection of fools and knaves as his subordinates. It is unlikely that this is the case.

Beaglehole pointed out that the *Bounty* men about whom Bligh was most vitriolic went on to pursue blameless and distinguished naval careers. Bligh, however, continued to be accused of the same faults wherever he went and whatever position he held. He added that Bligh never mellowed and that after his second breadfruit voyage in 1793, '. . . [he] made no more discoveries except, one is tempted to say, of his own limitations, and of those he was always incredulous'.

Mad to do it – or Mad?

Was Fletcher Christian very, very angry on the day of the mutiny, or was he insane? My research makes the latter likely, so the question his brother Charles asked becomes more relevant than ever: 'But who was it that has drove him into that unhappy state?'

The first suggestion of something more than anger was Madge Darby's 1965 theory that there was a homosexual relationship between Bligh and Christian and that this had gone wrong. The friendship between these two men had been especially close but it's likely that Bligh's preferments were because Fletcher was better at his job than others and because his professed ability to humour Bligh was thought by him to make Fletcher a friend and companion.

Fletcher Christian, ten years younger than Bligh, was the ideal protege, well-born and connected, loyal, charming and a quick learner. With his father dead when he was less than four, he grew up with a resident grandfather but without the interest of an older male member of the family, at least not of the father-figure type whom it is permitted to clasp emotionally and physically. This psychological void, combined with sudden financial betrayal and the practical need for a patron, would certainly recommend Bligh's interest as worthy of encouragement.

Bligh fits well into the role of a surrogate father to Fletcher Christian. The reciprocated and loyal interest of a bright young man from a good family, who was also a talented sailor willing to learn from him, would serve only to flatter Bligh. As a single child, Bligh needed, or enjoyed, the feeling of having a surrogate brother or son, too. Such psychological dependencies are more fragile and more explosive than the real thing but do not need to be expressed physically. The possibility that their special relationship might flower into a sexuality that would never be considered when ashore, ignores the absolute impossibility of concealment on such a cramped and crowded ship as *Bounty*. Bligh was noted as usually having his cabin door open, so if ever it were closed because he and Fletcher were sexually active it would have been obvious to all what was going on.

Homosexual sex of any kind was forbidden in the Royal Navy on pain of death, although it was only persistent sodomy that might be punished ashore. Bligh would have heeded such constriction absolutely and this should be enough to convince most that a homosexual relationship did not exist but there is more powerful contemporary support that submerges the idea. Every one of those later put on trial in England could have used the charge of homosexuality to damn Bligh and help towards saving themselves. Even the suggestion would have ruined Bligh, a guaranteed spiteful revenge for those who wanted Bligh to suffer. Just as none of the accused blamed Fletcher Christian for their situation, none of the accused used counter-charges of homosexuality against Bligh. This should have prevented such theories being aired. Madge Darby, Richard Hough and others should have researched more, thought deeper and written less.

Yet there's little doubt in my mind that the intensity of their friendship contributed to its breakdown. Young men must one day grow away from parents or parent figures and the wrench is more difficult for the latter, for whom it is a retrograde step to loneliness. After five months ashore, during which he matured in every way, including sexually, Fletcher came back on board no longer needing a father or any other substitute, whereas Bligh would still have expected Fletcher to be dependent. The new relationship would have been mutually agonising. Bligh bullied, insulted and nagged painfully at Christian, hoping to demean him back into his dependent role and soon Christian couldn't stand the sight of Bligh. Fletcher Christian had only one way to salvage his sanity. He followed the common pattern of resolving familial tensions, by doing the equivalent of leaving home.

In the notes William Bligh made in the open boat after the mutiny, he wrote that Christian was 'subject to violent perspiration and particularly to his hands so that he soils any thing he handles'. In another description written in Timor, Bligh describes 'violent perspirations'. The most likely explanation is that Fletcher Christian suffered from hyperhidrosis but there is no evidence to tell us how long this condition had existed, for no other person mentioned it. The genesis of most hyperhidrosis remains a mystery, except to say it commonly appears in puberty and it may improve or even disappear in the late twenties and thirties.

Hyperhidrosis is the medical term for excessive sweating and affects the palms, the armpits, the feet or the face and gets worse in times of emotional pressure or conflict. It's important to understand that the condition exists independently of other complaints; it does not have to be associated with or be a symptom of a physical or mental condition. To be clear, hyperhidrosis cannot be used to diagnose other conditions. There is a type of hidrosis that can also darken the skin and perhaps this contributed to Fletcher's acknowledged swarthiness.

Excessive sweating is also associated with opium taking. Drug addiction is impossible in Christian's case without also believing that Bligh condoned and accepted Christian using the opium in *Bounty*'s stores for recreational purposes. The confined living in *Bounty* would have made an addiction impossible to conceal and any unexplained shortfall of such supplies would have to have been explained to Fryer and eventually made up by Bligh as Purser.

We know Bligh used personal debt to wound Christian and that he would add insult to injury wherever he could, by mocking anything he judged different or less in others. If he ridiculed Fletcher's sweating, it was unforgiveable. Who can bear being humiliated for something they can do nothing about?

The conflict that developed after *Bounty* left Tahiti was ideal for making Fletcher's condition increasingly severe. In times of stress, sufferers of hyperhidrosis of the face can look and feel as though they have been rained on. The acidity of sweat pouring into their eyes can make these red with irritation and Christian is described as having eyes 'aflame with revenge' on the day of the mutiny. Apart from a sleepless night, they were as likely to be red because of reaction to violent perspiration. His long hair would have been sodden and his shirt drenched alarmingly from his armpits. Perhaps the rest of *Bounty* resisted Fletcher Christian so little because they thought these were signs of madness and feared for their personal safety.

The unpublished autobiography of Charles Christian gives unexpected illumination from Bligh, who eventually gave a different reason for the mutiny from any in his published works. Charles recorded a conversation between Captain Bligh and Major Taubman, the man responsible for putting Fletcher Christian aboard *Britannia*. When Taubman asked Bligh what could be the cause of Fletcher's defection, he replied: 'It was Insanity.'

'He spoke right,' says Charles. 'But who was it that had drove him into that unhappy state?'

Bligh always knew the answer, for he had been told by Christian as soon as he was arrested on *Bounty*. Charles Christian adds that when Fletcher was a boy, he was 'slow to be moved'. On board *Bounty*:

> Jealousy and Tyranny had produced Ill Usage to so great an Excess . . . and New call out to Revenge ensued as an Effervescence from the Opposition of good to bad Qualities.

In the 1930s, it was said that Christian's wild-eyed look and mutinous behaviour might have been caused by syphilis and he took the ship to escape into hidden disgrace. This is a twentieth century view of syphilis. Fletcher Christian was not suffering from tertiary or neuro-syphilis, the stage of the disease that can turn the mind and when death is imminent and inevitable. The most licentious of men is unlikely to have been in this state at 24 for, although this final stage can appear within five years of initial infection, it usually takes ten to 40 years and the longer time is the more usual by far. Anyway, there is no evidence of Fletcher Christian passing venereal disease on to Mauatua or to any other Tahitian woman. It wasn't subsequently a problem on Pitcairn Island.

The late Dr Sven Wahlroos was a practising psychologist and the first to use such professional skills to analyse the mutiny and to explore if Fletcher was insane on the day of the mutiny. Dr Wahlroos's *Mutiny and Romance in the South Seas: A Companion to the Bounty Adventure* (1989, recently republished) concludes that everything points to Christian suffering Borderline Personality Disorder. The clinical description, as defined by the American Psychiatric Association, is telling:

> Interpersonal relationships are often intense and unstable with marked shifts of attitude over time. Frequently there is impulsive and unpredictable behaviour that is potentially physically self-damaging and the borderline person will often go from idealising a person to devaluing him.

This and the following quote reproduced with permission from the *Diagnostic and Statistical Manual of Mental Disorders, Third Edition.* Revised. Copyright 1987 American Psychiatric Association.

The description might as well be of Bligh, but we are focusing on Fletcher Christian. Wahlroos's professional opinion is that Fletcher Christian suffered a brief reactive psychosis. He quotes the American Psychiatric Association again to support this:

> The essential feature is the sudden onset of a psychotic disorder of at least a few hours but no more than two week's duration . . . suicidal or aggressive behaviour may be present . . . Individuals with Borderline Personality Disorders are thought to be particularly vulnerable . . . situations involving major stress predispose to development of this disorder.

Clinical psychologist Paul J. Rodriguez agrees with Dr Wahlroos's basic diagnosis and adds that many people diagnosed with Borderline

Personality Disorder have commonly experienced childhood neglect, abuse and conflict, including the loss of one or both parents when young. Fletcher Christian's father died when he 3½ years old and he later lost his family home through a combination of mismanagement by his mother and profligacy by his older brothers, both of which can be construed as abandonment through neglect of his welfare.

Thus, explains Rodriguez, if Fletcher felt he was abandoned by Bligh or believed he was being neglected or demeaned by a man he once idolised, any inherent instability would have predisposed him to behave in extreme ways, especially during times of stress. In *Bounty* in late April 1789, there seemed to be stress everywhere Fletcher Christian turned and it was very clear that he had been abandoned, betrayed even, by Bligh. Rodriguez says:

> Fletcher Christian would have responded to events on Bounty with feelings of deep emptiness and may have had considerable difficulty controlling his anger. He would have dramatically altered his attitude towards the person whom he believed to be abandoning him, from intense admiration to intense devaluation.

> When faced with considerable stress the sort of events which almost anyone would find difficult to endure a Borderline person may suddenly lose touch with reality. This is usually short-lived and can involve deep feelings of detachment from events and people, or grossly inappropriate behaviour.

Brief Reactive Psychosis, the diagnosis by Dr Wahlroos of Fletcher Christian's condition during the mutiny, is now known as Brief Psychotic Disorder with Marked Stressors, a mental state that commonly includes paranoid or grandiose delusions and irrational behaviour. The duration of this sudden-onset condition varies but the sufferer always returns to his or her previous pattern of behaviour. This fits well with what we know of Christian's behaviour and I shudder to think how he felt when the Disorder disappeared and he realised what he had done. Was it hours, days or weeks after he arrested Bligh on 28 April?

If Fletcher Christian did suffer from this condition, I would expect to find a long-standing and inflexible pattern of instability in his relationships, emotions, self-image and control of his behaviour. Instead, every contemporary pre-*Bounty* account describes him as someone particularly affable, charming and socially sensitive, who went out of his way to understand others, especially those of lesser position.

The explanation of this dichotomy, says Rodriguez, is fascinating:

> Individuals with Borderline Personality Disorder may appear charismatic, which masks or makes acceptable behaviour which would otherwise have been judged unsuitable.

That is the final piece of the Fletcher Christian puzzle. The very characteristics that might today lead to a greater and earlier understanding of Fletcher Christian are precisely those that led writers and historians astray for over two centuries. His appealing personality and charisma were not signs of great confidence but clues to his fragility.

So, Fletcher Christian probably was insane on the day of the mutiny. The exact details of what went wrong between Captain Bligh and Fletcher Christian aboard *Bounty* cannot be known, except that men who were there thought the animosity between the two men was long-standing. To this we must add the well-chronicled fact that for most of his naval life Bligh had a reputation for bullying and mentally torturing other men, even those he considered friends, and that Christian was by every account a special target for such behaviour by a man who had once been seen by him as a hero and protector.

After sailing from Tahiti, Bligh worked Christian harder than justified and insulted him more. Bligh's failure to recognise approaching danger from Christian is not the only time he suffered because of his inability to see another man's point of view. He expected others to think the same way he did and could not understand it when they did not. These days he might be described as being in denial and he applied such selective thinking in his account of the mutiny. In *A Voyage to the South Seas*, published in 1792, Bligh wrote that until the day of the mutiny he considered 'the voyage had advanced in a course of uninterrupted prosperity', which anyone who was there would say was delusional. His belief in himself as a faultless administrator and captain was misguided and sorely exposed before and after the mutiny.

Here's what psychologist Dr Sven Wahlroos has to say about Bligh in *Mutiny and Romance in the South Seas*:

> Bligh probably did not have any clear-cut mental or emotional illness but he did show prominent compulsive, narcissistic, histrionic and somewhat paranoid tendencies. A major part of his interpersonal problems lay in his almost total lack of understanding of the impact he had on others. His focus was always on himself . . . he felt he had nothing to do with the misfortunes which befell him during his life.

Of all the many supporting sources for this view, including Beaglehole, Wahlroos quotes just one. In his 1976 book *Captain Bligh*, Richard Humble wrote:

> A man who is pathologically unable to accept imperfection is a permanent martyr to himself: he has an enormous cross to bear . . . [Bligh] was not only unable to face up to this [making mistakes], he recoiled from the very idea. From this mental block sprang his tendency to arrogance and diversion of the blame on to others; whatever went wrong it could never be his fault. Inconsistent though he was, he was never inconsistent in this.

On 28 April 1789 Fletcher Christian paid a terrible price for Bligh's self-deceit and inconsistencies. He had come aboard *Bounty* regarding

Bligh as mentor and special friend but was driven temporarily insane because he was abandoned and humiliated in front of others.

Whether or not Fletcher realised he was out of his mind on 28 April 1789, the consequences were the loss of everything he had gone to sea to recover, his family name and honour, his career, fortune and future. The result was exile, with men he is unlikely to have chosen and in a part of the world largely unknown.

The consequence for Bligh was to be abandoned in an overloaded open boat in the middle of the South Pacific, thousands of miles from any European settlement.

Bligh's Open-Boat Voyage

The last sight Fletcher Christian had of William Bligh was as he and his eighteen companions sailed for erupting Tofua. Here they were made anything but welcome and Quartermaster Norton was killed in a rock-throwing battle. *Bounty's* cast-off men jettisoned extra clothes and equipment as temptations to their pursuers, thus deflecting them so they could escape. Accepting the dangers of Pacific islands, Bligh announced he saw no safe succour closer than the Dutch East Indies settlement of Timor, 1,200 leagues/almost 7,000 kms away. This is Foul-Weather Bligh at his most magnificent. One sailing professional said to me, if you overlook the distance, he knew the general geography and all he had to do was go across quite a lot and then up a bit. Nevertheless, it was a truly heroic decision that few others then or now would be brave or confident enough to do.

The provisions were 150 pounds of ship's biscuits, 28 gallons of water, 20 pounds of pork (presumably salted), 5 quarts of rum, 3 bottles of wine, some coconuts and some breadfruit. In modern terms, this is 68 kgs of ship's biscuit, 127 litres of water, 9 kgs of salted pork, just over 5 litres of almost 100 per cent proof rum (about 50 per cent alcohol) as well as the wine, coconuts and breadfruit.

No one could lie down to rest, not even one at a time. Bligh never mentions what the men did to increase their comfort in the challenging closeness, how they coped with performing personal functions or any description of individual trauma except for bowel pain and constipation. He wrote that:

> . . . all agreed to live on one ounce [25g] of bread and a quarter pint [fewer than 150mls] of water a day. Therefore, after

examining our stock of provisions, and recommending this as a sacred promise for ever to their memory, we bore away across the sea, where the navigation is but little known and in a small boat twenty-three feet long from stem to stern, deep loaded with eighteen men; without a chart, and nothing but my own recollection and general knowledge of the situation of places, assisted by a book of longitudes and latitudes to guide us. I was happy, however, to see everyone better satisfied with our situation in this particular than myself.

Bedevilled by rain for 21 of 43 days, they laboured towards the eastern Australian coast. Bligh wrote:

> . . . so covered with rain and sea that we can scarce see or make use of our eyes . . . Sleep, though we long for it, is horrible . . . we suffer extreme cold and everyone dreads the approach of night . . . the least error in the helm would in a moment be our destruction. The misery . . . has exceeded the preceeding . . . The sea flew over us with great force and kept us bailing with horror and anxiety . . . another such night would produce the end of several.

On 25 May 1789 after almost a month on the open sea, Bligh cut rations further and four miserable days later negotiated the treacherous Great Barrier Reef, to land on the Australian coast. A change of mood overcame the men. Factions emerged with the majority supporting Bligh and the rest looking to Fryer. There were disagreements about the proportions served of an oyster stew and some pork was stolen. There were constant complaints about who was collecting the most food, who was eating too much, excusable petty niggles of men who, famished and dispirited, faced anonymous death for reasons not of their own making.

Further up the coast on 31 May, Purcell's temper erupted into mutiny when he said to Bligh he was as good a man as he and that, anyway, they would not be here if it had not been for Bligh. Bligh wrote: 'I saw there was no carrying command with any certainty or Order but by power, for some had totally forgotten every degree of obedience'. Henceforth, he always carried a cutlass but yet had the astonishing discipline to write regular reports, observations and sketches, noting details of current and coastline and fixing his daily position. Once they were north of Australia, Bligh noted it seemed as if they 'had only embarked with me to proceed to Timor, and were in a Vessel equally calculated for their safety and convenience'. Days later the men weakened alarmingly, with much of the terrible sleepiness that often precedes a predisposition to surrender. Bligh, too, was seriously ill.

After 41 more days, Timor was sighted on 12 June. Bligh refused when Fryer and Purcell demanded they should land immediately, perhaps unwise on an island both unknown and inhabited by tribesmen. All the men in the boat were filthy, starving, exhausted and probably in pain, so to be denied respite when so close to land must have been agonising. Bligh severely reprimanded Fryer, telling him 'he would be dangerously troublesome if it were not for his ignorance and lack of resolution'.

Something changed Bligh's mind. A few hours later Peckover and Cole were landed in a small settlement, where they learned that Coupang was just along the coast. A local agreed to tow the boat there once he had sight of Bligh's parcel of Rix dollars, the money the Admiralty had given him to buy additional plants for the West Indies and Kew Gardens from this Dutch dominated part of the world. That puts paid to the charge that Fletcher Christian stole *Bounty's* cash reserves.

The pitiful cargo was towed into Coupang, now Kupang, on the south-west coast of Timor, as day broke on 14 June. Even though he and his men were desperately ill, Bligh raised a pennant of distress and waited at sea for formal permission to land. The signal was quickly spotted and Bligh was astonished to be greeted in English. The mercenary-sailor's commander, a Captain Spikerman, organised an English breakfast with pots of tea and asked Bligh to invite his men up, too. Bligh ordered Fryer to remain to guard his belongings and so Fryer demanded that Bligh's servant John Smith also remain.

It was hours before Dutch soldiers told Captain Spikerman that there were two men still in the boat. Tea and bread were immediately sent, but only the tea was taken as the two felt eating could endanger their health further. With little else to do, Fryer shaved. Smith did not think himself capable, so Fryer did it for him, later saying, 'all this time I might have gone to the devil for my good friend Captain Bligh'.

Governor Adrian van Este put a big house at Bligh's disposal and his haggard crew had to share it. For two months the men convalesced but on 20 July the botanist David Nelson died of fever.

Bligh was convinced the mutiny was a conspiracy of many aboard and laid down the foundations of his defence, writing a full report of the mutiny, descriptions of the mutineers and letters of excuse, but to get home, he would first have to sail to Batavia, 1800 miles/2900 kms away. He bought a 34 foot/10.4 metres schooner named *Resource* that was armed with four swivel guns and stands of small arms because there were pirates in these waters and sailed on 20 August 1789, towing *Bounty's* launch and with locally collected breadfruit. After a month at sea, they reached Surabaya on the north-east coast of Java and Purcell and Fryer were misbehaving again. This time Bligh marched them below at bayonet point. It didn't help when Bligh sent for help from Dutch officials, because calumny had been spread in the township, suggesting Bligh would be hanged or blown from a cannon's mouth when he returned to England.

In a local court of inquiry Fryer accused Bligh of overcharging the Admiralty. Bligh countered by producing his receipts and vouchers that had been signed by Fryer and the boatswain as well as by two respectable residents of Coupang. Discovered, Fryer begged forgiveness, ending a note to Bligh, 'if matters can be made up, I beg you will forward it'. This was pointless, because Fryer had also blackened Bligh back in Coupang, suggesting no bill would be honoured by the Admiralty if it had only Bligh's signature.

Purcell and Fryer were put onto separate Dutch ships that would also be sailing on to Batavia. On 22 September the ships called at Samarang on the north coast of Java and there Fryer apologised properly and was released. Purcell remained in irons until they reached Batavia. Here, Bligh became feverish. His condition deteriorated, so he obtained an explanatory medical certificate and on 16 October 1789 sailed with his servants Samuel and Smith on the Dutch East Indiaman, *Vlydte*, leaving the rest of the men in Fryer's charge.

By now the cook Thomas Hall had died and before the rest of the group departed Master's Mate Elphinstone and Quartermaster Linkletter also perished, both possibly of malaria. The butcher Robert Lamb died during his passage home but the fate of Acting-Surgeon Ledward is not known.

Of the nineteen men Fletcher Christian turned off *Bounty*, twelve returned to England. The first was Bligh, who landed on the Isle of Wight on 14 March 1790 and days later arrived in London with his astonishing news.

The only first-hand account we have of a family member's reaction comes from Charles Christian, Fletcher's mutinous surgeon brother. By 1790 he was in Hull and wrote:

I was struck with horror and weighed down with a Sorrow to so extreme a pitch that I became stupified. It was hard to bear, but I thank God, strength was given to me equal to the burden.

I knew that this unfortunate occurrence, following so close on the heels of my late eventful and disastrous voyage [in Middlesex], would occasion the lies which had been spread abroad in consequence to assume the aspect of Truth. I have in bed perspired with agony of mind till I thought my nostrils were impressed with a smell of Death such was the peculiar sensation I experienced.

Later, Charles wrote to Dr Betham, William Bligh's father-in-law and:

> ... firmly prophecied that it would be found that there had
> been some Cause not then known that had driven Fletcher to
> this desperate step. I was enabled to form the just presage from
> what I had so recently observed possible to occur on Board
> of Ship where Strife and Discord prevailed. I told Betham
> that my feelings were so harrowed up with this unlooked for
> and unhappy intelligence that I would have him consider that
> instead of Ink, it was my Heart's Blood I wrote with.

There was similarly melodramatic, but more serious, reaction from
brother Humphrey. According to genealogical notes written in the
nineteenth-century transcript of the diary of the brothers' first cousin
Jane Christian Blamire, Humphrey, 'then at a station on the Barbary
coast of North Africa, being in very bad health, died shortly after
reading the account of the mutiny'.

There is no recorded contemporary comment from brother Edward,
who had been admitted to Gray's Inn in 1782, and called to the Bar
in 1786. In 1788, aged 30, he was named Downing Professor of the
Laws of England in Cambridge although the college was not to be
founded until 1800. After his noted successful 1791 prosecution of the
Earl of Lonsdale on behalf of William and Dorothy Wordsworth for
a substantial debt, he devoted much time to explaining his brother
Fletcher, as we will see.

It is incorrect to say that Fletcher's first cousin John Christian
XVII changed his name to John Christian Curwen because of the
mutiny. Ten days before Bligh landed, the *Cumberland Pacquet* for
3 March 1790 records:

> Mr Christian of Workington will shortly take the name of
> Curwen. His Majesty's Royal Licence and permission respecting
> same will probably be announced in the next Monday list.

John had been preparing for the change for some time and had formalised the Christian coat of arms in 1788; both the Christians and the Curwens had a unicorn crest and henceforth the Christian one was collared. John Christian Curwen was too well known as a politician to hide behind a name change and anyway always retained Christian as part of his surname. He was simply getting things straight between his two ancient families, the Christians and the Curwens; his wife Isabella was the last Curwen, one of the ten oldest families in England, and the change was to honour her by keeping the surname alive. John had a Christian heir from an earlier marriage.

The press had a heyday and soon most people knew about the mutiny and the boat voyage. Bligh had only adulation and sympathy.

Democracy at Sea

Fletcher Christian might not first have considered mutiny as a solution to his anguish, but he had certainly thought about what he would do if he were in charge of *Bounty*. To do so is typical of every second-in-command anywhere on land or sea. Many of his early actions as the new commander of *Bounty* show detailed forethought based on the Age of Enlightenment precepts he heard in London. When Fletcher had sailed in December 1787, the Americans had revolted and there was much revolutionary talk of France's future.

Avoiding comparison with Bligh's autocracy, he encouraged meetings of the men to decide broad issues and introduced voting to ensure that the basis for every decision was universally understood. This is extraordinary in every way. Technically a Royal Navy ship, *Bounty* was the first English ship totally free in the South Pacific and was being run democratically. It worked.

When even hard-line mutineers were given the choice, they demonstrated they understood the dangers of a sailing ship in uncharted waters and voted for the best man for the job, not the most popular. Hence, non-mutineer George Stewart was chosen as second-in-command; even though unpopular on board because of his severity, he was acknowledged as particularly efficient.

The twenty-five men aboard were certainly able, a community of craftsmen and tradesmen like no other. Most were tattooed, most were scarred. If their faces were not deeply pitted by smallpox, like Adams, Burkitt, McIntosh and Norman, they had wounds of old fights, of abscesses and accidents. They used Tahitian words and phrases, shouting *mamoo* rather than telling someone to shut up and calling women *vahine*.

Henry Hillbrant was Hanoverian and spoke little English and that with a heavy accent. Heywood had a broad Manx accent, Martin was American, John Williams was from Guernsey and spoke French as easily as accented English. Edward Young had played an active but quiet part in the mutiny, standing armed with a sword behind Christian and his prisoner. Always said to be one of the first to follow Christian, he was dark complexioned, probably because he had some West Indian blood, had lost most of his front teeth and those that remained were rotten. His slurred speech was flavoured with the argot of the West Indies. Heywood was described by Bligh as fair-skinned and well-proportioned although still growing. Stewart was bottle-shouldered and probably had an Orkney burr.

There is a shouty claim that Christian and his activists were not mutineers but pirates, even saying there was never a mutiny. Of course there was a mutiny. What then followed was not piracy because the dictionary definition is the taking of *another's* ship. To be fair, the misuse of 'pirates' and 'piracy' began early, whatever the true meaning. When Bligh wrote on 7 October 1790 to explain he no longer had the Kendall chronometer, he said 'it had been left in the said ship when pirated from my command'. Allowing that Christian had taken the king's ship, then I suppose this makes him and those who followed him pirates of a sort. In the late eighteenth century it seems to have been exciting and romantic to call them such, as was seen in the publications and theatrical productions based on the mutiny after the news got to London. Pirates and piracy are still seductive to some, even when there are none about.

Christian's use of democracy on board has been connected by the same voices with the voting used by pirates of Jamaica's Port Royal, because of his visits to the Caribbean. The profound fault with this stance is there were no pirates when Fletcher was there because piracy was an occupation of the seventeenth century. Their Port Royal stronghold at the mouth of Kingston Harbour was destroyed by earthquake on 7 June 1692 almost a century earlier. To demean Fletcher Christian in the twenty-first century by saying there was no mutiny and that he and his shipmates were merely wicked pirates is wearisome, not to say ill-educated.

Sources for the post-mutiny episodes have generally been accounts written by Adams on Pitcairn and by Peter Heywood and Morrison on their return to England. Other contemporary records include Captain Edwards' abstracts from journals kept on a daily basis by both Peter Heywood and George Stewart, which were lost with the foundering of HMS *Pandora*.

Two days after the mutiny, Fletcher Christian ordered the royals, the smallest sails used at the very top of masts, cut up so they could be made into uniforms for all hands. They were likely to be linen, which softens with age and use, so should have been comfortable to wear. With a nicety that reflected previous thought, he gave his navy-blue woollen officer's jacket so it could be cut into strips to use as edging, a design entirely new and creative. At that time only naval officers wore uniforms and these were dark blue with wide, white facings turned back over the chest. Seamen wore simple working clothes, known as slops. Morrison tells us Christian observed:

> ... that nothing had more effect on the mind of the Indians than a uniformity of Dress, which by the by had its effect among Europeans as it always betokens discipline especially on board British men-of-war.

The second part of the statement is Morrison's private observation, but it is acute and relevant. Christian's uniforms would bind his crew of mutineers and loyalists together both as equals on board and in the eyes of those encountered. It was an extraordinary idea on a Royal Navy ship, where difference had always been thought essential and is a further sharp example of Fletcher's revolutionary ideals.

As *Bounty* sailed east in the pleasant days of the early dry season, this newly free assortment of tanned and tattooed sailors sewing jackets under the probable supervision of tailor William Muspratt provides one of the few amusing pictures of the entire saga. Democratic and universally uniformed, *Bounty* was unlike any British ship that had ever sailed, naval or otherwise. On 1 May all but a few of the breadfruit plants were thrown overboard. On the 6th and 7th, the men divided 'the pleasing apparel of the People and Officers' who had preceded the breadfruit overboard. The curios, woven mats and tapa cloth were also divided, and Morrison says that those of Christian's party always got the biggest and best. The loot, there is no other name, was stored in the emptied greenhouse.

Fletcher Christian moved into Bligh's small book-lined cabin. He was 24 and there was absolutely no precedent for what he had done or for what he should do next. If any of the men had supported the mutiny so they could return to Tahiti, their seizure of the ship meant it was forever forbidden them. Fletcher Christian had to tell men who had broken the law that they had done so in vain. Fletcher didn't shrink from the inevitable and made his first unilateral decision. *Bounty* was to sail to Tubuai, 350 miles/565 kms south of Tahiti.

The announcement polarised some of the non-mutineers, who talked of getting rid 'of those we did not like by putting them on shore and that in all probability our design might be favoured by an extra allowance of grog'. If it were so easy, it is astonishing no attempt was made to do it. One author dismissively wrote that now Christian 'was incapable of keeping control of his men, just as he could not control his passions', citing the plot as evidence but totally misunderstands what it was like to be free men on a ship taken by mutiny, when everyone had been given permission to suspect others and plan new freedoms for themselves. To the plotters' 'unspeakable surprise', the whispers were discovered by Christian, who began carrying Bligh's pistol in his pocket at all times and ordered his followers to arm themselves. Churchill slept on the arms chest and, Biblically, whenever two or more of the plotters were gathered together, they were joined by one of Christian's men. The situation was never serious, and its discovery was a relief. Christian now knew who might be a threat.

Of course there was dissension and Christian's radical power-sharing was difficult for some to accept. Yet he did establish the first English colony of free men in the South Pacific, just a year after the first fleet of prisoner ships arrived in Sydney, so far west and on the Tasman Sea. When Tubuai was abandoned, he was alive and had maintained mastery over more than fifty Europeans and Polynesians as well as retaining ownership of *Bounty*, clear proof of the power and endurance of his command.

On 24 May *Bounty* made Tubuai and the next day prepared to move into the lagoon. Knowing nothing of the customs and conditions on shore, Fletcher Christian hove to outside the reef and ordered the small cutter to be launched so that George Stewart might locate an opening. The Tubuaians paddled across the lagoon to attack the cutter. Their threatening canoes were 30 to 40 feet/9 to 12 metres long, with a high prow carved into an animal's head and with a tall scroll at the stern. Painted red and decorated with pitch and with glittering fish scales and shells, each carried up to 20 warriors with long spears of dark wood.

After mobbing the cutter, some warriors boarded it, thus giving the Europeans a strange safety because at close range the islanders' 18 foot/5.5 metre spears were useless. The cutter's men had only a brace of pistols, one of which did not work. In the melee, one of the boat's crew was wounded and the working pistol misfired but wounded a Tubuaian. The cowed boarding party tumbled back into their canoes.

Undeterred, *Bounty* was carefully worked further into the lagoon, to anchor in 16 fathoms/30 metres, a quarter of a mile/400 metres off the unbroken ribbon of white sand that circumscribes most of the island. Tubuaians assembled from every district, crowding the beach and flocking about the ship in their canoes, wailing and hooting with great conch shells. The months in Tahiti had made Fletcher Christian and several of the ship's complement passably fluent in Tahitian and Tubuaian was close enough for the two parties to understand one another, as can Polynesians from anywhere in the vast triangle of Hawaii, Easter Island and New Zealand.

The islanders would not come on board but by their dress Fletcher knew battle was on their minds. Their fighting costumes were largely red and white and clearly took some time to don. First, pieces of red-dyed bark cloth or of woven coconut fibre were wound around the body and held in place at the waist with a plaited sash with coconut fibre tassels. The shoulders were bare and unencumbered and the folds in the cloth were used to carry stone projectiles, just as theatre tickets were once tucked into cummerbunds. Across the chest was suspended a pectoral, sometimes of pearl shell, always highly decorated. On his head each man wore a helmet of woven and matted coconut fibre shaped like a beehive. Some were covered with white cloth and crowned with black man-of-war bird feathers. Those could ward off a cutlass swipe but those with a pearl shell and a semi-circle of wild duck wings were more vulnerable.

Next morning, there were many more canoes on the white sands. At last, an old man, probably a chief, came aboard. 'He appear'd to view everything with astonishment and appear'd frightened at the Hogs, Goats, Dogs etc, starting back as any of them turned to him.' Fletcher discovered this was because Tubuai had no mammals other than rats.

Gifts were made to the man, who carefully and too obviously counted those aboard. He promised to return and in the meantime the ship's arms were got to hand, to counteract the islanders' armoury. Many carried a frightening weapon about 10 feet/3 metres long, worked into a club at one end, flattened and pointed at the other. A warrior clasped it with his arms spread and swung it, alternately clubbing and stabbing.

At noon on 27 May the canoes were launched. Among them was an unusual double canoe, carrying women decorated with flowers and pearl shells. They were young and handsome, with black hair that hung to their waists in waving ringlets, not something seen on Tahiti. The girls stood and beat time while one of them, seemingly a chief's daughter, sang a siren's song. Christian had ordered all hands to change into the new uniforms and mounted a guard spaced evenly around *Bounty*. The eighteen women and five of the men who had paddled them came on board so readily that his suspicions were further aroused. Sure enough, about 50 canoes containing perhaps 1,000 men had glided up to the other side of the ship and began blowing conch horns. The defensive precautions Christian had taken were heeded and the war party chose not to board, even though the odds were massively in their favour.

The men who accompanied the women on board were pests, stealing anything they could. The glass of the compass was broken. One man stole the compass card but was noticed by Fletcher Christian and in the struggle for its return it was torn. The Tubuaian disliked being thwarted and a hand–to–hand scuffle followed. Christian's well-documented strength got the best of the thief, who was sent smartly off to his canoe with several stripes from a rope end and then the women and remaining canoeists quickly followed. Once in their canoes, they brought out and brandished their hidden weapons.

Fletcher Christian noticed one of the buoys that marked an anchor being cut away. He fired a musket at the offender and ordered the firing of a cannon that had been primed and loaded with grape shot. Grapeshot was a canvas bag filled with grape–sized metal balls, that begin to spread as soon as fired and that also included a fuse and explosive designed to detonate when it hit its ultimate target. Christian pressed his advantage further. *Bounty*'s two boats were quickly manned with armed men and pulled to shore in pursuit. The boats were pelted with stones until muskets were fired. In a few moments, the beach was deserted.

Although they had seen only two men fall, eleven men and women had been killed by *Bounty*'s men, remarkably few considering grapeshot had been fired into open canoes at very close quarters. Was Fletcher Christian being bad tempered or undisciplined in firing at the Tubuaians? With so few men aboard, *Bounty* was extremely vulnerable, and survival was more important than relationships with unfriendly people.

In 1789 there were no published guidelines for Fletcher Christian about making initial contacts with Pacific islanders. When Tubuaians threatened the ship and damaged its equipment, *Bounty* had to assert itself. Even Captain Samuel Wallis, first European discoverer of Tahiti, had initially to defend himself with firearms. The ship agreed to call their anchorage Bloody Bay.

Bounty's two small boats sailed around the eastern end of the island showing a Union Jack and a white flag. Fletcher landed in several places and pushed through the thick fringe of undergrowth and trees to find houses and to leave gifts of hatchets but he saw no one. Unbeknown to him, many of the 3,000 islanders had come to the uncultivated swamp behind Bloody Bay. They watched *Bounty* there for several days and 'for want of their usual bedding they caught Colds, Agues, and Sore Eyes, Running at the Noses' which was interpreted as some sort of punishment from the men on the ship.

His determination was so fixed that he 'dream't of nothing but Settling on Toobouai', persuading himself that it could be induced to friendship, either by persuasion or force. *Bounty* weighed anchor and headed for the warmer welcome of Tahiti to gather supplies and, inevitably, women.

Fort George, Tubuai

Teina and Itia welcomed Titreano and *Bounty* back with such pleasure that it dulled their ordinary sense of curiosity. Christian fibbed that they had met Captain Cook, about whom Bligh had earlier lied, saying he was still alive. Cook was said to be furnishing a new settlement on the island of Aitutaki and had taken Bligh and his breadfruit to help. Now with *ra'atira Titreano* in command, *Bounty* had been sent back for supplies.

During two weeks in Matavai Bay, Christian kept an armed guard at all times and his crew was forbidden to tell the truth on pain of death. *Bounty* was loaded with 312 pigs, 38 goats, 9 chickens and the bull and cow left by Cook, which had either never mated or had done so to no effect. Dogs and cats were adopted and many of the empty pots in the great cabin were planted with flowers and tubers.

This time *Bounty* sailed with nine women. Adams had Teehuteatua-onoa, known as Jenny, McIntosh a woman he called Mary, and Fletcher Christian now had Mauatua, whom he renamed Isabella, presumably after the rich cousin he is thought to have wanted to marry; this is the first time she is mentioned in any account. Also on board were eight extra men and ten 'boys', probably energetic teenagers keen on adventure.

The voyage back to Tubuai held several surprises and, after much discomfort from bad weather, the bull died and was heaved overboard. Stowaways were discovered, including young chief Hitihiti from Bora Bora, who had once been especially friendly with Bligh and previously sailed as far as New Zealand with James Cook. Fletcher Christian was now responsible for more than fifty lives, at sea and ashore, some of whom were willing, some of whom were not.

By 26 June *Bounty* was once more anchored at Tubuai and landed the cow and 200 of the pigs. The locals were far more terrified of these than they had been of the firearms, the more so because, unlike Tahiti, their houses and gardens were not fenced. The loose animals ran uprooting, guzzling and even dining on the low hanging thatched roofs of their homes. The other livestock were landed on the small keys within the lagoon.

The mutineers of the party probably thought freedom was now upon theirs. On 5 July trouble began and on the 6th two were put into irons by a majority vote. Drunkenness, fighting and threatening of each other's lives meant that by 7 July matters were so bad that after a truce, Fletcher Christian and Churchill drew up Articles that specified mutual forgiveness of past grievances, which every man was obliged to sign. Only Matthew Thompson refused.

At first glance, the island of Tubuai did seem to offer Fletcher Christian the possibility of a settled future. It would indeed have been wonderful if a man so young, so beset by the threats of both mutineers and Bligh loyalists, perhaps also with pangs of conscience, was able to establish a settlement that satisfied everyone.

The natural glories of Tubuai by day were scarcely matched by its nocturnal features. None has ever described the misery better than Morrison:

> And when they go to sleep they beat the musquettoes out and make a fire at each Door to keep them out as they are very troublesome and together with Fleas and lice keep them employed till sleep gets the better of them and the Rats run over them all night in droves, but as we left several cats it is possible they may reduce their numbers.'

Tubuaians depilated but did not bathe regularly and did not tattoo. Although so different in comfort, hygiene and custom from Tahiti,

Tubuai was similar in the way it was ruled with no over-all chief but divided into three clandoms. That which included Bloody Bay, which is almost on the dividing line between east and west, was the biggest, making most of the western land. The chief was Tamatoa and he made great demonstrations of friendship.

Fletcher and Tamatoa went to fix on the site for a settlement but finding none suitable in Tamatoa's district, Fletcher Christian then went to the north-eastern clandom, smaller and poorer, and ruled by Taaroa.

Tamatoa was furious. Unable to get Fletcher Christian to change his mind, he and Tinarau, chief of the south-eastern district, joined forces and prohibited the people in their districts, the majority of the population, from going to the ship or having anything to do with the visitors.

The site Fletcher had chosen for his settlement was some miles east of the reef opening and Bloody Bay and the ship was laboriously kedged through shallow waters and over treacherous coral. By 10 July *Bounty* was anchored only 100 yards/90 metres from the shore. Fletcher then chose the exact site for his fort, probably having purchased it with red feathers.

Critics claim Fletcher Christian chose this site through ineptitude, misunderstanding the political balance and internecine tension on the island but none had bothered to go there. When I visited Fort George's site in 1980, I discovered he had chosen wisely, because there is an independent spring in the middle of the site. With no exposed contributing stream, the settlement's well of fresh water could not be interrupted or contaminated by others. It was an apt and practical choice.

When Christian returned aboard, he found Sumner and Quintal had gone ashore without permission and it was not until next morning that they returned. When they were called to explain their absence, they said, 'the ship is moored and we are now our own Masters'. Christian clapped the pistol he carried to the head of one, saying 'I'll let you know who is Master', and they were both put into leg irons. When they were brought up next morning the resoluteness of Christian's behaviour had convinced them he was 'not to be played with'. They begged pardon and promised to behave better. Fletcher hoped to prevent further such frustration by giving leave for two hands to sleep on shore each night. As many as pleased could go ashore on Sunday, as long as the animals on the keys were checked.

The forge was set up and armourer Coleman made iron rammers for the muskets and then altered axes for felling trees. Then Coleman and McCoy made spades, hoes and mattocks. Botanist William Brown, assisted by a Tahitian, cleared ground to plant yams. Hillbrant stayed on board as appointed cook, Byrne and Ellison with some of the Tahitian men cared for the boats but the majority were to build the fort. On shore, arms were to be carried but left under the care of a sentinel while ground was being cleared. To protect the ship from water, one of the cutters was anchored near the beach, one stayed close to *Bounty*.

The ground for the fortress was measured, a clod was turned as symbolic of possession, a Union Jack was hoisted on a makeshift flagpole and the place named Fort George for, although Fletcher had mutinied against Bligh, he remained a patriot, loyal to his king. Because the place was overrun with rats, several cats were brought on shore and let loose and then an extra allowance of grog was given and drunk.

Once the ground had been cleared, the fortress was laid out. This was not a Wild West fort of split timber as some illustrations have shown, although there might have been a palisade planned atop the earth walls. It was to be made of rammed earth and monumental in concept. The soil excavated to form a moat was to make the walls. The front was only about 50 yards/45 metres from the beach and Morrison says that overall it was to have been 100 yards/about 90 metres square, measured outside the surrounding ditch.

The ditch that became a moat was to be 18 feet/5.5 metres wide, enough to ensure it was not easily crossed, wet or dry. The walls were to be a monumental 20 feet/6 metres high, measured from the bottom of the ditch, 18 feet/5.5 metres wide at the base and 12 feet/3.5 metres wide at the top.

The exact height the walls reached has never been established but in 1902 they were 6 feet 7 inches/2 metres high and the ditch about the same depth, about two-thirds of the original target. The ditch seems never to have been more than 8 feet/2.4 metres wide.

Defence consisted of a drawbridge on the north side facing the beach, with a cannon on each corner and two swivel guns on each side, with two of the latter always in reserve for reinforcement. Each direction was thus protected by at least two cannons and four swivel guns.

Fort George was the most splendid vision imaginable for a romantically inclined adventurer brought up playing in the ancient fortifications of Moorland Close and Fletcher was no idle spectator. 'He always took a part in the most laborious part of the Work' and, to encourage his men to keep up with him amid the heat, rats and insects, he allowed an extra half-pint of porter, a strong, dark bitter beer, twice a day.

Early in August a party went ashore to take women by force and meeting with expected opposition shot a Tubuaian and wounded another with a bayonet. Fletcher's strict rationing of time ashore must have been relaxed for Morrison says:

> We remained quiet some days, but as the people were fond of
> sleeping ashore, some of them were decoyed by the Weomen
> into Tinnarow's district, where they were strippd.

This was vexatious and when Adams was imprisoned in Chief Tinarau's house, Fletcher was obliged to assert authority on behalf of his men. Once Adams was released and after trying to placate Tinarau, the chief's revered ancestor images were removed and his house was burned.

By September, work on the fort had slowed but the gate posts were fixed and three-quarters of the walls completed. Tinarau wanted his ancestors returned and on 2 September crossed the island with an entourage carrying baskets of food and befuddling *kava* as peace offerings. This was a Trojan Horse plan to get inside the fort and then attack with concealed weapons but Christian had discovered it. Tinarau swept away in a passion as at a pre-arranged signal cannons were fired onto the shore.

Morrison, Stewart and Heywood secretly entertained the idea of escaping back to Tahiti in the ship's large cutter, but Fletcher had ordered that the boats were not to be repaired until all were settled safely ashore. The trio thought of risking the voyage with the boat as it was. Morrison wrote:

> Tho the passage was short and it might perhaps be made with safety in 5 or 6 days, yet had we the Chance to Meet with bad weather our Crazey boat would certainly have made us a coffin . . .

The situation was soon to change and they were unable to make the attempt.

The Tubuaians came to believe the fort's ditch was to be a mass grave for them. Jenny says there was also a conspiracy between Tubuaians and one of the Tahitians to do the reverse, that is to murder all the Europeans and divide their goods.

The lack of women had never been solved. Tubuaian women would not join *Bounty's* men at the fort, although they were happy to sleep with them at their own houses, which was not thought good enough. One plan suggested the Europeans made slaves of the Tahitian women, men and boys, who would be distributed by casting lots. Another wanted Fletcher to lead a party to capture women by force. Fletcher would have none of these strategies, even though he was told those disaffected would do no more work until each man had a wife. Fletcher's objective was to persuade rather than to force the Tubuaians, which is hardly the decision of a man 'who could not control his passions or men'. The unrest was so general that work did stop and three days were spent debating. Exercising their tongues was as thirst-making as labouring with their bodies and the men demanded more grog but Fletcher refused what he considered yet another absurd demand, so they broke the lock of the spirit room on the ship and took it by force. He called yet another meeting of all hands to gather opinions.

After two days of talking, a proposal to move back to Tahiti where they might get women without force was accepted on a show of hands. Fletcher had lost Fort George.

Wanting never to be captured and taken home to shame his family further, he asked for *Bounty* in a speech that resounds with black despair:

> I'm resigned to sailing where the wind takes me. Somewhere, anywhere . . . but it will be to oblivion. Then one day, if it pleases God, you will forget me and what I have brought you to.

The best description of Fletcher Christian at the time was written by Bligh in the open boat. He was:

> . . . aged 24 years, 5 feet 9 inches/1.75 metres high, blackish, or very dark brown complexion. Dark brown hair, strong made; a star tatowed on his left breast tatowed on his backside; his knees stand a little out, and he may be called rather bow legged. He is subject to violent perspirations, and particularly in his hands, so that he soils any thing he handles.

His darkish complexion was probably exaggerated by tanning from months under the South Pacific sun but now Fletcher Christian would never again pale in English weather.

It took less than a minute for every man aboard to agree to Fletcher's request for the ship. He was supervising the daytime addition of water and lime juice to the high-proof Navy-issue rum when Matthew Quintal stepped forward, saying that he would be proud to sail with

Fletcher. Cornish Quintal, barely as tall as Fletcher's shoulder, was 21 and 'very much tatowed on the backside and several other places'. The first man Bligh flogged for insolence and mutinous behaviour, he too opted for a future with no boundaries except to wander the South Seas, forever hoping to avoid retribution.

William McCoy said he would sail wherever his mate Quintal went. McCoy was 25 and only slightly taller than Quintal. Fair-skinned with light brown hair and strongly built, he had a scar where he had survived a stab in his belly and another under his chin and 'had tatows in different parts'.

Then Isaac Martin volunteered, by now Jenny's new lover. Martin was taller than Fletcher by 2 inches/5 cms and another victim of Bligh's contradictory orders. He took twenty-four lashes for striking a Tahitian thief while he wrestled back things stolen from *Bounty*. One would expect him to have been rewarded for saving the ship's property, so Bligh's punishment can only be explained as inconsistency and muddled thinking. Sallow skinned, brown haired and raw boned, he too had a Garter star on his left breast.

Next was William Brown, the assistant botanist. A little shorter than Fletcher and from Leicester, he had been a career naval officer, working up to be an Acting-Lieutenant and a second-in-command but had then elected to become a botanist. He once refused to join the daily dancing on *Bounty* but wasn't flogged and merely had his daily grog ration stopped. He was tattooed and had a remarkable scar that contracted his eyelid and ran right down to his throat, the result of scrofula.

John Mills added himself. Slightly taller than Fletcher, the Gunner's Mate was a Scot from Aberdeen and at 40 was one of the oldest aboard. He went with Fletcher to arrest Bligh, who described him as strong made and raw boned. He was a bully, the self-deluding sort who excused sadistic taunting or physical abuse as 'only having a bit of a laugh'.

Then John Adams came forward. He was 22 and stood only as tall as Quintal and was described by Bligh as strong made, with a brown complexion, brown hair and a face pitted by smallpox. Widely tattooed, he had a scarred right foot, a feature that Fletcher Christian is supposed to have copied to hide his identity in Richard Bean's 2014 play *Pitcairn*, amidst other extraordinary notions that cannot be defended as dramatic license; in the play Tubuai is called Tubai, and Tahiti's *manahune* become *manahane*. Adams stood beside Fletcher from the earliest moments of the mutiny, was first to be tattooed and first to have a permanent Tahitian mistress and a *taio*.

Fletcher then accepted the offer of Williams, the French-speaking native of Guernsey aged 25 and another active mutineer. Black haired, slender and tattooed, he was as short as Quintal, Adams and McCoy. Williams received six lashes in False Bay, South Africa, when Bligh found fault with the way he heaved the lead, by which the ship knew how much water was beneath her hull.

Edward 'Ned' Young was the eighth to join Fletcher. Born on St Kitts in the West Indies, he agreed he was the worst looking man in the ship. His lilting, vowel-caressing Caribbean accent was made more indistinct by a mouth of teeth that were entirely rotten or well on their way, the result he explained of being brought up on a sugar island. 'You'll be wanting at least one other officer, Mr Christian,' Ned said. Somewhere Ned had black blood, but from whom he had never made clear. He was educated and claimed to be well-connected but wanted to get away from the Royal Navy and the endless taunts of 'nigger'.

'No. No you can't, Ned,' Fletcher protested. 'What's the future in that for you?'

'The future for me? Something better than the prospect of being strung from a yardarm on the other side of the world. I wasn't a mutineer but I did nothing to stop you. Bligh is bound to have it in for me.' Then Ned said something likely to encourage Fletcher more than anything else he had heard. 'We will never leave you, Mr Christian, go where you will.'

The details were quickly settled. Fletcher Christian was to have the ship in seagoing condition and the sixteen who elected for Tahiti

were to be given supplies including arms and a share of everything on
the ship. Among those who wanted to settle on Tahiti were Churchill
and Thompson. They were probably the most destructive of the Fort
George community and, from their later behaviour on Tahiti, Christian
was well rid of them.

A party including Hitihiti was sent to collect stock and to find the
cow but was ambushed, beaten and plundered. Hitihiti's chiefly status
was insulted and the islanders sent a message with the bruised men that
they would treat Christian the same way. Fletcher was not intimidated.
Twenty men were armed and with nine Tahitian men and four of the
boys, one of whom always carried the Union Jack, they marched off to
retrieve their roaming stock and to chastise the offenders.

They were confronted by a war party of about 700 who fought with
stones, clubs and spears but with more fury than judgment, retiring
with great loss. Some animals were collected but with further ambush
being expected, Fletcher issued each European with 24 rounds of
ammunition and Hitihiti, being an excellent shot, was armed with a
musket. Once safely back at Fort George, they found Chief Taaroa
with his aged father and young brother, Taaroamiva, who had come
to explain that *Bounty*'s animals were the bone, and the flesh, of
contention. Tinarau was determined that the animals that roamed into
his territory were his property and he was arming more men to ensure
he kept them. On an island that had only rats as mammals, pigs had
become an important status symbol, as well as being something new
and delicious to eat.

Fletcher now needed to show leadership to his own party as well as
to block Tinarau. If he had upset anyone on the island it was Tamatoa
but this chief had kept his distance. He drew up his war-party into
ranks with one Tahitian between two of his men, arming the former
with clubs. In silence they marched south through the thick woods
towards Tinarau's district. When they reached a path with dense bush
on each side, Burkitt, thinking he heard something stir, stopped to
look and received a spear wound in his left side. The Tahitian beside

Burkitt levelled his attacker and took his spear. In seconds there was bedlam as Tubuaian warriors rushed in with 'great fury and orrid yells'. Christian's party quickly faced different defensive directions and fired several times but the Tubuaians continued attacking.

Bounty's men retreated safely to rising ground a short distance to their rear, by which time their Polynesian men were armed with captured spears. The Tubuaians attacked the hillock with redoubled energy, not the least perturbed by the growing number of their own dead. The retreat back to Fort George had to be continued, for thick bush above *Bounty's* men was excellent cover for the attacking Tubuaians. Several Tahitians were now wounded, and Christian had injured his hand on his bayonet.

They fell back through the bush to a taro ground 200 yards/180 metres away, keeping up a constant rear-guard fire. There they protected themselves behind irrigation banks, in a sort of trench warfare. The Tubuaians followed hotly and then halted to throw stones from the edge of the bush.

Fletcher saw that although the furious fighting seemed without order, the Tubuaians were organised into parties of twenty to twenty-eight men, each of which had a leader whose orders were followed. One of these rallied his men by venturing from the cover of the bush but even at that distance he was shot dead. Seeing that each man who came into the clear was killed or wounded, the Tubuaians retreated. Burkitt was growing faint so Skinner, whose musket had been disabled, helped him back to *Bounty*, while the rest waited to be attacked again. It was soon apparent that guns and Fletcher's leadership had beaten the local warriors, who outnumbered them by over ten to one and he was given three rousing cheers.

Burkitt had had the narrowest of escapes and healed in a short time. Morrison says the affair gave them a very mean opinion of their bayonets for although several men had fallen by them, the blades always broke off and remained in the body. The length of the Tubuaians' spears meant that bayonets were no use against them. If they had not had firearms, everyone in Fletcher's party would certainly have died.

On the 14th, the day after the bloody battle, the cow was slaughtered and proved excellent meat. For safety, everybody now lived on the ship and while they were feasting young Taaroamiva came aboard to tell them sixty Tubuaian men had been killed (fifty according to Heywood), including Tinarau's brother, as well as six women who had been supplying them with spears and stones; many more were wounded. Taaroamiva had been so loyal to Christian that he feared for his life and asked if he and two friends could join *Bounty*. Fletcher agreed and they were doubly pleased when told the ship was bound for Tahiti.

Bounty weighed anchor and made her way relatively easily to the opening, being lighter than before. When clear of the reef, they lay by and:

> ... filld Saltwater to keep her on her legs and at noon made sail, leaving Toobuai well Stockd with Hogs, Goats, Fowles, Dogs and Cats, the Former of which were increased to Four times the number we landed ...

Fletcher Christian's settlement had not failed because of lack of leadership, as he is so fatuously accused. Morrison, who was there, says the greatest enemy of Fort George was the determination of the priests of Tubuai that Fletcher Christian would never live on their island. Once the priests saw the Europeans were, as Morrison observes, 'Common Men and liable to accident like themselves' they could not bear to see 'such Superiority as the Europeans in general usurp over those who differ from themselves'. Because Fletcher and his party ignored and ridiculed their authority, the priests used every means to prevent the three chiefs making friends with them, believing that if the visitors remained their own power would be lessened, which Morrison adds 'in all probability would have been the case'.

If Fletcher Christian had not led so resolutely on Tubuai, the people who came with him aboard *Bounty* would have been slaughtered. Any who moaned about Christian's restrictions lived only because of them.

Fletcher Christian's plan succeeded in persuading a group of over fifty mutineers and non-mutineers, including Polynesian men, women and boys, to labour to build a moat and enormous earthen fortifications in tropical conditions, while pestered by rats, insects and Tubuaians. That seems a personal triumph through leadership by example and by fair decision making or democracy. Frustrated but not beaten, he had lost no men or women and still had the ship. What was missing was his future.

The remaining trade goods, arms and ammunition, alcohol, clothes and practical goods were divided on board and on the 22nd, *Bounty* drifted into the lagoon of Matavai Bay and those headed for shore were unloaded before nightfall.

Did Fletcher Christian go on shore in Matavai Bay that day? He is quoted as saying he could not face the chiefs to whom he had lied on his last visit. Heywood said Christian took him to one side on the black sands of Matavai, absolved him of any complicity in the mutiny and told him to give himself up to the ship that was bound to arrive in search of *Bounty*. Heywood said he was also entrusted with a message to pass on to Christian's family, relating circumstances that might extenuate, though they could not justify, the crime he had committed.

Heywood kept the meeting secret until well after his subsequent trial in 1792. It was only sensible to distance himself from Christian, who had been such a close friend that Bligh regarded Heywood as Fletcher's ally.

Oblivion

Early on the morning of 23 September 1789, two days before he would turn 25, Fletcher Christian cut a cable, leaving a second anchor at Tahiti. No one knows why he suddenly fled, but it has been said Mauatua discovered those who had been landed were planning to take the ship from him, now that they had arms and ammunition.

Bounty slipped through the reef, carrying Fletcher's eight companions, plus six other men, nineteen women and a baby girl. One woman immediately jumped overboard and swam for the reef. Late in the morning *Bounty* made the atoll of Tetiaroa, where some women jumped when they saw canoes coming that would rescue them.

Fletcher Christian possibly did mean to ignore any protest by the women aboard, but things changed, perhaps through a combination of the noise made by the 'much afflicted' women and because each of the white men had quickly found a willing companion. Fletcher turned *Bounty* to Moorea, where a canoe put out and six 'rather ancient' women were rescued by canoe. Any other of the women aboard could have left at Moorea, so it's clear none was kidnapped, not one was forced to leave Tahiti. Abandoning Tahiti was what the twelve remaining women most wanted. Fletcher Christian was not a kidnapper because there was no need. The women who remained aboard were spirited individuals who welcomed the opportunity to escape their oppressed lives in Tahiti.

The men who wrote history about men had never thought about Tahitian women as any different from Tahitian men and hadn't recognised that even their physical appearance had been changed to please men. Daughters permitted to live had their faces deformed by massage when new-borns, so they had flat noses that would create awful breathing problems. Their fingers were constantly rolled so they became extended and pointed. Sons had their foreheads flattened and their skulls tightly bound to make them elongated and pointed, so they looked bigger and fiercer in battle.

Facially deformed from birth, women were prevented by abortion or murder from normal motherhood, were imprisoned by daughters, risked that any warrior son might be sacrificed by priests, could be divorced at whim, were forbidden to eat or even touch most foods, were shared sexually by a husband's family and friends and prevented from taking part in religion although profoundly oppressed by it.

So, universally kidnapped? I don't think so. Grateful for the opportunity to be women on their own terms? I *do* think so.

If you were an eighteenth-century Tahitian woman, might you not see Fletcher Christian and *Bounty* as a way of escaping its vicious, male-dominated culture, especially to sail away with pale-skinned men who were first thought to be gods and who had metal and writing and who let you eat the same food as them and let you keep your babies?

Rather than being kidnapped, it seems more likely that Mauatua and Jenny, at least, actively encouraged Fletcher to sail suddenly and at first light, before either Europeans or Tahitians tried to take back *Bounty* and frustrated their chance of freedom. Anyway, why would women have to be kidnapped only from Tahiti? Whatever the men's destination, there were bound to be other islands from which women could be invited or inveigled.

When Fletcher Christian put *Bounty* about and sailed away from the turreted twins of Tahiti and Moorea, neither he nor the ship would see them again. The fates of *Bounty* and those aboard were unknown for almost twenty years.

The ship now had only one truly seaworthy small boat, many of the sails had been cut up or given away, booms and spars had been lost at Tubuai. Long months under the tropical sun, thinking the ship would be abandoned, meant her decks needed recaulking because the planks would have shrunk. In storms or a heavy sea, water would drip through the deck, creating mould and stink below, adding to the constant assault of the smell of the animals and of the filthy bilge waters. Ahead was to be no South Pacific cruise of comfort and ease; indeed, considering the voyage *Bounty* made, the inexperienced Ma'ohi men and women had must all have had to co-operate to manage a sailing ship like this or they would have perished. It was as well their ship had been designed to be crewed by only thirteen.

In his search for a home Fletcher Christian guided *Bounty* over nearly 8,000 miles /12,990 kms of Pacific waters, equivalent to sailing a third of the way around the globe. *Bounty's* crew was Edward Young, John Adams, William McCoy, Matthew Quintal, John Williams, Isaac Martin, John Mills and William Brown. Six Ma'ohi men were clearly on board willingly, too. The noble Tararo was from the sacred island of Raiatea and is said to be a relative of Mauatua. The lesser noble Tubuaian Titahiti (previously Taaroamiva), younger brother of Chief Taaroa, was on board by choice, as was his friend Oha. Niau was a younger cousin of Tararo but Tahitian, as were Teimua and Manarii.

The route Fletcher sailed *Bounty* was pieced together only in 1958 and even now is so little known that books still show *Bounty* somehow taking four months to sail south-east from Tahiti to Pitcairn, a distance of 1,200 miles/1930 kms. Professor H.E. Maude of the Australian National University, Canberra, spent some years on Pitcairn Island during the Second World War and helped to set up its philatelic service. Using his knowledge of Pacific history to locate and interpret new sources of material, much of it records of oral tradition, he finally pieced together the extraordinary journey of *Bounty*, corroborating previously misunderstood or ignored references made to islands and incidents by the Tahitian Jenny, when she told of Fletcher's search for a hiding place.

Remembering the conflicts of Tubuai and now that he had responsibilities for others, including Mauatua, Fletcher Christian had to find an island that was uninhabited, difficult of anchorage and well off the beaten track. The last is the simplest to achieve. The

Polynesian triangle shaped by New Zealand, Hawaii and Easter Island is 10 million square miles/25 million square kms, just slightly less than the continent of Africa and most of it was utterly unknown, even to those who lived there.

Fletcher Christian thought of sailing up to the Marquesas, hoping on the way he might find a suitable island that was close to Tahiti but realised this invited early discovery and instead allowed the prevailing westerly winds to sail *Bounty* towards the Tongan archipelago, where he had mutinied five months before.

On board both Europeans and Polynesians had much to learn of each other's customs, because each South Pacific island had different customs and *taboos*. Ten of the women were Tahitian, one was from Tubuai and one from Huahine. The six men were from Tahiti, Tubuai, Raiatea and Huahine. The Ma'ohi men probably had greater problems with the liberation of taboos on what fish and meat women could eat but the difference in personal hygiene must have very difficult for all to bear. Where were the running rivers to bathe in daily and to flush away their waste? Rather than scented breezes they had to endure the stink of *Bounty's* bilge; being downwind of any sailing ship meant it might be detected before it was in view.

Professor Maude deduced that *Bounty* passed through the Cook Islands. Several accounts of floating islands with rivers and taro swamps had been collected in 1814 and 1823 and led Maude to the conclusion that Fletcher Christian was the European discoverer of Rarotonga. *Bounty* introduced the orange to the island and the export of that fruit's juice became a twentieth-century mainstay of its economy. There was bartering on Rarotonga and *Bounty* sailed on to an island Jenny calls Purutea, which seems to be what is now Mangaia. Jenny says a canoe came from the island bringing a pig and some coconuts. One of the canoeists came aboard and was delighted by the pearl-shell buttons on Fletcher Christian's jacket. Christian gave the jacket to the man, who then stood on the gunwale to show it to his friends, when one of the mutineers shot him for no reason and he fell into the sea. With loud lamentations the body was put into the canoe and the islanders who came bearing gifts paddled back to shore with only a dead companion as thanks. Christian was indignant but Jenny said, 'He could do nothing more, having lost all authority, than reprimand the murderer severely'.

The context in which this statement was made and by whom must be very carefully considered. Jenny gave her interviews around 1818 and whatever her understanding of Europeans was later in her life, it cannot have been very great in 1789. To a Tahitian woman, authority meant autocracy and as Fletcher Christian did not flog the miscreant or put him in irons the way he might have done even on Tubuai, he would undoubtedly appear to have lost authority in her eyes.

From a European view it might be considered differently. What should Fletcher have done? Killed the murderer? Locked him up? There were not enough capable people on board for him to have done either and I think to have done so would have been dangerous. Considering they were less than half way through their voyage and were anyway quite free of Royal Navy or any other regulations, Fletcher was running the ship in a sensible pragmatic way, for the greater good. Few men could have done better. The other mutineers would know this. Neither Jenny nor anyone else who was on board ever supplied other examples of lost authority. Fletcher was commanding in a way Tahitian Jenny did not understand.

With superior navigational skills supported by having one of the world's first chronometers on board and with experience as a Master's Mate that had trained him in best ship-management practice, as well as his professed delight in doing every task on a ship, no-one else was remotely as capable of sailing *Bounty* safely. He also had the traditional navigational skills of the Polynesians aboard, who could read the waves and winds and birds seen in a way Europeans could not.

Fletcher sailed *Bounty* on to Tongatabu, the main island of the Friendly Islands and of today's Kingdom of Tonga. Jenny said they stayed two days, then continued further westwards until they were more westerly than Tofua and collected birds' eggs on Vatoa or Ono-i-Lau, in the Lau Group in the south of the Fijian islands, where the inhabitants were thought to be cannibals.

It was two months since they had left Tahiti and they had been at sea almost all the time. The ship, although protected from worm by its expensive copper sheathing, would be deteriorating further. The animals and plants on board needed constant water and feed and, without the meticulous hygiene and care of Bligh, the ship was more noisome and unhealthy than ever. After so long at sea without the inhibitions of dress required by their ex-captain, the Europeans had probably already adopted the free and comfortable Tahitian *pareu* or loin cloth or, like many modern sailors on the Pacific, wore nothing at all.

Fletcher Christian's searches in the books left in Bligh's cabin at last suggested a solution, somewhere called Pitcairn's Island, over 3,000 miles/4,900 kms east as a bird flies. Choosing Pitcairn and then convincing twenty-seven companions to accompany him there required enormous courage by Fletcher Christian and tremendous faith in Christian by the others, once again dismissing ill-informed claims he was not firmly in command. Pitcairn meant well over a month more at sea and there would be no respite because they would not encounter land.

It took even longer and *Bounty* probably sailed closer to another 4,000 miles/6,400 kms. For two exhausting and dispiriting months *Bounty* tacked into the chill teeth of the south-east trades. It's not surprising some of the dispirited party 'therefore thought of returning to Tahiti'. They were cold and bored and even the wines of Tenerife couldn't temper the fatigue and the monotony. There was no escape from the whine of the wind in the rigging, none from the wretched complaints of the spent timbers on the slow rhythm of the South Pacific. Neither could there be respite from duty, no refreshing uninterrupted sleep. Christian could never relax his vigilance. Sighting the sails of a faster ship, and most were faster than his ex-coastal trader, could signal the end of *Bounty*'s voyage.

Bounty headed deep into the cold southern reaches until she was far south-east of Pitcairn and could then turn north-west and up to the warmer waters in which Pitcairn was promised. Days after the dawning of the new year of 1790 there was sudden hope born of unexpected disappointment. When Fletcher Christian sailed *Bounty* to the spot where Pitcairn was promised to be, he found nothing but more water, further horizons of anguish and unkept promises to those on board. To Fletcher this was the most encouraging event for months.

The 1767 description he had read of Pitcairn by Carteret, whose 15-year-old crew member Robert Pitcairn had been first to spot it, made the island sound perfect for Fletcher's needs. Isolated by unimaginable stretches of water, Pitcairn's smallness makes it even more difficult to find or stumble across than most islands. It has no protective lagoon, so is pounded by violent unhindered surf, which makes landing treacherous. It was said to look fertile, had running water and seemed uninhabited. But where was it?

Fletcher Christian realised at once that, as was common at the time, the island's longitude had been charted incorrectly. If he could find Pitcairn, he would have sailed *Bounty* and himself right off the face of the known earth and into the oblivion he wished. He would be invisible.

Christian zigzagged eastwards along the line of latitude for 210 miles/330 kms. On the evening of 15 January 1790, he sighted Pitcairn at last. It was pitifully small to be the object of such excitement, a lonely rock only about 1 mile by 1½ miles/ 1.6 kms by 2.5 kms, like the discarded plaything of a forgetful Leviathan.

After a four-month voyage criss-crossing the South Pacific for almost 8,000 miles/12,875 kms there was to be no simple finale. For 48 hours he and *Bounty* were hurled about in a violent swell that made every thought of landing impossible. Yet, because they saw no signs of life on the thickly-clad peaks that loomed or on the lofty sea cliffs, each hour's delay made the island only more attractive.

A truly safe and calm day for landing at Pitcairn occurs only a few times in the life of most men. At last Fletcher Christian took advice from his Ma'ohi companions that conditions had subsided to the point where an attempt was worthwhile. The wind must have been blowing from the cold south or the east for they rowed through the surf on the west of the island. Here was the only possible alternative landing site to what became known as Bounty Bay on the eastern side and where, incidentally, a new quay has been built, which now makes it easier and more likely for cruise-ship and other visitors to land.

Christian, Brown, Williams and McCoy, together with three Ma'ohi men, guided their boat through the sea to land on sharp but slippery boulders, perpetually drenched by surf. They pushed their way through the resistant undergrowth and began climbing the slopes, a glissade of rotting leaf and viscous red mud. For two days they fought their way around the towers and secret passages of this fortress and must have seen most of the island in their uncomfortable, tense exploration. Ancient paths, made by someone or some animal long gone, were overgrown, narrow and easily lost. The mid-summer air would be humid and enervating and there was the constant fear of angry animals or attack by inhabitants.

By the time Fletcher was back in *Bounty*, he knew Pitcairn was everything that he could wish for. There were paper-mulberry trees for making tapa cloth, candle-nut trees for light, pandanus palms for thatching. There was water. Fruit and vegetables grew wild and there were no animals, no mosquitoes. There were coconut trees in abundance and breadfruit, too. With the mangoes and plantains, oranges and sweet potatoes, hogs, goats and chickens aboard *Bounty*, Fletcher and his companions would live like tropical kings. With *Bounty's* cannon mounted atop the cliffs they would also be unassailable.

It was simple to follow the example of the unknown earlier inhabitants and choose to settle on the easier slopes that stretch a short distance along the north-east coast, beginning just above and to the west of the comparatively safer anchorage they would call Bounty Bay. The remains of old gardens had rich red earth, were well drained and had water close. Bounding one side was a high peak, from which a lookout could be kept.

Much later it was discovered the island had attracted stone-toolmakers from all over Polynesia, for here there was every practical material, including black, glass-like obsidian, that could be flaked to extraordinary sharpness. These artisans never settled permanently but had created the gardens and carved the idols the newcomers found. The last of them had probably left the island in the mid-seventeenth century, 150 years before *Bounty* arrived.

Everything Fletcher Christian had identified as crucial to his survival was here. The island was solitary, almost impregnable and uninhabited. It was also fertile, comfortably more temperate than tropical and its whereabouts was unknown. Pitcairn signalled a new beginning for them all, far beyond practical expectations. It promised the return of all Fletcher cherished, all he had abandoned. Here on Pitcairn with Mauatua as his wife, with land, friends and freedom, he might live with dignity, even as a fugitive from the Royal Navy and Crown.

In January 1790, Pitcairn must have felt like Paradise found but it was a fragile Paradise and it would shatter.

The Second Breadfruit Expedition

S ir Joseph Banks was not happy. There was no breadfruit in the Caribbean, a Royal Navy ship was missing, and Bligh was deluging him with begging letters of self-justification. *Pandora* had been sent to bring back the mutineers, but no-one knew if it would succeed, or what those who returned might have to say about the mutiny. Banks's solution was a second breadfruit expedition by HMS *Providence*, again led by William Bligh, now promoted to Captain.

Providence sailed on 2 August 1791. This was not the relief to Bligh that it was to Banks. Bligh was suffering from intense and recurring headaches and fever and should have stayed home in bed. It was the health of his patronage and expectation of promotion that must have persuaded him, because it was cruel of Joseph Banks to send the sick Bligh on the second breadfruit expedition, who probably wagered this would minimise harm to himself because Bligh could not then be present and cross-examined if there were to be *Bounty* mutineers' trials.

HMS *Providence* carried discipline-keeping marines and the brig *Assistant* sailed as a tender.

On 7 August 1793 the second breadfruit expedition arrived back from the West Indies and docked in The Royal Naval Dockyard, Deptford. The venture was a resounding botanical success, apart from the exasperating refusal of the West Indian slaves to eat the stuff. When *Providence* and *Assistant* were paid off at Woolwich, the *Kentish Register* of 6 September 1793 reported that Bligh was cheered, which made a good impression on everyone. Sailors know it pays to be nice to superior officers in public and, as far as the complements of *Providence* and *Assistant* knew, Bligh was still a hero. Not for long.

The mutineers' trials in 1791 (and perhaps the discreet circulation of Morrison's Memorandum) and the publication of a letter from Heywood blaming Bligh and not Fletcher Christian for the mutiny had radically changed opinion about Bligh throughout the Royal Navy, where it counted. He found he was neither welcomed nor given audiences at the Admiralty. His lieutenants aboard *Providence* found his recommendations for promotion were often useless.

When researching in the National Library of Australia in Canberra, I discovered a document related to the second breadfruit voyage that, while known to a few, had never been used in any biography of William Bligh. It is the 1792 draft of a letter to his brother by Lieutenant Francis (Frank) Godolphin Bond, first lieutenant on HMS *Providence*, written during the late days of the expedition. Bond had not sailed with Bligh before and was a relative through marriage, the son of Bligh's half-sister Catherine Pearse, the daughter of his mother's first marriage to Richard Pearse. Other officers included the excellent water-colour artist Lieutenant Tobin and midshipman Matthew Flinders, off for his first look at a part of the world he would make very much his own.

What follows is first-hand evidence, not hearsay and not written years later.

It is not surprising it had been ignored by Bligh supporters.

> To say a southern voyage is quite delectable is also to say you have every domestic comfort; but on this score I must be silent, for at present I mean to say but little of our Major Domo (i.e. Mr. Bligh) . . . Yes Tom, our relation has the credit of being a tyrant in his last expedition, where his misfortunes and good fortune have elevated him to a situation he is incapable of supporting with decent modesty.

The very high opinion he has of himself makes him hold everyone of our profession with contempt, perhaps envy: nay the Navy is but [a] sphere for fops and lubbers to swarm in, without one gem to vie in brilliancy with himself. I don't mean to depreciate his extensive knowledge as a seaman and nautical astronomer, but condemn that want of modesty in self estimation. To be less prolix I will inform you he has treated me (nay all on board) with the insolence and arrogance of a Jacobs: and notwithstanding his passion is partly to be attributed to a nervous fever, with which he has been attacked most of the voyage, the chief part of his conduct must have arisen from the fury of an ungovernable temper.

Soon after leaving England I wished to receive instruction from this imperious master, until I found he publickly exposed any deficiency on my part in the Nautical Art etc. A series of this conduct determined me to trust to myself, which I hope will in some measure repay me for the trouble of a disagreeable voyage in itself pleasant, but made otherwise by being worried at every opportunity.

His maxims are of the nature that at once pronounce him an enemy to the lovers of Natural Philosophy; for to make use of his own words, 'No person can do the duty of a 1st lieut who does no more than write the day's work of his publick journal'. This is so inimical to the sentiments I always hope to retain, that I find the utmost difficulty in keeping on tolerable terms with him. The general orders which have been given me are to that purport I am constantly to keep on my legs from 8 o'th'morning to 12, or noon, altho' I keep the usual watch. The Officer of the morning watch attends to the cleaning of the Decks; yet I am also to be present, not only to get it done, but be even menially active on those and all other occasions.

He expects me to be acquainted with every transaction on board, notwithstanding he himself will give the necessary orders to the Warrant Officers, before I can put it into execution. Every dogma of power and consequence has been taken from the Lieutenants, to establish, as he thinks, his own reputation what imbecility for a post Capn! The inferior Warrants have had orders from the beginning of the expedition, not to issue the least article to a Lieut. without his orders so that a cleat, fathom of log line, or indeed a hand swab, must have the commander's sanction. One of the last and most beneficent commands was that the Carpenter's Crew should not drive a nail for me without I should first ask his permission but my heart is filled with the proper materials always to disdain this humiliation.

Among many circumstances of envy and jealousy he used to deride my keeping a private journal and would often ironically say he supposed I meant to publish. My messmates have remarked he never spoke of my possessing one virtue tho' by the bye has never dared to say I have none. Every officer who has nautical information, a knowledge of natural history, a new call out to taste for drawing, or anything to constitute him proper for circumnavigating, becomes odious; for great as he is in his own good opinion, he must have entertained fears some of the ship's company meant to submit a spurious Narrative to the judgement and perusal of the publick.

Among the many misunderstandings that have taken place, that of my Observing has given most offence, for since I have not made the least application to him for information on that head, he has at all times found illiberal means of abusing my pursuit; saying at the same time, what I absolutely knew was from him. Tir'd heartily with my present situation, and even the subject I am treating of, I will conclude it by inserting the most recent and illegal order. Every Officer is expected to deliver in their private Logs ere we anchor at St Helena. As our expedition has not been on discoveries, should suppose this an artibrary command, altho the words, King's Request, Good of the Country; Orders of the Admiralty &c &c &c are frequently in his mouth—but unparrelled [sic] pride is the principal ingredients in his composition.

The future will determine whether promotion will be the reward of this voyage: I still flatter myself it will, notwithstanding what I have said. Consistent with self respect I still remain tolerably passive; and if nothing takes place very contrary to my feelings, all may end well: but this will totally depend on circumstances; one of which is the secrecy requested of you concerning the tenor of this letter. My time is so effectually taken up by Duty that to keep peace I neglect all kind of study; yet the company of a set of well informed messmates makes my moments pass very agreeably, so that I am by no means in purgatory . . . The 2nd August [1791] we left England and had pleasant w[eather] to Teneriffa, where Captain B. was taken very ill, and from particular traits in his conduct believe he was insane at times.'

Lieutenant Bond's son, the Rev F. H. Bond, had a paper that summarised what he had been told by his father about Bligh and supported this with quotations from notes, which have not been made public. Most of what follows are now the words of F. H. Bond.

Though a prime seaman, however his [i.e. Bligh's] passionate temper and violent language were so uncontrolled that he was hardly ever employed without exasperating his officers and ship's company. The story of the Mutiny on the Bounty, the immediate causes of which were an outburst of temper on his part and grossly insulting words to one of his officers, and the marvellous voyage of the Bounty's launch for 4,000 miles are so well known that they need only be referred to here. This extraordinary feat of seamanship was now on everybody's lips and Bligh was universally commiserated. He had of course told his story in his own way and was, like many violent tempered men, perhaps really unconscious of the amount of provocation he had given. He had represented the mutiny as the result of his crew's experience of the delicious climate and the life of the island of Otaheite.

The most perfect harmony was luckily maintained among the Lieuts throughout [the Providence voyage], a matter of immense importance for a reason which must unfortunately be presently noted . . .

During the voyage to the Cape of Good Hope, Bligh transferred Bond to *Assistant*, a much smaller ship and something of an insult. Once at the Cape, Bond was returned to *Providence*. His comments in notes made at the time were full and hasty and his son declines to quote them as Lieutenant Bond had written under the influence of strong feeling. He merely wrote of the notes:

It will be enough to show that there was great cause for discomfort. Hardly had the voyage commenced when Cp. Bligh's arbitrary disposition and exasperating language began again to render his ship a most unfortunate one for his officers and especially for his First Lieutenant [Bond] who from his position was brought into closer contact with him. Orders of an unusual nature were given with haste and in a manner so uncalled for and so devoid of feeling and tact as to occasion very great irritation.

The short exchange with the Assistant was felt at the time quite a relief and his resumption of duties as First of the Providence was attended with discomfort which he speaks of as frightful. A dictatorial insistence on trifles, ever-lasting fault finding, slights shown in matters of common courtesy, strong and passionate condemnation of little errors of judgement all these stung the hearts of his subordinates and worked them up into a state of wrath which would probably have much surprised Bligh himself had he known it.

Instances are given of his want of courtesy. At a ceremonial visit to the Governor of the Cape, Bligh takes the opportunity of snubbing Lieuts Portlock and Bond by presenting them after a junior Lieut, and the Commander of the Assistant last, quite against the rule of etiquette. At Teneriffe he refused to present two of his officers to the Governor, who thereupon corrected the intentional blunder and presented themselves. The Governor, it is added, received them well.

Refusals of leave to land, apparently without cause, which annoyed at the Cape, were felt still more strongly at Otaheite, when frequent leave was naturally expected during their 3 month stay. One other point was very trying to Bligh's nephew, the great inconsistency of his conduct. He says that in prosperity Cap. Bligh was all arrogance and insult, despotic insistence without explanation, advice or show of kindness; often an hauteur and distance which utterly ignored the nephew as well as the rank of his First Lieut.

In time of real danger what a change to cordiality and kindness! The Devil's Hole for example! 'Oh Frank! What a situation; into what a danger have I brought you! God grant that we may get safe out of it.'

HMAV *Bounty* is believed to be the first Royal Navy ship to sail for neither warring, ruling nor exploring purposes, but to profit from them. She carried an unprecedented crew of only voluntary sailors, which might have contributed to the later mutiny in the South Pacific.

Is this what Fletcher Christian looked like? Based on the many known portraits of Fletcher's ancestors and eighteenth century uncles and cousins, it was painted by the late John Lockett, an expert in facial form and structure, as a commission by Adrian Teal to illustrate his thesis on the many ways Fletcher Christian is portrayed in literature.

Moorland Close, Fletcher Christian's birthplace, is seen outside a defensive enclosure of ancient brick. In his time the walls and towers enclosed the remains of a medieval 'part-castle' and other outbuildings; an evocative adventure playground.

Milntown, in the parish of Lezayre, Ramsey, in the north of the Isle of Man, became the Christian family seat in 1511. The original buildings were replaced by a severe five-bay Georgian house that Fletcher would have known. It was enlarged in the 1830s, when fashionable Gothic battlements were added.

Ewanrigg Hall had been the Christian family seat in Cumberland since the mid-1600s. First little more than a fortified Pele tower, it was extended in the 1680s. In 1778-8, new rooms and a new façade doubled its size; the two low wings were added in 1782-3. This is where Fletcher Christian's father, Charles, was born and brought up, and it became the first seat of Fletcher's first cousin John Christian XVII, the head of the family. The last vestiges have gone and the grounds are now a housing estate.

Ewanrigg Hall.

An engraved copy of a William Bligh portrait painted after his return from the South Pacific and his courageous open-boat journey. *Bounty*'s launch and an erupting Tofua are depicted in the background.

(Courtesy HMAV Bounty Museum, Weinfelden Switzerland)

The breadfruit greenhouse and small cabins for Captain Bligh and Master Fryer took almost a third of the lower deck, where all living and cooking took place without portholes. Two cockpits below this added airless, darker accommodation and storage.

(Courtesy HMAV Bounty Museum, Weinfelden, Switzerland)

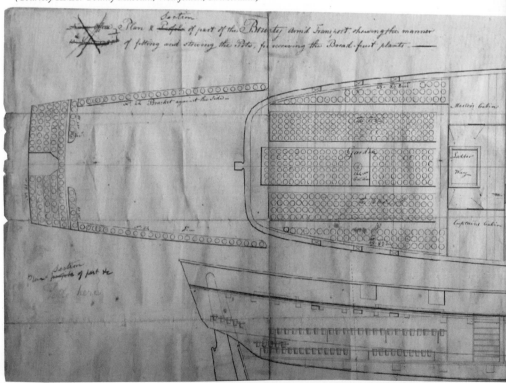

Matavai Bay 1980: it seemed little different from what Fletcher Christian would have seen when he stepped out from the breadfruit camp.

The print is not romanticised as dancers did use coconut shells like this, and men and women draped tapa cloth like togas.

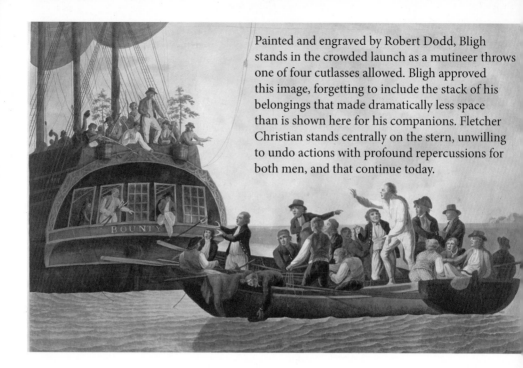

Painted and engraved by Robert Dodd, Bligh stands in the crowded launch as a mutineer throws one of four cutlasses allowed. Bligh approved this image, forgetting to include the stack of his belongings that made dramatically less space than is shown here for his companions. Fletcher Christian stands centrally on the stern, unwilling to undo actions with profound repercussions for both men, and that continue today.

After the mutiny, Fletcher Christian sailed *Bounty* almost 8,000 miles (12,990 km) in search of a home before finding Pitcairn Island, which at the time was incorrectly mapped 210 miles (330 km) from its true position; they were invisible.

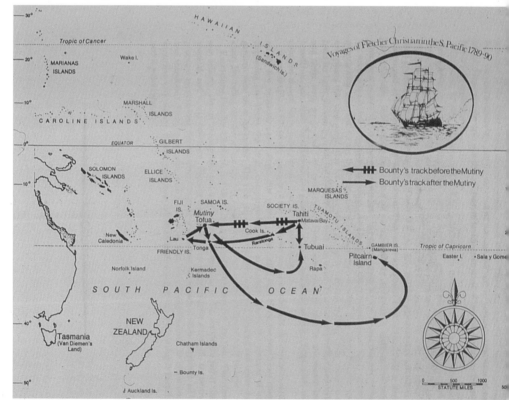

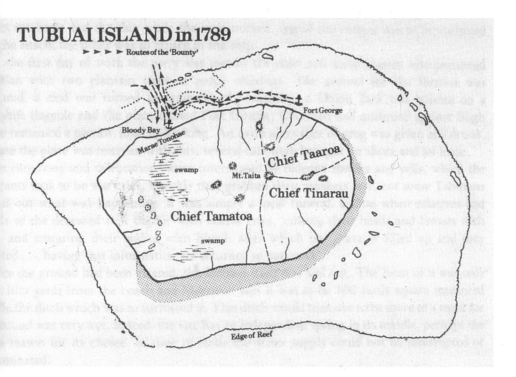

TUBUAI ISLAND in 1789

▶ ▶ ▶ ▶ Routes of the 'Bounty'

Fort George

Bloody Bay

Marae Tonohae

swamp

Mt. Taita

Chief Taaroa

Chief Tinarau

Chief Tamatoa

swamp

Edge of Reef

letcher Christian settled in Tubuai's lesser district of Taaroa after finding a site with safe, fresh water, around which Fort George was built. Although incomplete when he abandoned Tubuai, emnants of the massive walls and the deep, wide moat survived into the twentieth century; I tood in it.

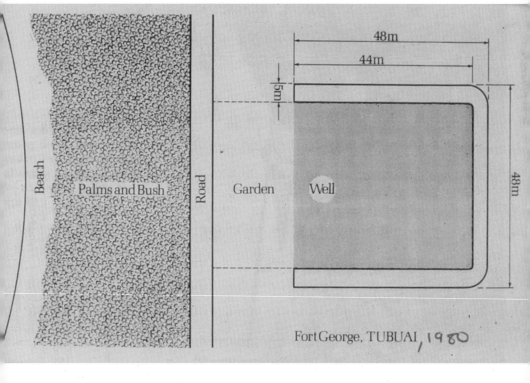

48m

44m

5m

Beach

Palms and Bush

Road

Garden

Well

48m

Fort George, TUBUAI, 1980

The Fort George site in 1980. There are no walls, but remnants of the moat are just beyond the flat area.

Looking at the breadfruit on the Fort George site during my sailing expedition to Pitcairn Island in 1980.

Pitcairn's Island. S. Pacific

A B C

A. Bounty Bay. Here the Bounty was ran on shore & afterwards burnt
B. Village
C. Water Valley - Round the first Point is the landing Place

n Fletcher and Mauatua's day their hideout was called Pitcairn's Island. After they sighted it on
5 January 1790, it was eighteen years before the fate of *Bounty* and her crew was discovered.

Bounty Bay has no protective coral reef and calm waters are almost unknown; to the right is Ship Landing Point.

Thursday October Christian. His birth nine months after *Bounty* arrived is a potent but long unrecognised clue to the hidden independence of Pitcairn's Polynesian Foremothers.

een from the top of Ship Landing Point is the small ledge where *Bounty* was unloaded before
he was burned and sunk.

ounty Bay in 1980, with the sticky red earth of the Hill of Difficulty winding up to Adamstown;
is now concreted and the jetty much enlarged. A safer landing has been built at Tedside,
eaning cruise visitors can land more safely.

Views of Christian's Cave
PITCAIRN ISLANDS **20c**

Views of Christian's Cave
PITCAIRN ISLANDS

Christian's Cave dominates Adamstown and was featured on one of Pitcairn's many famed stamp issues. I climbed the steep rock face to sit and think on the cave's ledge, overlooking the village and with Bounty Bay in the distance, just as my gt-gt-gt-gt grandfather Fletcher did.

Views of Christian's Cave
PITCAIRN ISLANDS **5c**

Is this where Fletcher Christian is buried? Two early visitors said they were shown his grave beside a pool: this dried pool is close to his supposed house, on land he was working to be close to Mauatua, who was expecting their third child at the time.

This 1795 print of Belle Isle in Lake Windemere, surrounded by bare hills, proves there were no trees in which Fletcher Christian could hide.

letcher Christian's porcelain Chinese bowl, decorated with peonies and pheasants, was given
y Mauatua to Captain Mayhew Folger, who 'found' the Pitcairn community in 1808. The bowl
now owned by the Nantucket Historical Association and displayed in the Nantucket Whaling
Museum.

This *tu'i* or pestle of carved
granite, its handle worn
smooth, is believed to have
come to Pitcairn with *Bounty*.

The tombstones under the banyan tree are where Mauatua and her son Charles are believed to lie. Long covered by the village hall, the site has now been cleared.

Tom Christian beside the living-rock pool believed to be carved by Fletcher Christian for Mauatua; it is fed constantly by cool water.

I replied, 'No sir, we shall do very well; I don't see that there's any real danger to the ship.'

The event which called for this conversation is not given but there is the hint that the danger was caused by the helm being put the wrong way through mistake.

> . . . The serenity of the weather gave us the most flattering hopes of a safe passage; but several affairs have lately occurred to prevent the cordiality which should have existed between my commander and myself, and his remarks tended to deprive me of self-confidence. I was e.g. reproached and threatened because my men on the Fore Tops yard were beaten by Tobin's and Guthrie's, the carpenter was abused for acting on my orders and ordered to take the skippers out; the boatswain was similarly treated. The usual etiquette in our respective positions was quite set aside.

There is that charge of inconsistency again, that lack of firm, universal boundaries on which sailors and their safety rely. Who can doubt that Lieutenant Bond tells us the truth about Bligh and gives us a concise picture that is also relevant to his behaviour on *Bounty*?

Bond did not mutiny on *Providence* because he was not in purgatory. Unlike Fletcher Christian he had peers aboard and he had no close ties of friendship with Bligh. On later ships there were continuing complaints about Bligh's manner of command, his constant inconsistency and insensitivity but he never learned, never changed. When commanding HMS *Warrior* in 1804 he was court-martialled for using abusive language to an officer and behaving in 'a tyrannical and oppressive and unofficerlike behaviour contrary to the rules and discipline of the Navy'. The charges were found largely proven and he was reprimanded.

The second breadfruit expedition kept Bligh well away from any trial of *Bounty* mutineers and the perils of cross-examination or of counter claims being accepted by the court. It did not prevent Fletcher's eminent brother Edward and many others doing what had been impossible in court. They wanted to know the cause of the mutiny, what happened *before* 28 April 1789, which had been the only date that interested the trial judges.

Pitcairn Pioneers

PITCAIRN'S FOREFATHERS – January 1790

Fletcher Christian: Sailed as *Bounty's* Master's Mate, promoted to Acting Lieutenant and second-in-command; led mutiny, 28 April 1789. Presumably murdered 23 September 1793

John Adams: Able-bodied seaman. Died 5 March 1829

William Brown: One of *Bounty's* gardeners, had previously served as a lieutenant. Murdered 23 September 1793

Isaac Martin: Able-bodied seaman. Murdered 23 September 1793

William McCoy: Able-bodied seaman. Supposedly committed suicide when affected by alcohol distilled on Pitcairn

John Mills: Gunner's mate. Murdered 23 September 1793

Matthew Quintal: Able-bodied seaman. Killed by Edward Young and John Adams, probably in late 1799

John Williams: Able-bodied seaman. Murdered 23 September 1793

Edward Young: Acting Midshipman. Died of asthma, Christmas Day 1800

Manarii: Tahitian also known as Menalee. Killed by Quintal and McCoy when he hid with them after shooting Teimua

Niau: Tahitian and a younger cousin of Tararo. Shot by Edward Young

Oha: From Tubuai. Shot by Niau in 1790 or 1791

Tararo: Also known as Talaloo, a noble or *ra'atira* from Raiatea, possibly related to Mauatua. Shot by Niau in 1790 or 1791

Teimua: Tahitian. Shot by Manarii while playing his nose flute for Teraura sometime after Massacre Day

Titahiti: Originally Taaroamiva. From Tubuai, younger brother of Chief Taaroa and thus also *ra'atira*, perhaps even *ari'i*. Killed by Teraura, then the wife of Edward Young, later wife of Thursday October

PITCAIRN'S FOREMOTHERS – *Te Tupuna Vahine* – January 1790

Mauatua/Mrs Christian: (Isabella, Mainmast, Maimiti) Tahitian consort of Fletcher Christian (two sons, one daughter), then of Edward Young (one son, two daughters). She remembered Cook's visits to Tahiti and is said to have left at least one child on Tahiti: see Tamahere in MRS CHRISTIAN – *BOUNTY* MUTINEER (Amazon). Older than Fletcher Christian but by how much is unknown. It's not known when Fletcher began to call her Isabella; Mainmast is a nickname given because of her very upright height and posture. She was never known as Maimiti during her life time as this was adopted by Nordhoff and Hall for their Bounty trilogy – see *Mrs Christian* – Bounty *Mutineer*, Author's Notes – and was then popularised by the 1936 movie starring Clark Gable and Charles Laughton.

In *The Pitcairners* (Angus & Robertson), author Robert Nicolson said Mauatua and Fletcher Christian were married on Tahiti, but when I met him he said he had no evidence but had presumed this, so this can safely be ignored.

Faahotu (Fasto): Tahitian first consort of John Williams. Died childless 1790/91 of a disease of her neck, possibly scrofulous. Williams' demand for another woman started Pitcairn's long descent into strife

Mareva: Shared Tahitian consort of Manarii, Teimua and Niau. Later lived in Adams' household. No children. Died between 1808 and 1814

Puarai (Obuarei): Tahitian, first Pitcairn consort of John Adams. Childless. Fell from a cliff while gathering birds' eggs 1790/91, creating the second shortage of a wife amongst the mutineers

Sully (Sally): Arrived on Pitcairn as a baby, daughter of Teio and an unknown Tahitian father; married Mauatua's second son, Charles, known as Hoppa. Four sons, four daughters. Died 7 March 1826

Teatuahitea (Sarah): Tahitian consort of William Brown. Childless, she died between 1808 and 1814

Teehuteatuaonoa (Jenny): Tahitian consort of John Adams, then of Isaac Martin. No children. Only Ma'ohi woman to leave Pitcairn but not until 1817, and she did not return to Tahiti; death date uncertain

Teio (Mary): Tahitian, first consort of McCoy and later of John Adams, mother of his only son, George. Died 14 March 1829. Arrived on Pitcairn with a baby girl, Sully, who married Mauatua and Fletcher Christian's second son, Charles

Teraura (Susannah): Youngest Tahitian woman, first consort of Edward 'Ned' Young, then of Matt Quintal (one son). Married Mauatua's oldest son Thursday October when she was over 30 and he was 16 (three sons, three daughters). Died 15 July 1850, so was present with Mauatua in 1838 when Pitcairn passed laws giving women the vote and made education compulsory for girls

Tevarua (Sarah, Big Sully): Tahitian, first consort of Matt Quintal (two sons, two daughters). Died 1799

Tinafanea: From Tubuai, first the shared consort of Titahiti and Oha, then given to Adams. No children. Died between 1808 and 1814

Toofaiti (Nancy, Hutia, Toohaiti): From Huahine. She was first the consort of Tararo but then given to Williams. After Massacre Day she was one of Ned Young's consorts (three sons, one daughter). She died in the Tahiti flu epidemic 9 June 1831

Vahineatua (Prudence, Balhadi, Praha Iti): Tahitian, first the consort of John Mills (one daughter, one son) and then of Adams (three daughters). The Pitcairn Island Register says she died on 29 April 1831 in Papeete, another epidemic victim: see *Mrs Christian – Bounty Mutineer*:

Because both of Mauatua and Fletcher Christian's sons married older Tahitian women, their grandchildren were three-quarters Tahitian, the only such on Pitcairn. When other first-generation Pitcairners (all half *Ma'ohi*, half English) married one another, their children were still half-*Ma'ohi* and half-English but if they married a descendant of Fletcher and Mauatua, their children were $^6/_8$ Tahitian. Thus, Mauatua and Fletcher Christian's descendants were and are still more Tahitian than English if they married Pitcairn or Norfolk Island partners with no outside blood.

My Christian great-grandfather Godfrey was more what we now call Polynesian than European. He, my grandfather and my father all married 'out', thus explaining my lack of Tahitian colouring and features – and height!

The early days of 1790 on Pitcairn, 1200 miles/1900 kms south east of Tahiti, were hard. Although the January temperature on Pitcairn rarely exceeds 90°F/32°C in the shade, this is burden enough when you are quickly relieving a vessel of animals, plants, provisions, fittings, tackle and, eventually, even its copper sheathing and timbers. Teio's baby daughter, Sully, one of my great-great-great grandmothers, came ashore in a barrel.

A tense two-way watch was being kept. On the island signs of habitation were everywhere, and some of the island was so densely forested, so rugged, there was no sure way of knowing who or what might be hiding. They watched the sea too. While they were unloading the tattered ship, they were at their most vulnerable should they be spotted by another, for the masts and spars of a square-rigger are etched all too obviously against even the roughest lines of nature but to remove them too soon would make escape impossible. The longer the ship rode the unpredictable South Pacific swell, the greater the risks both of being spied and of losing her, so *Bounty* was run on to the rocks some way to the left of the beach, directly below a 700 foot/215 metre peaked cliff they named Ship Landing Point.

There was no need to build a fort here, so shelters had quickly been made of palm fronds and *Bounty*'s sails, hidden in the trees well back from the cliff edge. After more than three months at sea, the pioneers could again enjoy true privacy, eat fresh fruits and vegetables, bathe, drink fresh coconut milk or water from the spring that gardener Brown discovered close to the camp. Pitcairn's seas were full of fish, the rocks encrusted with shellfish and alive with huge saltwater lobsters, the cliffs with sea birds and their eggs. Now that the animals could be fed, fattened and bred properly, they could regularly slaughter a pig or goat for a pit-oven feast. Twenty-eight mouths, even if one was an infant, could easily eat a whole animal at one sitting.

On 23 January, less than a week after they had landed on the 17th or 18th, *Bounty* was stripped and emptied but then ablaze, her sun-bleached and warped timbers spurred to greater conflagration by the tar used on her decks and caulking. Was it an accident?

Quintal is blamed for the fire, over-anxious about discovery and retribution, possibly because there was some discussion about preserving the vessel; Fletcher Christian was thought to be entertaining ideas of sailing it away so he could give himself up. Fletcher's Brief Psychotic Disorder was well behind him, but Pitcairn was the first time since the mutiny that he was free of the heavy burdens of commanding the ship, of responsibility for over fifty other men and women on Tubuai, and then through the difficult search for a home. Only now could he consider the consequences of taking *Bounty*, what the repercussions might be and what he should do about them.

Was it really Quintal who set fire to the ship? I no longer accept this as plausible. He always denied it and had just the sort of personality that would make him boast about doing it. If not Quintal, who?

If *Bounty's* masts led to early discovery or if Fletcher Christian sailed away in her, inevitably revealing the Pitcairn settlement, *everyone* would be at risk. Consider how much the Ma'ohi women had changed about themselves, the huge helpings of freedom they were experiencing and the new future they could imagine. I believe they would be the most determined that their new way of life was not put at risk. There are facts that prove this, facts overlooked for over two centuries of men retailing history as only what men made it. It's an insight of which I am especially proud, because in an instant it changes everything ever said or thought about the Pitcairn settlement.

It escaped the notice of hundreds of *Bounty* writers and theorists that, after eight months of searching for a home after the ship last sailed from Matavai Bay, not one of the twelve Ma'ohi women was pregnant when they arrived at Pitcairn, something well beyond the norm. It's not true that South Pacific Polynesian women ovulate less and that this makes them less likely to conceive. That's merely a way to avoid facing the facts of abortion and infanticide.

So, no babies were expected when *Bounty* finally discovers Pitcairn. Then, the boss and his wife, Fletcher and Mauatua, produce Pitcairn's first child almost exactly nine months after arrival, implying an agreement between the women and an accepted hierarchy, just as there had been on Tahiti and in *Bounty*. Quietly and secretly, these freed women were in control of their bodies and had a vision of their futures that they would protect from the influence of men, all men.

These women knew little of contraception but had three methods of abortion – deep massage, herbal and extraction – so must have been terminating pregnancies until they knew they had a safe, secure and permanent home. Ma'ohi believed a person's spirit returned after death to the burial place of its placenta. What would you safely do with a placenta at sea or any impermanent settlement but damn that spirit to perpetual unhappy wandering?

For Pitcairn's women pioneers neither permanency nor pregnancy was possible on a ship at sea. These women were determined they would escape the brutality of their previous lives, so I believe it was to protect the safer, freer future they could now see as women and mothers that they burned *Bounty*, just as I reckon it was they who had urged Fletcher Christian to flee unannounced from Matavai Bay. Invisible from the world in which they had grown, they would create a world safer for women and all their children. There was never a full-blooded Ma'ohi child born on Pitcairn and this can only have been by design of women who wanted nothing of their male-dominated Polynesian past.

The continued implementation of Fletcher Christian's ideas of democracy and equality were soon shattered. At an early stage, voting was used by the mutineers to divide most of the island between Fletcher Christian and the other eight white men. Each was allotted a space to build in both the settlement and gardens elsewhere. The six men from Tahiti, Tubuai, and Raiatea, two of them high-born, were given no land and became servants forever.

Fletcher's authority was not needed for their safety, so the other mutineers expected a greater say in things and had a majority anyway. An entirely new social order was emerging and dealing with it was difficult for a young officer and a gentleman, who at sea had always known where he was with these men. As simple seamen they had never had much to lose because they never thought to own much but now saw new horizons. As the landed gentry of a new Pacific kingdom, they had everything to gain by questioning the authority and position of Fletcher Christian and could vote for or against what he or they wanted.

The work involved in building, fencing, fishing and farming initially prevented most quarrels on Pitcairn. The six black men worked land for the white men and appeared largely to acquiesce, even though beaten with knotted ropes and threatened with guns.

Mauatua gave birth to the first Pitcairner on a Thursday in October 1790. It was a son and Fletcher named him Thursday October, which might well be something he learned in the Caribbean, where African slaves refused to give their children traditional names until they were freed. It is a clue to the discomfort Fletcher felt.

Quintal and McCoy fathered sons, and Mills fathered Pitcairn's first daughter; called Elizabeth she is another of my great-great-great grandmothers. In 1792, Mauatua bore another son, Charles, named for Fletcher's father and the brother from whom he learned about mutiny.

Charles's birth was a Pitcairn Epiphany, an extraordinary event, the resonance of which has been overlooked for centuries, including by me, even though Charles is one of my great-great-great grandfathers.

Charles was born with a club foot, something common in South Pacific islands but Fletcher Christian would never have seen it in Tahiti. Club-footed babies had their skulls crushed before their first breath. When Mauatua decided in a few heartbeats that Charles would live, she traduced and dismissed centuries of priestly domination of women. She rejected all she had been taught was proper for a Tahitian woman, choosing to tread a path no Tahitian woman had known. Allowing Charles to live with a club foot demonstrated the depth of the revolutionary thinking that Fletcher Christian and *Bounty* had released in Pitcairn's women.

Mauatua's decision to let her second son live put every man and woman, black and white, on notice that Pitcairn was different from anything they knew or expected and should be seen as a marker for all that followed.

20 September 1793: Massacre Day

When the American sealer *Topaz* captain Mayhew Folger accidentally found Pitcairn in 1808, he quickly suspected that something Biblical and bloody must have happened. Isolated for eighteen years, the community had only one white adult male, nine Polynesian women and twenty-six mixed-blood children, the oldest about eighteen. The Pitcairners were welcoming and gentle and everyone spoke English of a sort and were practising Christians.

The adult man was John Adams, now in his early forties and he was in a real dilemma. He was a suspected mutineer with new scars, tattoos and wearing beaten bark as clothing. How much did the visitors know about events aboard *Bounty* and his part in them? What had happened to Bligh and the men in the open boat? Was he party to mass murder as well as mutiny? Was what had happened on Pitcairn likely to be judged under English law? In short, was he liable to arrest and punishment?

He believed that as he was now a practicing Christian and effective pastor of the island, he had atoned for any crime, protesting he was innocent of complicity in the mutiny because he was in his hammock at the time. The women would also have wanted to protect their children and to hide their involvement in wrongdoing. Pitcairn's children had only been told what they needed to know. Who could love a mother who admitted to murdering your father?

During this and other early visits once Pitcairn's true geographical position was known, the women were forbidden to speak Tahitian and didn't speak English, using instead a confusing mix of eighteenth-century English and Tahitian. Their children spoke better English but merely repeated they had been told. *Ha'avere* still ruled. This was one of the customs brought to Pitcairn by the Ma'ohi women, a part-serious, part playful habit of lying for the sake of amusement or for deflection of harmful truths.

On Pitcairn *ha'avere* was not to enliven boredom as it had been on Tahiti. It was to bury all the women had done to protect their children. There can be no question that Mrs Christian, Mauatua, ensured the game was played for maximum blame on the black men and as little possible mention of Fletcher Christian. If European men did not want to talk to her, she was very happy not to talk to them.

On the other hand, Mauatua, who always introduced herself as Mrs Christian, did what she could to put Fletcher Christian and the community the best possible light. She gave Captain Folger the K2 chronometer, saying it should be returned to the king.

It took Adams and his flock seventeen years fully to believe he would not be arrested and taken off the island, something dreaded by the community. When Captain Beechey arrived aboard HMS *Blossom* in 1825, Adams was certain that any cross-examining about his past was academic rather than incriminatory and began to give fuller and more accurate accounts, while drawing a veil over his own involvement in the horrors that emerged.

One other eye-witness account is by Jenny, who had first been with Adams during the Tubuaian experiment and then gone with *Bounty* to Pitcairn as partner of Isaac Martin. She was always fiercely independent and a leader of the women, but she had never been a mother and left Pitcairn in 1817 aboard *Sultan*. Subsequently, she talked to a Captain Peter Dillon who translated her account from the jumble of Tahitian and English in which it had been given. The details she remembers are about people rather than dates and places, and thus are more believable. They helped me discard much generally accepted history as fable.

There is conflicting opinion about the behaviour of Fletcher Christian on Pitcairn. He is either morose and brooding or a happy, active, natural leader. Both pictures were given by Adams. The former was probably what the upright and sermonising nineteenth-century interviewers wished to hear but Fletcher Christian was a believer in deeds, not words. A busy organiser, digging his garden, building his house, delighting in physical activity of any kind is the more likely picture. Yet Fletcher was human, and he had done something quite spectacular. He would have been less than human if he had not sometimes yearned for the privileges of his life back in England, the conversations, the feeling of being part of a greater, fast-changing world. At such brooding moments, he was said to retire to a cave high in the sheer side of Lookout Point. There he had erected a small watch house and kept a store of provisions. Beechey thought it so difficult to access that a single occupant could hold off a party whatever their size as long as there was a supply of ammunition.

Bounty arrived with fifteen men, twelve women and a baby girl; six of the men were black and nine were white. Five of the Ma'ohi men shared two women because Tararo was allotted one of his own, reflecting his high rank. Although sharing women was something Tahitians might ordinarily have done by choice, here it was a further underlining of the lowly status forced on these men. Not owning land was particularly lowering to the two nobles amongst them, Tararo from Raiatea and Titahiti, brother of Chief Taaroa of Tubuai. Slowly their position as nobles, friends and accomplices was eroded. They became slaves. Even Pitcairn's women regarded them as second best and none gave birth to a child from them, an important illustration of how little these women wanted of their past lives.

Ma'ohi men and women grew up learning about fishing and gardening for food and on Pitcairn only they who knew where each crop would do best, which banana variety did well up a hill or better on a plain, which fish was safe to eat, which caused hallucinations, even how to make the best fishing lines and hooks. The rich and fertile soil of Pitcairn quickly rewarded them, but the European men expected their black servants and slaves to do most of the work. In some mitigation, eighteenth century English sailors has probably seen black men only working as slaves or servants to white men.

The women had much to learn. On Tahiti, men did the cooking in pits or by roasting animals and fish in front of open fires. Here women were expected to cook in metal *over* fires while disregarding the *tapu* that had restricted them touching men's cooking and eating implements. That would have begun on board *Bounty*, where they would also have been introduced to baking in closed ovens.

These women's determination to make Pitcairn their own is shown not only by what they learned but what they abandoned of Tahiti, Huahine and Tubuai. Infanticide was no longer decreed by men. Baby girls no longer had their face massaged to make flat noses and boys did not have their skulls flattened and pointed. Profane dancing for men's sexual excitement ended, as did all food restrictions. There was no tattooing, mothers did not become slaves to daughters or fear the long hoots of conch-shell trumpets that might mean a son would be beaten to death as a sacrifice for priests who forbade women to take part in their religion.

What Pitcairn's foremothers did with tapa cloth is the most telling example of their determination to break with the past. On Pitcairn it was once known as *ahu* and it can be beaten from the bark of different trees, including breadfruit, and the various colours and qualities ranged from floating gossamer to tough floor coverings. Brought up to copy the painted and stencilled patterns their mothers and grandmothers and countless other generations had always used, Pitcairn's women universally turned their back on these. Instead, they created patterns of their own, sometimes clearly trying to copy designs of Georgian fabrics presumably carried aboard *Bounty*. This dismissal of powerful feminine traditions of their pasts demonstrates, just as much as allowing a club-footed boy to live, a united determination to create new identities and futures.

Lengths of Pitcairn's *tapa* were given or sold to visitors with such ease and in such quantity that it's difficult to believe they held residual sacred or spiritual meaning to Pitcairn's women, dead or alive. This stance ignores that the founding foremothers, *te tupuna vahine*, had fully embraced the Christian religion well before the island was rediscovered and this alone would have negated any otherworldly Ma'ohi spiritual connection tapa had to them. It seems to me that they regarded their tapa as resources, just as relics of *Bounty* and her crew were sold and traded.

The greatest collection Pitcairn's tapa is held hidden by the British Museum and there are many who believe that carefully curated collections featuring their unique designs are potentially valuable resources that could be used to raise independent funds for the island. This would also increase awareness of these extraordinary foremothers, whom I feel would take pride that their designs would support the survival of the community they founded with so much heartache and tragedy.

At very least, reproductions of Pitcairn's unique declarations of female independence should be displayed on Pitcairn and Norfolk Islands, as should the extraordinary collection of pre-*Bounty* stone tools held at *Tāmaki Paenga Hira*, Auckland War Memorial Museum. Neither collection contributes to the good when stored in impersonal darkness.

The greatest challenge Pitcairn's pioneer women had was learning how to handle men who drank alcohol, too generously and too often. The *'ava* the women had known on their islands made men talkative but relaxed, befuddled but not challenging. *Bounty's* alcohol changed men's moods and made them aggressive and brutal.

Alcohol fuelled the most poisonous of the several serpents in Pitcairn's apparent Paradise, the determined pursuit of guaranteed sexual intercourse, which soon exacerbated the imbalance between the black and the white men. With a year of arrival, Jack Williams' consort Faahotu died of what seemed to be a scrofulous eruption on her neck. Williams demanded one of the women shared by the Ma'ohi but Fletcher blocked this, suggesting Williams wait for Sully, the infant who had come ashore in a barrel. She was possibly as old as three, but Williams was not prepared to wait, even if she was given to him before her puberty. The white men capitulated, and lots were cast for the three 'spare' women shared by the Ma'ohi men. The die chose Toofaiti from Huahine, known as Nancy, who welcomed the outcome.

This was the worst possible result because she was the exclusive consort of Tararo. Tararo was deeply wounded that Toofaiti preferred the increased status of having a white husband and weeping with anger and humiliation he took to the hills. Three days later he returned and by force or sweet words took Nancy back and they set up home in a cave below a cliff, still known as Talaloo's Ridge.

Next to lose his wife was John Adams. Puarai was killed when she fell while gathering eggs from a Pitcairn cliff. He was 'given' Tinafanea, who had been shared between Oha and Titahiti. Three of the six Ma'ohi men had had wives taken from them. The other three now had one between them. Like Fletcher they had been pushed too far and were going to do something about it.

The women knew this but curiously are said to have let their white husbands know only by incorporating clues into the songs they extemporised as they went about their daily tasks: 'Why does black man sharpen axe? To kill white men.' Fletcher seized a musket and went to find the conspirators, first heading to the large house at The Edge above Bounty Bay, where five of the six Ma'ohi men once lived communally. Oha was the first he met, and Fletcher discharged his gun straight at him but it had been loaded only with powder, as a deterrent; Fletcher was not willing to jeopardise his position by killing in anger. Oha misunderstood and mocking Christian's bad aim ran to join Tararo and Nancy in their hideout.

When the four remaining Ma'ohi plotters realised their plan was discovered they quickly extracted a promise of forgiveness from Fletcher and the others in return for an act of treachery. They agreed to kill Tararo and Oha. First, there was an ineffectual attempt at poisoning. Anxious to break the tension so all could sleep easily, Christian ordered the men to be shot. He chose Niau, the youngest of the men, to do this, saying that if he failed, he would be shot. Once Niau succeeded,

Pitcairn was thought safe once more. Nancy returned to live with Williams and a couple of years of relative tranquillity ensued.

In late September 1793 there were five children. The Christians had two boys, McCoy and Quintal each had a son and Mills a daughter. Fletcher's wife Mauatua was due to have another baby shortly and Mills's wife was pregnant again.

The widely accepted narrative blames Quintal and McCoy for pushing the four surviving Ma'ohi to murder because both were cruel and thoughtless towards the men they treated as slaves. If Quintal's man did not prepare his food sufficiently quickly or well, he was severely flogged. When the man was bleeding and whimpering, unable to defend himself, Quintal would rub brine into the lacerations. McCoy was just as free with the clout and lash. On 20 September 1793, the four black men are said to have had enough and did something about it. That date is still remembered on Pitcairn as Massacre Day.

Is it happy coincidence that the same day nine of the ten women left the village to collect eggs in the hills? Their European husbands were left working in the plantations that were part of their properties. Fletcher worked close to their house at the request of Mauatua, who had not gone with the other women because she expected the birth of their third child and according to Jenny wanted Fletcher to be within call, an important point when interpreting what happened where.

Posing as a thoughtful servant, Tetahiti borrowed a gun from Martin saying he wanted to shoot a pig for the white men's dinner. Teimua and Niau joined him. Williams was the first victim of the black men. When he heard the shot, Martin exclaimed they could all expect a glorious feast that night, believing it was meat and not man that had fallen. The three murderers then asked if Manarii, who was working with Mills in his garden, could help them carry the animal they had supposedly shot. Now a quartet, they moved to the yam plantation where Fletcher Christian was working. As he struggled to remove roots from some newly cleared ground he was shot from behind and fell down. To finish the job, he was disfigured about the head with an axe, and left for dead.

As he was shot or as he lay bleeding in the freshly turned red earth, Fletcher Christian groaned loudly. McCoy recognised it as the cry of a dying man, but Mills contradicted him, saying it was only Mauatua calling her children. Reassured, McCoy went back to work with Mills.

The Ma'ohi were still outnumbered and feared meeting the Europeans if they discovered the truth and banded together against them, so they separated McCoy and Mills. Teimua and Niau hid in McCoy's house and Tetahiti told him that his house was being ransacked. When he burst in, he was shot at twice but neither bullet hit him. He escaped to raise the alarm, but he ran into Quintal and the two ran to hide in the bush.

The two would-be assassins of McCoy then shot Mills but as he was only wounded they chopped off his head. Martin was shot next but managed to get to Brown's house. He fell after a second shot and was beaten over the head with a hammer by Manarii until he was still. Teimua had a good relationship with Brown and supposedly shot him with a blank charge, telling him then to pretend to be dead once he fell in his garden. He moved too soon and Manarii beat his brains into Pitcairn's already red earth. Five white men were now dead, and the numbers were even. One or two more deaths would make masters of the Ma'ohi.

Adams had been warned of the troubles by Quintal's wife Tevarua and took precautions to secrete himself in the bush with a supply of provisions. He exposed himself precipitately and was shot in the shoulder. As he fell, he was attacked with the butt of the gun and broke two fingers warding off the murderous thrusts. The gun was put to his side but misfired twice. Shocked but stimulated by fear, Adams leapt to his feet and found enough strength to outstrip his would-be assassins.

Finding themselves unlikely to prevail, his pursuers offered Adams protection. Exhausted, Adams accepted and was helped to Mauatua's house, where most women had sheltered after returning to the village. Adams was not the only one the women championed. Young was said always to have been a special favourite of the women and protected from the start. He has equally been suspected of helping plan the massacre, just as he has been blamed for suggesting Fletcher's mutiny, because one of the black men pursuing Adams is supposed to have apologised, saying he had forgotten Young had said Adams was not to be harmed.

When a truce was agreed, there were plenty of women for the remaining eight men. Yet plenitude brings its own complications. The Ma'ohi quarrelled as to who would have which widow. They doubtless had competition from Young and Adams, too. The most troublesome of the victors was the Tahitian Manarii, a man clearly comfortable with murder. About a week later, he shot Teimua at point-blank range while he played his nose-flute for Young's wife Teraura, Susannah. He had to shoot twice because the first didn't kill Teimua. Susannah had been fond of the murdered musician and as the youngest of the adult women was a keen prize for all the men. Tetahiti made a competitive point of consoling Teraura, so jealous Manarii attacked again. This time the women intervened to protest against his brutality and Tetahiti survived.

Fearful of retribution from black and white alike, Manarii escaped into the mountains to form an unlikely alliance with McCoy and Quintal, who were still too frightened to reappear. There's a thought that both these men should have been the first targets and their survival must have been a blow to whoever planned the killings.

Who did plan the killings? Why did Tevarua tell Adams about it and why was Young's name mentioned by one of the Ma'ohi men? It's hardly likely the black men would have shared their plans yet some of the women clearly knew them.

My view is that the women planned the murders, wanting to get rid of the drunken white men while plotting together to save Young and Adams, the men who behaved most reasonably and were the least threat to them and to their children. But why was Fletcher Christian murdered?

There are no stories of alcohol-fuelled brutality by Fletcher Christian that would justify him being included in the slaughter, but it should be remembered that Mauatua was alive when Pitcairn was discovered in 1808 and would easily have controlled what was said, particularly to protect the ears of the next generation, who had no idea who had spilled the blood that eventually led to their idyllic lives.

We simply do not know if Fletcher Christian was equally brutal when drunk or if a type of insanity had again claimed his mind. What we do know is that one of Nature's most powerful emotions is that of mothers protecting their young and I feel this must be included in any of the many weavings of theory and possibilities.

With McCoy and Quintal still alive, no one had won and from now on lives were bargained and spent recklessly. First either Adams or the women got a message to McCoy and Quintal that there would be truce if they disposed of Manarii. They shot him and delivered his severed hands into the village at night to prove it. Anxious to have the treachery and fear over with, Jenny agreed to take Tetahiti to bed. While they were together, Teraura, still only about 18 years old, attacked him with an axe. According to some stories the slash to his throat was not enough and she had to split his skull with a further blow of the axe. Outside, Young was showing Niau some of the finer points of loading and firing a musket but then shot him. McCoy and Quintal wanted proof the last of the black men were dead and so body parts of Tetahiti and Niau were sent to them. They agreed to return to the village on 3 October. Nine men had been slaughtered, five white men and the last four Ma'ohi men. There would never be black children born on Pitcairn.

On the day of the first massacre, a girl had been born to Mauatua and called Mary Ann. Not long after her birth, John Mills II was born. Now there were seven children on Pitcairn and the oldest, Thursday October Christian, turned three a few days after the murders ceased. The situation was now reversed. The Ma'ohi women could choose their men. Adams and Young were each joined by three women, McCoy and Quintal each had two.

In December of the same year, Young began a journal, which only Captain Beechey reported seeing. Most of the details are domestic and banal. Houses were rebuilt for the newly expanded families, new divisions of land were fenced off and gardens were protected from the pigs by digging pits to trap them. It must have been hard work with only four men, none of whom before had proven much interest in labour. The women weren't always available because in the next five years thirteen children were born. Several of the women were almost constantly pregnant, a definite change from the first years.

If there was any discontent, it appears to have been among the women, some of whom lived promiscuously with the men and changed their abodes regularly. Judging by Young's journal, the changes may have been accounted for by unhappiness and ill-treatment rather than sexual boredom. In fact, Pitcairn Island was now a distinctly unpleasant place to be. The bodies of those who had been murdered remained where they were killed but some had had their heads removed by the women.

On 12 March 1794, Young wrote that he had seen Jenny with a skull in her hand, and discovered it was that of Jack Williams. When he insisted it should be buried, the women with Jenny refused, asking him why he wanted such a thing when the other white men did not. Young conferred with the other three and said he thought that 'if the girls did not agree to give up the heads of the five white men in a peaceable manner, they ought to be taken by force and buried'. There was no way he could be certain one was not that of a Ma'ohi. What happened to the five skulls, whoever they had once belonged to, is not known. The incident exasperated some of the women so much it changed all previous resolves. Some wanted to leave Pitcairn and sail in a small boat back the huge distance to Tahiti, something so incomprehensible it serves to show their desperation.

On 14 April, they were so urgent in their demands that the men began building them a boat. The childless Jenny tore off the planks of her house for the craft and endeavoured to persuade her countrywomen to do the same. It was astonishing that the men should cooperate with such a scheme but in mid-April, the vessel was launched. 'According to expectation' it upset and although saved from a certain death during their attempt to return to Tahiti, the women became even more despondent and dissatisfied. After this, the defeated women were treated badly and frequently beaten by Quintal and McCoy; Quintal bit off most of Tevarua's ear when she returned from fishing with a catch he thought too little.

The day after the abortive escape, the bones of the murdered people were gathered and buried. The impression given in most accounts is that Fletcher Christian, at least, was buried in his own garden, close to where he fell. Although there is a definite Ma'ohi tendency to forget someone once he is dead, it is, nevertheless, an appalling thought that the fathers of the foremothers' young children, had lain rotting and exposed throughout the southern summer of 1793-94.

Quintal was showing signs of mental distress and had seriously proposed that the men should not 'laugh, joke, or give anything to any of the girls', yet on 3 October, he gave a party to celebrate the death of the black men a year before.

Only a month later the women were desperate enough to plan to kill the four men as they slept. Once found out, the women were not punished but the men agreed the first woman to misbehave in the future would be instantly put to death. So would each subsequent offender until the 'real intentions of the women' could be discovered.

Talk meant nothing to the unhappy women, who made a physical attack on the men on 30 November. More threats were made but now the women seemed to have the upper hand. Whenever they were displeased, they collected their children and some firearms and hid in a remote or fortified part of the island until it pleased them to return. By such mercurial behaviour, the women were able to keep their men in a constant state of suspense. More important, they and their children were safe from physical abuse.

Nevertheless, Quintal fathered five children and Young, having had four by Nancy, then had three by Fletcher Christian's widow. McCoy only managed one further child and Adams, after a slow start, fathered four.

By 1796 there was a more sociable atmosphere, with the men entertaining one another in their houses and making life a little more comfortable for their women, possibly because by now there was little or none of *Bounty's* wine and rum remaining. That was not to last. McCoy had once worked in a Glasgow brewery and on 20 April 1797 he finally succeeded in distilling raw alcohol from the sweet syrup of the ti-root, *cordyline terminalis*. Drunkenness was once again added to promiscuity.

The raw spirits inflamed the fragile minds of McCoy and Quintal. By the end of the year McCoy lost control totally and threw himself off the cliffs just below Christian's house. By 1799 Quintal was threatening to kill Fletcher Christian's children unless he could have Mauatua as his wife and that same year Tevarua fell or, more probably, jumped from a cliff. The final solution was as bloody as all that had preceded. After Quintal threatened them too, Young and Adams attacked and killed him with axes. Now, there were two white men left. Young lived until Christmas Day 1800, when he died of asthma. Adams almost died of alcoholism and after visions of an avenging archangel, destroyed the still and converted Pitcairn to Christianity, the first religion its women could share.

This is broadly what is believed to be the history of Pitcairn's early days but it's a history collected by men and written about by men, who would have little regard for women, especially men who spent so long at sea that they hardly knew women. In the early 1800s, Queen Victoria's reign was decades away. Jane Austen's books that featured strong-minded young women were published anonymously between October 1811 and December 1815, a world away from that of anyone sailing in the South Pacific. Women simply didn't count in the lives of Pitcairn's early visitors from Europe and America.

It is this misogynistic mind-set against which we must assess early stories of Pitcairn, seeing them as yet more history written by men about men. I believe Pitcairn's women actively encouraged the death of most men, partly for their own relief but mainly for the safety and future happiness of their children. What emotion is fiercer in any community?

Isn't it suspicious that women sang songs rather than telling such as Fletcher or others that they knew the Ma'ohi men were plotting murder? This is classic 'it wasn't me' strategy, used later somehow to absolve them of any blame. And how about them all being absent from the village on Massacre Day? That made it easier for the black men to kill and for the women to claim they knew nothing about it because they were not there. Once you stop accepting men's versions of history and start asking about the women who were there, Pitcairn's past, including Massacre Day, can be caste entirely differently. The true story of the long-invisible blood of Pitcairn's foremothers is overdue for telling, something I hope I have done in *Mrs Christian* – Bounty *Mutineer.*

These were women who had gone on *Bounty* to be independent women and mothers, who sought a life of fulfilment rather than one truncated by men. Many endured serious physical and mental abuse on Pitcairn, yet eventually nurtured a gentle community of mixed European/South Seas blood, on an island marooned in scarcely imaginable tracts of ocean. That part wasn't new to them, for they were of the generation that first knew about other lands. Their ancestors had lived isolated for generations.

What was new was the constant terror of brutish drunken men, who would never change their attitudes to women. Why were the women discovered planning to kill the remaining white men? Why did they constantly leave the village with their children to live apart from the men? It would be nice for me to know that Fletcher Christian's background made him less likely to be a bully and wife-beater but what if *Bounty's* huge stores of alcohol and another mental breakdown made life dangerous for Mauatua and her children? If nothing else, Fletcher must daily have been profoundly disillusioned that his ideas of a community based on equality had foundered almost as soon as they had arrived on Pitcairn. A loving wife might not have been enough to douse any rage he felt. Imagine your fears as a pioneering

Ma'ohi woman when your island was discovered by ships only of men, who had no conception of what life might have been with constantly drunken and demanding mutineers or of what life was really like for women, any women. Imagine the protective responsibility the women felt towards their children, some of whom might remember the last of the murders but couldn't possibly understand why they had happened. Like Adams, not knowing what outsiders might think or do, might not the women have continued with *ha'avere* and lied to protect themselves and their children?

Apart from suspecting that visitors might be judge and jury on them, would Teraura want her younger husband Thursday to know she had murdered Tetahiti with an axe? Would Quintal's children or Edward Young's children benefit by knowing Edward had murdered Quintal because he was a drunken brute? The community of those born on Pitcairn looked up to Adams as a faultless leader. Knowing Adams had also wielded an axe to kill Quintal could have removed the security they felt.

Of course those women would hide the truth and intentionally deflect the truth of the past. It's very telling there are no contemporary records of how Fletcher Christian treated Mauatua. Was he another drunken brute who threatened her and their children? Did his mental state break down again or was he the only one of Pitcairn's settlers who behaved with dignity and fairness before Massacre Day? Why was so little recorded about the man whose mutiny and criss-crossing of the Pacific discovered Pitcairn and who fathered its first son? Perhaps no-one asked the right question, but I believe that, if they did, they were certain to get no answer. Why? Because Mauatua was alive and could control what was said.

Why the truth might matter after so long was much less important than what the truth would do to their children, the oldest of whom was only eighteen. Some of this new generation might have appreciated knowing men had been killed for their protection but it's not as simple as that. If the women were largely responsible for the deaths of most mutineers, wasn't it better their children were ignorant of this? As I say in *Mrs Christian* – Bounty *Mutineer*: 'Could you love a mother who you knew had killed your father?' The women were safer from suspicion than they might be in the twenty-first century, when questioning would be more determined. In the early nineteenth century visitors had a bigger question than anything to do with women, black women at that.

Where was Fletcher Christian?

HMS *Pandora*'s Box

On 24 March 1790, ten days after Bligh returned with his story of South Seas mutiny, George III ordered the pursuit of Fletcher Christian. The Admiralty appointed Captain Edward Edwards, and in classic deprecatory mode, Bligh doubted Edwards' ability even to find his way to and from Tahiti.

Bligh was court-martialled but acquitted of any blame for losing his ship. On 7 November 1790 Edwards' expedition sailed in *Pandora*, a frigate of 24 guns and 160 men. After months of searching in the South Pacific, it apprehended a few of the fugitives on Tahiti but overall the voyage cost almost as many men as had originally sailed on *Bounty*. It was a far more horrid illustration of barbarity than anything aboard *Bounty* had been.

Edwards is not a reliable source for details of the voyage. Both Morrison and Heywood furnish us with accounts of their treatment at the hands of this man, treatment that John Barrow, Second Secretary to the Admiralty, described as having 'a rigour which could not be justified on any ground of necessity or prudence'. Edwards based his justification on something other than necessity or prudence, fear of another mutiny. He had already been the victim of one aboard HMS *Narcissus* in 1782. Six of those mutineers were hanged, one sentenced to 500 lashes and another to two hundred.

Pandora anchored in Matavai Bay on 23 March 1791, after rounding the Horn and sailing close enough to Pitcairn's Island to have warranted investigation but Edwards ignored it or perhaps couldn't find it.

The success of his mission seemed assured in the first hours after Edwards arrived in Tahiti. Coleman put out in a canoe and climbed aboard. To his astonishment he was arrested. No-one could have suspected that Edwards was ordered to treat all *Bounty's* men he found as mutineers.

Next George Stewart and Peter Heywood arrived in a double canoe. They asked for Thomas Hayward, *Bounty's* lazy midshipman, now a 3rd Lieutenant, whom they had discovered was on board and expected him to plead their innocence. Heywood wrote later, 'he (like all worldlings when raised a little in life) received us very coolly and pretended ignorance of our affairs!' Stewart and Heywood were clapped in irons. Then the unsuspecting Skinner arrived and joined them in bondage.

Ten more *Bounty* men remained, all acting as mercenaries for Teina and helping prepare for a major massacre. Their arms and ammunition helped permanently change the social structure of Tahiti, enabling Tu eventually to become the first king of Tahiti, an unrecognised repercussion of Fletcher's mutiny.

Once all *Bounty's* men had been arrested, they were treated insufferably. Perhaps because Edwards was terrified that his own crew would be persuaded to mutiny, they were chained and forbidden to speak in English or Tahitian under pain of instant death. The hammocks they were given were verminous and they were unable to change their clothes because they were bound so tightly. The foul air and enervating temperature of their floating prison must have been torture enough to men who had so recently been free in the perfumed air of Tahiti. Enforced silence and lice made it intolerable.

Still not certain the prisoners were fully secure, Edwards ordered the construction of his infamous *Pandora's* box. On the after part of the ship's quarterdeck, it was 18 feet by 11 feet/5 metres by 3.4 metres. Only just taller than a man, the box was entered by a scuttle less than 2 feet/61 cms square and had only two holes 9 inches/23 cms square for ventilation. Iron grates in these effectively halved the amount of air that could pass. This unshaded box held fourteen men who were constantly protected by a musical comedy trio. Two guards stood on top and a midshipman marched around the four sides.

When the weather was sunny the heat was so intense that sweat ran from the suffering men in streams to the scuppers. When it rained, they were soaked. The prisoners could have the food friends brought them, but the foul conditions must have killed much of their appetites. There were two open basins for their wastes.

George Stewart was so shaken by the tormented cries of his wife he begged she should never be allowed to come aboard again. When McIntosh's leg slipped out of irons as he slept, everyone's irons were tightened. When their wrists began to swell, they were told the handcuffs were 'not meant to fit like gloves'.

The torture continued in Tahiti for two months before *Pandora* sailed on 8 May 1791, but the prisoners were still confined in the box. Edwards hoped to find Fletcher Christian and *Bounty* but in early August he gave up and ran for home. When near the Great Barrier Reef, he foolishly made inadequate safety precautions one night and *Pandora* ran aground, tumbling her manacled prisoners upon one another. Somehow, they managed to shatter their irons, but Edwards ordered them manacled again and as the water rose higher and higher, more guards were placed over the prisoners and Edwards ordered they be shot or hanged if their irons were broken again.

By six-thirty in the morning it was apparent that *Pandora* was lost. Edwards gave the order to abandon ship and jumped over the side with his officers, at last saying the prisoners could be released. An armourer's mate scrambled into the box to unlock their shackles. Muspratt, Skinner and Byrne struggled out but then *Pandora's* Master-at-arms, more heartless than Edwards and unaware of his orders, secured the hatchway once more. The moment he did this, the ship lurched and threw him overboard. The prisoners were locked in again with the man who was to release them. The ship was sinking but the Armourer's Mate worked in a frenzy to unshackle the men. At the last minute a sailor named William Moulter shouted that he would release the prisoners or go down with them and wrenched the bolt off the hatchway. Amazingly, everyone escaped but Hillbrant, who drowned while still fully shackled.

When Edwards arranged a rollcall on a sandbank three miles from the wreck he found thirty-five of his men had been lost including the prisoners George Stewart, Henry Hillbrant, Richard Skinner and John Sumner, but Edwards' vile treatment continued. The escapees from *Pandora*'s box were naked but he refused them permission to shelter from the tropical sun under a sail, so to avoid sunburn and sunstroke they buried themselves in sand. As scapegoats for the entire disaster, *Bounty*'s men were cruelly and ruthlessly treated as Edwards then led a hungry and thirsty flotilla of four open boats containing 99 men to Coupang. For the odious Hayward it was his second such arrival there.

Only in March 1792 when the prisoners were aboard HMS *Gorgon* in Cape Town, were they treated with any humanity. They arrived at Spithead on 19 June and were rowed through the foul waters to HMS *Hector* in Portsmouth Harbour.

Courts Martial and Defences

Of the twenty-five men left on *Bounty* when Bligh was turned off, only ten were to be tried. Some should not have been, but Bligh had forgotten to speak up, or did not do so loudly enough. For three months the suspected mutineers were confined aboard HMS *Hector* in Portsmouth harbour and there they were allowed writing paper, ink and visitors. Morrison composed his Memorandums, wrote his own defence and helped others construct theirs. With help from his companions, he was also working on his Journal, a detailed record of his experiences since December 1787. Heywood worked on his dictionary of the Tahitian language.

Two days after Edwards' court martial for the loss of *Pandora*, during which it was clearly shown there was no sympathy for the men of *Bounty*, not even the ones Bligh conceded were innocent, the ten survivors were brought to trial aboard HMS *Duke* on 12 September 1792. If they were found guilty, death was the sentence, but it was the practice that recommendations for mercy could and would be heeded. Each was charged with 'mutinously running away with the said armed vessel [*Bounty*] and deserting from His Majesty's Service'.

There was no mention of piracy and, as is often overlooked, there was no interest in any contributing causes of the mutiny. The trial was only about what happened on 28 April 1789. Did each man mutiny or did he not?

It was over a year since Bligh had sailed away in *Providence*, so he could not be cross-examined, which made it difficult for the prisoners or their counsel to plan suitable defences. Bligh's Narrative was admissible as evidence because it was 'official' and, not being able to contradict or to add what had been omitted, this meant the prisoners could be disbelieved on major issues. Public opinion was decidedly against them.

Peter Heywood was doubly damned by acts of commission and omission, especially when Bligh did not publish some lines from his original manuscript in his public versions of the mutiny. The most relevant omission was: 'As for the officers . . . they endeavoured to come to my assistance, but were not allowed to put their heads above the hatchway.' If Bligh had published that sentence, his story that everyone left on board was associated with the mutiny could not have been sustained. Suppression of that sentence was spiteful but there was just enough suspicion of collusion, based mainly on the extraordinary idea that as an officer this comparative boy should have led a counter-revolt. He was found guilty but recommended for mercy. An enormous effort was made on his behalf, led by his sister Nessy, something criticised as the upper classes conniving to protect and save one of their own but what is surprising about that?

The king granted Peter Heywood a free pardon on 24 October. Later legal wrangles resulted in the declaration that the King's Warrant was not so much a pardon for a crime committed as a quashing of the conviction.

Morrison was found guilty but also given a free pardon. It is likely that copies of his Memorandum, subtitled *Vedi et Scio* (I saw and I know), which was written while he was awaiting trial, was circulated discreetly amongst senior members of the Royal Navy during the trials and was one of the 'various reasons' contributing to his pardon. There was plenty of precedent for counter charges at mutiny trials and it was precisely this kind of nastiness that Banks would want to avoid. Read in conjunction with the trials' evidence, Morrison's outline of what could be said in reply (even if not substantiated), showed it would be troublesome to convict men about whom there was any possible doubt. They, then having nothing to lose, would counter claim. In some cases, the captains against whom counter charges had been made were found guilty and dismissed from the service. Banks could not afford to let this happen to Bligh because it would ruin them both.

Morrison's Narrative was not published until 1935, but even so details of what Bligh had not said were repeated in and out of the Royal Navy and helped consolidate views about him.

Norman, Coleman and McIntosh were acquitted, as was the fiddler Byrne, but none was given compensation for their appalling treatment by Edwards aboard *Pandora*. Muspratt was convicted but discharged because of a technical irregularity.

Ellison, Burkitt and Millward were sentenced without a recommendation for mercy. On 29 October 1792, the three men were hanged publicly aboard HMS *Brunswick*. Seamen from every other Royal Navy ship in the port were present. Millward is said to have made the following stirring and penitential speech to the assembled tars. It sounds unlikely but several people vouch for its veracity and perhaps it was penned by Morrison.

> Brother seamen, you see before you three lusty young fellows about to suffer a shameful death for the dreadful crime of mutiny and desertion. Take warning by our example never to desert your officers, and should they behave ill to you, remember it is not their cause, it is the cause of your country you are bound to support.

The shameful death the onlookers were about to see was an example indeed. Royal Navy hangings were not a sudden drop to break your neck. Instead, a cohort hoisted you aloft from deck level, so that the slow choking and the facial discolouration, the bowel and bladder voiding and the futile struggling against suffocation were public and prolonged.

Once the trials were over, quite different stories emerged. Heywood quickly told Fletcher Christian's family the truth about *Bounty*, as he had promised Fletcher he would in Matavai Bay. He sent a moving letter to Edward Christian that was also published in the *Cumberland Pacquet*, the first intimation the public received that they might not have been told the whole truth by Bligh. Writing from Great Russell Street in London on 5 November 1792, he said:

> SIR, I am sorry to say I have been informed you were inclined to judge too harshly of your truly unfortunate brother; and to think of him in such a manner as I am conscious, from the knowledge I had of his most worthy disposition and character (both public and private), he merits not in the slightest degree; therefore I think it my duty to undeceive you, and to rekindle the flame of brotherly love (or pity) now towards him, which, I fear, the false reports of slander and vile suspicion may nearly have extinguished.
>
> Excuse my freedom, Sir: If it would not be disagreeable to you, I will do myself the pleasure of waiting upon you; and endeavour to prove that your brother was not that vile wretch, void of all gratitude, which the world had the unkindness to think him; but, on the contrary, a most worthy character, ruined only by the misfortune (if it can be so called) of being a young man of strict honour, and adorned with every virtue; and beloved by all (except one, whose ill report is his greatest praise) who had the pleasure of his acquaintance.
>
> I am Sir, with esteem
>
> Your most obedient humble servant
>
> P. Heywood

Edward Christian must have been astonished. Although his brother Charles thought there were extenuating circumstances, Edward, like everyone else, must have believed Bligh's version. Now he was told that 'the dreadful mutiny on the Bounty originated from motives, and was attended with circumstances different from those which had been presented to the world'.

Edward's legal chambers were in Gray's Inn, where he had been since 5 July 1782, but he went to see Mr Romilly of Lincoln's Inn and then took advice from a more senior legal man who had been present at the trial, probably Sir Archibald McDonald, Attorney-General. Bligh's servant John Smith went to see Edward Christian of his own accord, clearly wanting to tell a different story. *Bounty's* sailing master John Fryer visited Joseph Christian of No. 10 Strand and he said Fryer also told a new and different story. Heywood, Smith and Fryer acted with speed but Edward Christian, acting with the caution of all good legal men, took his time to do anything about publicly defending his brother Fletcher.

The *Cumberland Pacquet* published Heywood's letter and other papers reprinted it. Bligh was far away at sea, so Banks cut the reprinted piece out of a newspaper, the name and date of which he omitted to note, and kept it to show him. This is part of the preface, written by a newspaper:

> Though there may be certain actions which even the torture and extremity of provocation cannot justify yet a sudden act of phrenzy, so circumstanced, is far removed in reason and mercy from the foul deliberate contempt of every religious and virtuous sentiment and obligation excited by selfish and base gratifications. For the honour of this county, we are happy to assure our readers that one of its natives FLETCHER CHRISTIAN is not that detestable and horrid monster of wickedness and depravity, which with extreme and perhaps unexampled injustice and barbarity to him and his relations he has long been represented but a character for whom every feeling heart must now sincerely grieve and lament . . .'

Heywood's letter then followed but, apart from saying the author was an officer on *Bounty*, his identity was not revealed. The article went on to say that Edward Christian had since spoken to three officers and two seamen from *Bounty* who were in the London area. McIntosh alone is named, having said about Fletcher: 'Oh! he was a gentleman, and a brave man, and every officer and sailor on board the ship would have gone through fire and water to have served him.' The newspaper article concluded by saying the mystery was soon to be solved and that shame and infamy would be in the proportions it had been earned.

Edward Christian now went about collecting evidence that would explain his brother's mutiny. It is common for Bligh apologists to demean Edward Christian, citing a line from the *Dictionary of National Biography*, where he is said to have died in full possession of 'his incapacities'. This might be true but does not represent who he was in 1791 and without the respect and status he then had he could never have gathered the evidence that he did.

Admitted to Gray's Inn in 1782, Edward was called to the Bar in 1786, after which he was permitted to act as a barrister. In 1788, aged just 30, he was named Downing Professor of the Laws of England, although the college was not to be founded until 1800, after which he was a Fellow of Downing from 1800 to 1823. He was appointed Law Professor at the East India Company College from 1806-18 and then was Chief Justice on the Isle of Ely.

In June 1791, the year of his great success prosecuting on behalf of William and Dorothy Wordsworth, Edward renewed his lease of chambers at 3 Coney Court at 3 Gray's Inn Square but by 8 December assigned the balance to another member of the Inn. From now on he must have spent much time in researching and writing in defence of his brother Fletcher, including his extensive correspondence with Sir Joseph Banks.

If there were anything suspicious, devious or dishonest about Edward's research and writing that was published in 1794 as part of Stephen Barney's *Minutes of the trial of the Bounty mutineers*, it is unlikely that Gray's Inn would have appointed him to their Bench, its managing committee in 1809 or to their most senior rank, that of *Thesaurarius* or Treasurer in 1810. A stained-glass image of his unicorn-crested arms commemorates this in the west window of Gray's Inn Hall. If he were to have been twisting facts it is equally unlikely he would have retained his position with Downing College.

What else would Edward Christian have done but gather those he felt would support his cause? What balances the supposed imbalance found by Bligh apologists is that he published the names and addresses of them all, inviting Bligh and others to confront them directly if they disagreed or suspected foul play. To my knowledge nobody did, because there was none.

Edward's equally qualified older brother John might have helped but he was dead. As a second wife he married the widow of a sugar merchant, twenty-three years older than him and, presumably, a great deal richer for they lived in Pall Mall, steps away from St James's Palace. He was only 39 when he left her a widow a second time in 1791. According to a document kindly sent to me by Caroline Alexander (*The Bounty: 2003*), the cause was 'a slow decline'.

It was to be almost 18 months before Edward Christian's revelations were published. He had no need to hurry, for others were equally interested in telling versions other than Bligh's.

It is naïve to call everything written by other men simply an attack on Bligh. Why shouldn't Fryer and Morrison and Heywood wish to defend themselves more publicly than the trial allowed? If Bligh was entitled to publish his opinions, why should not others be heard? Whatever was being said in public was different from that said in private. Charles Christian spoke to a captain of marines from *Providence*, who said 'from Bligh's odious behaviour during the voyage, he would as soon shoot him as a dog, if it were not for the law'. Lieutenant Bond wrote much more in that vein, but he did not do so in public, so it had no immediate effect.

Sir Joseph Banks received a welter of correspondence and documents concerning the *Bounty* affair from Edward Christian. Banks asked Bligh to answer the allegations and questions they brought up. For 18 months after returning in *Providence,* Bligh had little else to occupy his time. He was on half pay, with no offer of a command. It is not clear why this should have been so. He had promised Betsy that if he was returned safe from the *Providence* voyage, he would forswear the sea but that was ages ago and promises were the blight of his life. His long furlough may also have been an unofficial punishment or expression of displeasure after the publication of alternative versions of Bligh's Narrative.

The Mitchell Library in Sydney holds Bligh's draft replies to Banks concerning three separate sets of documents. I cannot think why these notes have not been given more importance, except they are not indexed and so take days to read and few authors on the subject want to spend so much time.

First, Bligh sketched answers to three letters addressed in December 1791 to Banks by Edward Christian in which he revealed the information he had collected from ex-*Bounty* men in London to which the newspaper article alluded and that he wished to publish. It was an act of fairness by Edward to present them to Banks before publishing, not the actions of a man who wanted to defend his brother Fletcher at any price.

Wishing to keep the interest of Banks, Bligh carefully moves for the first time towards allowing the possible veracity of other men's stories, indeed in places he positively contradicts his public statements. Perhaps he realised that to retain his position he had to resort to the truth, except Bligh asserts he was Fletcher Christian's sole patron and had employed him in the Merchant Service for three years, a lapse as the correct length was nine months.

Bligh scratchily makes the major confession to Banks that the mutiny might possibly have been caused solely by Fletcher Christian's desperation but then dismisses this because he was not aware of it:

What Mr Christian calls his Brother's being drove to desperation must have been a very sudden impulse, for it is certain that Capt. Bligh's usual invitation to dinner and supper with him was sent to him the day before the mutiny happened.

Fletcher Christian's mutiny against him was a sudden impulse? Bligh saying so is utterly inconsistent with his determined view that the mutiny was planned in advance. He dismisses the idea by believing a dinner invitation is proof enough that Fletcher Christian was not driven to despair. Elsewhere in the notes, Bligh finally admits he had words with his officers and men about coconuts but does not elaborate, another case where silence was his only defence. His inconsistency on shore equals that at sea.

Bligh also reveals that he argued with Christian after they left Tahiti, another important new admission and further proof his Narrative was by no means exhaustive, balanced or truthful. He shifts his ground on other points too but keeps his paranoia firmly in place. He constantly says to Banks that many of the men now criticising him should have done so at his court martial for the loss of *Bounty* in 1790. The fact they did not proved to Bligh they had no just complaints and had subsequently been suborned. On the other hand, Bligh had not prosecuted Fryer or others when he could but he ignores this. He also moves the theory of concerted action against him first from Tahiti to *Bounty* and then to England.

Once the prisoners from *Pandora* arrived back in Britain, Bligh claims they and their friends formed connections to prevent the mutineers from being hanged. And why not? It would have been very silly for Fryer and Purcell, for instance, to have attacked Bligh at the first court martial without the supporting evidence of others who were involved. Why is it thought strange if there was a degree of collusion among the defendants and possibly the prosecutors? It's what accused men do, especially when threatened with death if found guilty.

There are two more points about the trial. First, Bligh did not accept those men had any right to defend themselves, citing his Narrative as 'sacred truths', even though he knew this was not so. He had defended himself and dissembled and he should have expected others to do so, except he might then have been revealed as a liar or withholder of the truth. Bligh also overlooked that if the prisoners were plotting to save their lives, they could have done so by uniting to blame everything on Fletcher Christian but nowhere was Christian blamed. They could have made him a temperamental, inconsistent and disloyal second-in-command and Bligh would have had to support them, making him appear on their side. If as desperate and groundless as Bligh thought, they might also have played the homosexual card.

Bligh said Peter Heywood's evidence from the court martial incriminated Fletcher Christian in the fullest manner. That Heywood went on to write the letter to Edward Christian simply confirmed Bligh's belief that evidence had been tampered with. Bligh was sure that Edward Christian and Peter Heywood believed Fletcher was innocent, but this is untrue. Edward Christian knew his brother was a mutineer, said so in print and did not defend this. He his brother Charles and many others wished only to know the reasons the crime had been committed. If Bligh's reputation was damaged that was unavoidable, and had not Bligh already done this to almost everyone aboard *Bounty*? Professor Beaglehole is not the only one to say that the low opinions Bligh had of everyone who sailed with him were subsequently shared by very few others, yet that the low opinion of Bligh was extensive in and out of the Royal Navy for the rest of his life, when he was commonly that '*Bounty* bastard'.

In Bligh's letters to Banks about the court martial, he refers once more to the conspiracy he thought was planned on Tahiti, certain that Fletcher did have a particular female on Tahiti. He said Coleman remembered her and that Lebogue, who had gone out again with Bligh in *Providence*, had actually seen her at Otaheite on that visit. 'She went with Christian always untill his last Departure, which was sudden and unknown'. If Lebogue and Bligh agree that Fletcher's favourite was abandoned, this casts doubt on why Mauatua went with Christian to Tubuai and then to Pitcairn.

It is noteworthy that Bligh never asked this 'favourite' or any Tahitian for information about Fletcher Christian or any other ex-*Bounty* man when he was again in Tahiti.

In the Mitchell Library's notes to Banks, Bligh adds new information about Fletcher. First, he writes that aboard the *Britannia*, '*Christian stood godfather to Peter Roger's child my boatswain who was a very low man and was connected in plundering sugar belonging to Mr Hibbert £17 as Mr Lamb reported.*' Presumably Bligh is attempting to show that Christian was also 'low' because he stood godfather to the son of a dishonest man. Christian's act was a form of patronage and a telling example of how well he was regarded. Bligh was possibly jealous, never having been asked to stand as godfather to anyone's child. Bligh adds that '*Christian also had a hoard of provisions aboard Britannia*', perhaps supporting his belief that Fletcher was likely to steal coconuts. A private store of comforting provisions is almost the first thing any prospective long-distance sailor does. Why Bligh thought this worth mentioning is a desperate curiosity.

A Brother's Defence

Edward Christian had asked permission to reprint the Admiralty's official minutes of the *Bounty* court martial but was refused on the grounds that public records could not be released for private publication. So, Edward presented himself to Stephen Barney, the counsel for Muspratt. He had taken copious notes throughout the proceedings and although they were incomplete, with discrepancies and mistakes, they were better than nothing for Edward Christian's project. He would be able to publish men's words spoken under oath.

Having seen Edward Christian's evidence and answered Banks' questions, it was typical of Bligh's constant inability to judge other men that he did not foresee what was about to happen. In mid-1794 you could buy Stephen Barney's *Minutes of the Proceedings of the Court-Martial Held at Portsmouth August 12, 1792 on TEN PERSONS charged with MUTINY on His Majesty's Ship BOUNTY* [sic] *with an APPENDIX containing a full Account of the real Causes and Circumstances of that unhappy Transaction, the most material of which have hitherto been withheld from the Public.*

The Appendix was Edward Christian's work and at last the rumours, gossip and contradictions in private and naval circulation were suddenly public.

The introductory page of *The Appendix* is dated 15 May 1794 and Edward thanks Barney, acknowledging that his notes had been taken with no thought of future publication. Edward declares that he alone is responsible for the accuracy of what he says in *The Appendix* and that the information was obtained exactly how and from whom he says.

The Appendix is unequivocal about how abhorrent was the crime of mutiny and Edward pointed out the trial's concern was to establish

only who did what on the morning of the mutiny and had no interest
in preceding events that might have been contributory. This unknown
background to his brother Fletcher's mutiny is what Edward was
now presenting. Society was transfixed because, except for mutineer
Muspratt, all the nice things said to Edward Christian about his brother
Fletcher were from Bligh loyalists.

> He was a gentleman; a brave man; and every officer and seaman
> on board the ship would have gone through fire and water to
> serve him.

> I would still wade up to the arm-pits in blood to serve him

> As much as I have lost and suffered by him, if he could be
> restored to his country, I should be the first to go without
> wages in search of him

> Everybody under his command did their duty at a look from
> Mr Christian

> Mr Christian was always good-natured, I never heard him say
> 'Damn you' to any man on board the ship.

As a legal man, Edward Christian had collected a group of men of
impeccable reputation and almost every time he spoke to someone from
Bounty, one or more of these men were present. Just as sworn witnesses
in court, these eminent and successful men were prepared to be named
and to bear testimony that what they heard first-hand was faithfully
represented in *The Appendix*. The list further averts any charge of
falsehood because each could be contacted for verification, as their
addresses or official capacities were printed:

John Farhill, Esq., 38 Mortimer Street
Samuel Romilly, Esq., Lincoln's Inn
Mr Gilpin, No. 432 Strand

The Rev. Dr Fisher, Canon of Windsor
The Rev. Mr Cookson, Canon of Windsor
Captain Wordsworth, *Abergavenny* [an East Indiaman]
Rev. Mr Antrobus, Chaplain to the Bishop of London
John France, Esq., Temple
James Losh, Esq., Temple
Rev. Dr Frewen, Colchester
John Atkinson, Esq., Somerset Herald at the College of Arms

Most of the men had connections with St John's, Cambridge and with William Wilberforce, the great opponent of slavery, whom Edward befriended there. There is considerable circumstantial evidence in C. S. Wilkinson's *The Wake of the Bounty* to support the claim that Edward Christian was able to gather these men because they were opposed to the slavery-related business interests of Bligh's earlier patron and relative by marriage, Duncan Campbell. It may have been one of the things they had in common but what was the relevance here? If an anti-slavery campaign was their motive, they would have said so. Many of the men had connections with the Wordsworths, too. Edward had won their famous case against the Earl of Lonsdale in 1791 and William Wordsworth was also a St John's man. Both the Canons of Windsor were very close to the king, far too sensitive a position in which to join in perjury. Dr Fisher was known, according to one source, as the 'King's Fisher'. Antrobus was from Cockermouth and Romilly, later Sir Samuel, became a famous law reformer. What else would Edward Christian have done but gather those he felt would support his cause? What balances the supposed imbalance found by critics is that he published the names and addresses of them all, inviting Bligh and others to confront them directly if they disagreed. To my knowledge nobody did.

Edward's investigating committee must have been formidable to meet and perhaps some of *Bounty*'s sailors did alter their stories slightly 'to please the gentlemen'. It was not just able seamen who were interviewed, and Edward Christian also published the whereabouts of each man to whom he spoke. The only thing he hid was who said what and there were very good reasons for that, as shown when McIntosh was threatened in the street. The *Bounty* men interviewed who had returned with Bligh were:

John Fryer, the Master
Thomas Hayward, Midshipman
William Peckover, Gunner [who lived with some nicety in Gun Alley, Wapping] William Purcell, Carpenter
John Smith, personal cook to Bligh
Lawrence Lebogue, Sailmaker
Joseph Coleman, Armourer, tried and acquitted
Thomas McIntosh, Carpenter's mate, tried and acquitted
Michael Byrne, Musician, tried and acquitted
Peter Heywood, Midshipman, pardoned
William Muspratt, able seaman, might have been convicted but for a legal error
James Morrison, acquitted and who wrote to Edward Christian.

Edward Christian's Appendix re-tells the whole story, which because it is first-hand has been used in this book as authoritative. A particular paragraph in which Edward Christian discusses his brother's relationship with women has always created problems. The sentence continuously misinterpreted is one in answer to Bligh's assertion that Christian had a favourite female and that his mutiny was based entirely on his desire to return to her.

Fletcher Christian was on shore all the time *Bounty* was first in Tahiti, yet not one man on the same duty agreed he had a female favourite or any attachment or particular connection among the women. Even if Fletcher did, Bligh then tells us that this was not the woman who went away with him. So, either Fletcher had nothing to do with women on Tahiti or, as Edward said, Fletcher did but had no regular or favourite female companion and that thus for either of these reasons could not have mutinied for the sake of a woman.

Edward's last paragraphs are impressive:

> The writer of this Appendix would think himself an accomplice in the crime which has been committed, if he designedly should give the slightest shade to any word or fact different from its true and just representation; and lest he should be supposed to be actuated by a vindictive spirit, he has studiously forborn to make more comments than were absolutely necessary upon any statement which he has been obliged to bring forward. He felt it a duty to himself, to the connections of all the unfortunate men and to society to collect and lay before the Public these extraordinary circumstances.

> The sufferings of Captain Bligh and his companions in the boat, however severe they may have been, are perhaps but a small portion of the torments occasioned by this dreadful event: and whilst these prove the melancholy and extensive consequences of the crime of Mutiny, the crime itself in this instance may afford an awful lesson to the Navy, and to Mankind, that there is a pressure, beyond which the best formed and principled mind must either break or recoil. And though public justice and the public safety can allow no vindication of any species of mutiny, yet reason and humanity will distinguish the sudden unpremeditated act of desperation and phrenzy from the foul deliberate contempt of every religious duty and honourable sentiment; and will deplore the uncertainty of human prospects, when they reflect that a young man is condemned to perpetual infamy, who, if he had served on board any other ship, or had perhaps been absent from the Bounty a single day,

or one ill-fated hour, might still have been an honour to his country and a glory and comfort to his friends!

Bligh's best response would have been suitably edited and published extracts from the letters I discovered from him to Banks in response to Edward Christian's questions. Instead, he published a series of miscellaneous correspondence and orders that have no cohesion and upon which he does not comment. Some of them even tell against him, such as Heywood's letter to Edward Christian, which Bligh does not counteract by comparing it with Heywood's evidence in court. The few comments Bligh made were meant to debunk Edward Christian's method of collecting statements. Bligh suggested he withheld facts about who said what to obfuscate the truth and to prevent perjurers being brought to justice. This was a dangerous thing to claim about a Gray's Inn barrister and reckless to say about two Canons of Windsor or a Somerset Herald. Bligh was publicly calling them liars and plotters but Edward was only protecting his sources, then and now an acceptable part of collecting fact for publication.

Next, in 1795 Edward Christian published *A Short Reply to Capt. William Bligh's Answer.* Even Christian's foes admit it is brilliantly argued for it removes absolutely any suspicion that Edward Christian kept his quotations anonymous for any but the most noble reasons; without a guarantee of anonymity the men would not have spoken at all. McIntosh had been threatened for what he had said to Christian and whoever else was present.

The Short Reply is one of the rarest and most expensive pamphlets in the world. Only 150 were printed and in 1982 only three are known to exist. When *A Book of the BOUNTY* was published in 1938, it collected all contemporary documents, including Bligh's account of *Bounty* and his open-boat voyage, the minutes of the mutineers' trials, *The Appendix* and Bligh's *Answer.* Edward Christian's *A Short Reply* is not included and this must be why so many authors have overlooked its important substantiation of everything in *The Appendix*. Could it be they just don't want to know?

Edward Christian and his eminent colleagues worked together to publish facts that otherwise would have been suppressed. Journalists get prizes for that today.

Kennedy and others suggest that *A Short Reply* was meant to sting Bligh into taking legal action. Bligh could then have been cross-examined, hoping to disprove the allegations in *The Appendix* and their corroboration in *A Short Reply*. They could not be disproven, so once again William Bligh said nothing.

In April, just months after publication, Bligh was given command of HMS *Calcutta* and supervised her conversion from the East Indiaman *Warley* to a 54-gun fourth rate and in October sailed in her with 200 troops to put down a mutiny aboard HMS *Defiance*.

Once again, he was far less trouble to the authorities when he was at sea than ashore, yet he had learned nothing from his South Seas ordeals.

Pitcairn as Establishment Pawn

Once news got around about the idyllic Christian community on Pitcairn Island, the Anglican Church couldn't keep its suffocating hands off it. Here was living proof that, quite as the Christian family motto proclaimed, there was salvation through Christ. Establishment Anglicanism and arrogant Colonialism combined to know both better and best for Pitcairners, as they did for any peoples neither white nor British nor of their religion.

In 1831 Pitcairn Island had 87 inhabitants and was well able to support itself. John Adams, who died in 1829, had disagreed and written to London requesting the Pitcairners be transported to Australia, although this appears to have been ignored. Missionary Henry Nott convinced the Colonial Office they should instead be transported to Tahiti, so they could then be used to proclaim his religion throughout the South Pacific, about as dehumanising an idea as it is possible to imagine.

Another interfering missionary called Crook convinced Governor Darling of New South Wales to speed up moving the Pitcairners to Tahiti.

With no advance knowledge or opportunity for discussion on the island, the ships *Lucy Ann* and *Comet* suddenly arrived and told the community they were to leave. Painful as this was, they agreed and sailed on 7 March 1831, being promised land and other benefits. Once on Tahiti, none of these was realised. The king of Tahiti who had offered much was dead. His successor, the wilful young Queen Pomare, was trying to cope with civil war and a difficult lover and knew little of previous undertakings to the arrivals.

Although the British Government was behind their removal to Tahiti, it didn't even have a consul in Tahiti and the three representatives of the London Missionary Society took little responsibility, even though Pitcairners were planned to be their future proselytisers. Together with French missionaries, they were busier smothering and burning Tahitian heritage more fully and shamefully than any other Polynesian culture; it was even forbidden to wear flowers.

Pitcairn families were separated and billeted out to households that had different or no morality and spoke a different language. The unwilling refugees were mocked for their ragged clothes and curious way of speech, had no concept of money or deceit, and some adopted the alcohol and the immorality of Papeete's waterfront. Eventually they were crowded into one large house in Papeete. Proud and independent at home, they were reduced to living on hand outs and what little some of the men could earn labouring. Then an influenza-like pestilence hit them, another desperate challenge from their unwanted new world.

On 21 April, Mauatua's eldest son Thursday October was first to die. Three days later Lucy Ann Quintal died, only months old. On the 29th it was Vahineatua, one of Pitcairn's foremothers. On 6 May George Young died. Kitty Quintal was 12 when she died on 15 May. Next day Thursday's daughter Polly (Young) died. A day later 9-year-old Jane McCoy was lost. On the 8th Catherine Quintal died and then so did Toofaiti, another of the foremothers. Next month Thursday's son Charles died, so did Daniel McCoy and Hugh McCoy. In less than ten weeks, twelve had died, almost one in seven. The food supplied to them was dumped on their doorstep, as though they were lepers.

The Pitcairners resolutely raised funds to charter the *Charles Doggett*, Captain William Driver, using a combination of donations and the sale of personal possessions, including copper from *Bounty* they had taken for bartering anyway; even the three missionaries from the London Missionary Society contributed, as well they might.

The Pitcairners arrived back in Bounty Bay in September 1831, only to discover that their homes had been raided by the Royal Navy and that, amongst other things, the lovingly hand-made lead-and-oak gravestone of John Adams had been stolen—it is in the National Maritime Museum, London.

The tragedy of the migration to Tahiti was not the end of being bullied by egotistical Englishmen. Between 1832 and late 1837, the Pitcairners suffered appalling interference by an unauthorised mad man called Joshua Hill, who created competing churches and schools on the tiny island and threatened death to a girl who harvested from the wrong sweet-potato patch. He had been thrown out, but the island was vulnerable to drunken crews of whalers and sealers who thought the island fair game for lawlessness because it belonged to neither Britain, France nor the United States.

On 29 November 1838, the two oldest Mrs Christians, Mauatua and Teraura, helped persuade Captain Russell Elliot of HMS *Fly* to accept Pitcairn as a British Crown Colony. He had no such authority but, by his official 'approval' of an extraordinary list of laws and punishments, he legitimised the island enough for others to believe it.

The unique regulations Captain Elliott stamped into law included very clear rules about raising hogs, not killing white birds, who could pick fruit from which tree, the forbidding of claims against the past sins of others and made killing a cat one of the worst temporal sins.

Included in the long list was the Island-Council's remarkable decision to give the vote to all women over 18 and to make education compulsory for girls. Both were world firsts by a very long way. Considering Pitcairn's isolation and the type of visitor that generally called, the inspiration can only have come from within the island. To me that means Mauatua continued the voting legacy of long-dead Fletcher Christian, the man who had made her new life possible. It was a revolution, bloodless now, but with its roots first in mutiny and then in massacre and it was the first to benefit women. American and French women didn't earn the vote after their eighteenth-century revolutions.

My Tahitian great-great-great-great grandmother Mauatua must have been over 80 when she became one of the few women in history who had lawful voting power, even though this was barely acknowledged by the men who continued to visit and interfere with Pitcairn. After surviving all she had, Mauatua/Isabella/Mrs Christian died a victim of yet another introduced influenza epidemic. On 19 September 1841, she was buried on a site until recently covered by Pitcairn's village hall. My great-great-great grandfather Charles 'Hoppa' followed her to his grave in the same ground early the following year; his wife Sully had died in 1826. The village hall has now been removed and the burial site preserved as open space, which allows her descendants to be closer to Mauatua than has been possible for almost two centuries.

In September 1855 Pitcairn's population was 187 and for mixed reasons it was decided the island should be abandoned. Queen Victoria had always been keen on them and approved a move to Norfolk Island, until recently a British penal colony with a reputation at least as cruel as France's Devil's Island. Once again, the entire island voted to move. On 2 May 1856 they began an uncomfortable voyage of 3,700 miles/6,000 kms westwards across the South Pacific with as many of their possessions as practical aboard the 830-ton *Morayshire*. It was 8 June before they landed but it was not until the 26th that they were alone; the last of the convicts and penal officers helped them settle in and showed them how to use the tools they were leaving.

Norfolk Island is not Pitcairn closer to 'civilisation'. It is temperate rather than sub-tropical and had grown no breadfruit or coconut palms, meaning a major temperature and dietary change for the settlers. After a few years some returned to Pitcairn. They were mainly descendants of Fletcher's older son Thursday October, while those choosing to remain were largely descendants of Charles. My grandfather William was born there and was a whaling hand-harpoonist at the age of twelve.

The Pitcairners were promised independence on Norfolk Island but this never fully happened. Recently Australia has largely annexed the island, which seems to be of little advantage to the islanders, the majority of whom are *Bounty* descendants. It will be a continuing fight for them to maintain their unique culture and language, a version of Pitkern, itself a creation of eighteenth-century English and Tahitian.

It is a sad and unnecessary case of third-time-unlucky for *Bounty* descendants.

A greatly extended version of life on Pitcairn, including the forced move to Tahiti, is in my historical-fiction novel *Mrs Christian* - Bounty *Mutineer*. Although dramatized, it is based on solid research into Tahitian custom and gives deep insights into the thoughts and customs of Pitcairn's Polynesian Foremothers, co-founders of the first British colony in the South Pacific.

Fletcher Christian's Fate - I

C ould Fletcher Christian have escaped from Pitcairn Island and returned to Cumberland? Until I began my research in the late 1970s, the circumstantial evidence seemed as strong for a dangerous undercover return to his birthplace as for his demise on Pitcairn. My determination to find the answer led to important discoveries in many parts of the world, not least when I walked through conflicting stories on the red volcanic soil of Pitcairn Island.

My first extraordinary find was an unknown 600-year Christian family history put together by the last Mrs Christian and Miss Christian who lived at Milntown, over the turn of the nineteenth to the twentieth century. These spectacular volumes are now in the Manx Museum collections by courtesy of Ewan Christian, who inherited them from Milntown's genealogists through his father, John Monsell Christian. Over decades the two women copied by hand every document associated with the family for many centuries, some now lost or destroyed such as those burned with the Dublin Public Records Office in 1922. Their copy of Charles Christian's otherwise lost autobiography was part of this trove of family history.

In their entry about Fletcher Christian, whom the authoresses dub the undoubted black sheep of the family, they write:

> It is . . . extremely unlikely that the Pitcairners should have been deceived in the matter of their leader's death. Moreover, had Fletcher got back to England the only motive worth the risk would have been to see his family and of such an event no tradition has been preserved.

I find this completely persuasive, considering its provenance. If there had been the tiniest glimmer of gossip from sources in or close to the family, Vio Christian and her daughter, Rita Christian Browne, would have found it and recorded it.

It *is* equally unlikely that the Pitcairners could have been deceived about the death of their leader. If Fletcher Christian had not died on Pitcairn but escaped, some mention must surely have slipped out in conversation with early visitors. Whatever the answer there was no danger to them, so I believe Pitcairners' first questions would have been about whether or not Fletcher had succeeded, if he had survived. Surely Mauatua could not have resisted asking?

No hint of an escape has ever come from Pitcairn but because Adams told different stories about the island's past, he created a mystery that led others to infer such a possibility.

Only two ships accidentally found Pitcairn after *Bounty* did. Both thought it uninhabited. One sent men ashore to collect coconuts but did not detect any sign of habitation. Neither did the other ship, which was prevented from landing by violent swells. The next day was apparently the calmest since *Bounty* had arrived but fortunately the intruder had sailed off. The habit of having no fires during the day still kept Pitcairners safe.

On 6 February 1808, the Boston sealer *Topaz*, Captain Mayhew Folger, chanced upon the incorrectly charted rock. For reasons never explained but probably connected with the younger inhabitants' mixture of naivety and curiosity, the Pitcairn community made itself known to the ship.

When Thursday October, wearing cock feathers in his hat, led other Pitcairners to board the *Topaz*, Folger was astonished that he spoke English and claimed to be English, saying all their fathers were English. He didn't know about America and asked if it was in Ireland. He knew Bligh's name, was frightened by a dog and didn't know how hinged doors worked – on Pitcairn doors and windows slid. Folger stayed only for one day during which Adams gave one of his many versions of the island's history and what had happened to Fletcher Christian. Thursday's Tahitian mother Mauatua was still alive, although Thursday said she wasn't. The obfuscations of inaccurate memory and self-protecting *ha'avere* had begun.

That something awesome and Biblical had happened between 1790 and 1808 was certain. Pitcairn was not the expected group of middle-aged men and women and their children. Instead, the island was populated like an embryonic Eden, largely by children and teenagers. Fletcher Christian's older son Thursday October had turned 18 the previous October and was already a father. There was one adult European male, corpulent, pig-tailed, tapa-swathed John Adams. There were nine adult Ma'ohi women, seven from Tahiti and one each from Huahine and Tubuai. The other fourteen white and black men who sailed from Tahiti were not to be seen. Everyone told a different story about how and when Fletcher Christian died. This soon made men wonder if he were dead.

The Pitcairners didn't want King George to think them thieves and in exchange for a silk handkerchief Mauatua gave Folger the Kendall K2 chronometer and azimuth compass, trusting him to return it. After many adventures K2 is now displayed at the Royal Observatory, Greenwich. Mrs Christian also gave Folger Fletcher's Chinese porcelain bowl decorated with peonies and pheasants, which went home with him to Nantucket. Now owned by the Nantucket Historical Association, it can be seen in the Nantucket Whaling Museum together with the piece of *Bounty's* copper sheathing I had been given during my 1980 expedition to Pitcairn.

Folger sent news of his discovery back to England via the Consul in Valparaiso, but few were interested. France and Bonaparte were causing trouble again. It was not until 17 September 1814 that men again sighted the peaks of Pitcairn where none should have been. This was an altogether more serious encounter as these were British naval frigates,

Briton, Captain Sir Thomas Staines, and *Tagus*, Captain Pipon. The ships had been hunting for an American man-of-war, *Essex*, which had been worrying English whalers.

In 1817 Boston-based *Sultan*, Captain Reynolds, raised Pitcairn and was the last ship that did not previously know of the island. After that the publication of the visit of *Briton* and *Tagus* was causing a sensation and callers became increasingly common. They thirsted for gossip about the mystery of what was vaunted as the world's most perfect community and were also assured of excellent water and good meat, fruit and vegetables, a blessing in remote South Pacific waters. In return, they were expected to behave, to keep their libido, blasphemy and innuendo to themselves and to give such as nails, tools, clothes and religious tracts. These early visitors besieged the islanders with questions. The fate of Fletcher Christian and *Bounty* had been a favourite topic in the inns of ports and the wardrooms of naval ships for two decades. The enquirers learned much, except for the truth.

The world had been fed with possibilities of Fletcher's escape from self-inflicted exile since as early as 1796. That year the British public was tempted with a slim volume with a long title: *Letters from Mr. Fletcher Christian, containing a narrative of the transactions on board His Majesty's Ship Bounty, Before and After the mutiny, with his subsequent voyages and travels in South America.* On Tuesday 13 September 1796, *The True Briton* devoted half a column to a report based on the pamphlet, saying that Fletcher Christian, this 'extraordinary Naval Character', had at length transmitted to England an account of himself. It said that after seizing *Bounty* he had visited Juan Fernandez and other islands off the west coast of South America before being shipwrecked while rescuing Don Henriques, Major-General of the Kingdom of Chili [sic]. Suitably grateful, the Spanish Government lucratively employed Fletcher Christian, who was shortly to sail from Cadiz to South America on their behalf.

The True Briton, an evangelical weekly magazine printed in London, says that Fletcher's Letters were published in Cadiz and that:

> ... we are candidly told by this enterprising mutineer that the revolt ... was not ascribable to any dislike of their Commander but to the unconquerable passion he [Christian] and the major part of the ship's crew entertained for the enjoyments of Otaheite... "It is but justice that I should acquit Captain Bligh in the most unequivocal manner. . ."

Extracts from the Letters were published everywhere. The gentlemanly defence of Bligh makes one think that perhaps the commander himself, or someone close to him, had encouraged the publication, perhaps as an overdue response to Edward Christian's damaging texts. A copy was sent to Bligh by his publisher, a Mr Nicol. On 16 September Bligh wrote to Sir Joseph Banks:

> Mr Nicol has been so good as to send me down a pamphlet called Christian's Letters - is it possible that wretch can be at Cadiz and that he has had intercourse with his Brother, that sixpenny Professor, who has more Law about him than honour—My Dear Sir, I can only say that I heartily despise the praise of any of the family of Christian, and I hope and trust yet that the Mutineer will meet with his deserts.

Clearly the 1794 pamphlets of Edward Christian had wounded Bligh more than he had publicly admitted. Bligh was quite prepared to accept the Letters as authentic and the passion of his correspondence with Banks is thought by Gavin Kennedy to prove that the work did not come from Bligh's camp. That is unproven but it does show that memories of the mutiny stung and that Bligh's defence was still only to attack others rather than publish facts.

Among the journals that published extracts from the Letters was *The Weekly Entertainer,* seen by William Wordsworth at Racedown, Dorsetshire. The November 1796 issue of this 'agreeable and Instructive repository' published a letter from him that has excited much conjecture, now if not then:

> Sir, There having appeared in your Entertainer (vide the 255th page of the present volume) an extract from a work purporting to be the production of Fletcher Christian, who headed the mutiny on board the Bounty, I think it proper to inform you, that I have the best authority for saying that this publication is spurious. Your regard for the truth will induce you to apprize your readers of this circumstance. I am Sir, Your Humble servant, William Wordsworth.

This was not the only rebuttal of the Letters' authenticity. On 23 September, *The True Briton* wrote:

> Letters pretended to have been written by Mr Fletcher Christian having been advertised and an extract from them having been inserted in some of the Public Prints, it is necessary to assure the Public, as we do, from the best authority, that since Christian landed at Otaheite in September, 1789, that part of the ship's company who were afterwards brought to England by Captain Edwards, neither he nor the Bounty has ever been heard of. In a matter of so great seriousness, the Public ought not to be trifled with nor imposed upon by idle fabrications and scandalous falsehoods.

The authority quoted by William Wordsworth was undoubtedly Edward Christian, the family mouthpiece who had so successfully acted as counsel for William and his sister Dorothy in 1791. The Christian family had not heard from Fletcher Christian and although shamed by his mutiny it was unthinkable that he would not write if he were in Spain: his argument was not with them.

On 15 April 1815, *The Aberdeen Chronicle*, reporting the visit of *Briton* and *Tagus*, said:

> The mutineers were unheard of for several years. At length, some accounts, which we do not distinctly recollect, represented Christian, the ring-leader of them, to be subsisting by piracy; but this was contradicted, upon the authority of his family, who knew him to be dead at that time, 1804 . . .

That was a worrying thing for me to find. How did they know he was dead in 1804? They did not even know where he was, let alone possess details of his mortal state, unless he really had managed to be get back to Europe, returned to his family and died there. Was it true or was the anonymous Aberdonian journalist, lacking access to family information, simply filling an empty column, an unromantic but far more plausible theory?

Not everyone who read or heard about the Letters would know they were thought a forgery and another such narrative, with an even longer title, was successfully published only two years later in 1798. So convincing are the accounts I am sure they led to the belief in 1808 and 1809 that Fletcher Christian was back in Cumberland. There is no contemporary evidence to support this and it wasn't mentioned publicly until 1831, so the rumour was never substantiated, then or subsequently.

In February 1810, the *Quarterly Review* reported Folger's discovery of Pitcairn Island. Fletcher Christian's children were from then on the subject of great interest and represented as 'very handsome, their features strongly partaking of the English: the beauty of one of them, a girl named Mary Ann Christian, for which she is termed "the maid of the South Seas" is said to invite the same admiration which is offered to the most favoured of our own fair country women'. The news was barely noticed except by Mary Russell Mitford. Helped by Samuel Taylor Coleridge she wrote *Christina, The Maid of the South Seas: A Poem*, published in 1811. The first stone of an avalanche of romantic Pitcairn trivia had been dislodged. Late in 1815 a man called Porter published his narrative of a cruise that included the call of *Briton* and *Tagus* at Pitcairn. *The Aberdeen Chronicle* introduced three long extracts saying 'we are now enabled to complete [the mutineers'] history and to describe their present condition'. The truth was further away than ever.

The history of the Pitcairn community will never be known in full, for from the start there was a deliberate campaign to smudge the past that provided fuel for romantics and purveyors of conspiracy theories. Much of this was done by the surviving women and their art of *ha'avere* as well as by Adams protecting himself against arrest and extradition.

The first two visits resulted in different versions of Fletcher Christian's death. Folger stayed at Pitcairn only ten or so hours and we must suspect both the reliability of those who told the tales and those who reported them. There wasn't much opportunity to cross check. Captains Pipon and Staines fared little better.

Two of Fletcher's deaths were supposedly by murder, one a suicide, one a natural end. Only Adams and Ma'ohi foremothers knew the truth but they were the ones lying. The visitors had been told:

- Six years after Bounty arrived their servants, the Ma'ohi men, attacked and killed all the English except Adams who was injured
- Four years after they arrived, the same revolt of the six Ma'ohi occurred, with only Adams being spared, although injured
- Christian became insane shortly after their arrival and threw himself off rocks into the sea

- They all lived in tolerable harmony for several years under Christian's government and then he became sick and died a natural death. This was followed by two massacres when the Ma'ohi men killed the Europeans, and were in turn killed by the Ma'ohi women

A further enigma arose about Fletcher Christian's wife. Several stories said Fletcher was shot because he seized the wife of a Ma'ohi after Mauatua died giving birth to their first son. This was given credence by Lieutenant Shillibeer, who interviewed Pitcairners on board *Briton*. Fletcher's son Thursday said he did not know his mother, for she was dead. No Pitcairners contradicted him.

These confused and inconsistent stories about the possibility of Fletcher being murdered would bring little comfort to his brothers Charles and Edward, who were still alive, as was his mother, Ann.

So, since 1796, there had been rumours that Fletcher Christian was alive but not in the South Seas. Peter Heywood is one man who would have agreed wholeheartedly with the possibility, but his opinion was not published until 1831 after he and all the Christians were dead.

Sometime in 1808 or 1809, Peter Heywood was walking down Fore Street in Plymouth Dock when his attention was caught by the appearance of a man whose shape so reminded him of Fletcher Christian that he involuntarily quickened his pace. Both men were walking very fast and the rapid steps behind him roused the stranger's attention. He turned, looked at Heywood, and immediately ran off. His face was as much like Christian's as his back and Heywood, exceedingly excited, followed. Both ran as fast as they were able, but the stranger had the advantage and disappeared. That Christian should be in England Heywood considered highly improbable, though not out of the realm of possibility for at that time no account had been received of him. The resemblance, the agitation, and the efforts of the stranger to elude him were too strong not to make a deep impression on him. His first thought was to investigate but on reflecting upon the pain and trouble such a discovery could give to Fletcher Christian, he considered it prudent to let the matter drop.

There is nothing sinister about Heywood not following up this intriguing encounter, or in its not being made public for twenty years. The reports from *Topaz* made it clear that the Pitcairners considered Fletcher Christian dead. If he was not, then the 'pain and trouble' Heywood feared would fall mainly on his old shipmate. Anyway, Fletcher Christian could not have long been in England before finding out that it was Heywood who set into motion the endeavours of Edward Christian to expose Bligh and to publish alternative stories about the mutiny. My opinion is that if the stranger really had been Fletcher Christian, he would have embraced Peter Heywood, rather than fled, and I am sure Heywood thought so, too.

Or had he really seen Fletcher Christian in Devonport?

Fletcher Christian's Fate - II

There is one overriding proof Fletcher Christian did not leave Pitcairn that would have been clear to any British sailor, if they had thought to ask, or if they had known to ask.

If Fletcher Christian sailed secretly from Pitcairn, he must have taken *Bounty's* invaluable Kendall K2 chronometer and the azimuth compass, although I do recognise that to be useful, he would have had to keep it wound and working. K2 was still on Pitcairn when Mayhew Folger discovered Fletcher's hideout in 1808, and then Mauatua gave it to him, together with some of Fletcher's other possessions. She wanted them returned so that the Pitcairners were not thought to be thieves of the king's property.

It's probable that in the early nineteenth century, even Royal Navy visitors didn't know the K2 chronometer had been on board *Bounty* so many decades ago, and so wouldn't have asked about it. If they did know, no naval man would retail the idea of Fletcher Christian escaping without it or the compass.

Peter Heywood is supposed to have seen Fletcher Christian in Fore Street in Devonport, Plymouth in 1808 or 1809, but the man he called out to ran away. This is blown out of all proportion by the very thing that was supposed to do the opposite, that it was kept secret until after Heywood's death in February 1831. Only then did Sir John Barrow publish *The Mutiny of the Bounty* in 1831 and the public heard this.

In Plymouth in the early nineteenth century there would have been many a man who would run from a naval officer, or any other man, uniformed or otherwise. Press ganging was diminishing but was still used to man Royal Navy ships. In such a port there were also shipmates and captains to fear, as well as cut-throats and footpads.

Perhaps Heywood saw another member of the Christian family, possibly Charles, for there was said to be a widespread disability of the knees among males of the clan, which contributed to the peculiar gait imputed to Fletcher. Anyway, if Fletcher's head and shoulders had been axed on Massacre Day it's very unlikely that anyone would have recognised him at a distance. No-one who repeats this story considers this and that alone makes the idea of Heywood's sighting very flimsy.

In *The Wake of the Bounty*, C.S. Wilkinson promotes the idea that Fletcher Christian's escape was the inspiration for *The Ancient Mariner*. The author admits he has no new information to offer and that he began his research only because he found the signature of an F. Christian in a scrapbook in a Charing Cross bookshop. He was not able to compare this with the mutineer's autograph but because it was associated in the scrapbook with the Losh family, who had assisted Edward Christian, he thought it might be the long-lost key to proving the return of Fletcher. He also mentions the existence in a notebook of Coleridge in the Public Records Office in which is the scribbled note, 'The adventures of Fletcher Christian'.

It is absurd to think the latter is anything other than the most basic aide-memoire. I subsequently found two signatures of Fletcher Christian on *Bounty* documents that have survived, which can be seen in the earliest edition of *Fragile Paradise*, but was unable to arrange to compare them with that held by Wilkinson.

Then there is the paper delivered by William Fletcher MP in 1867: *Fletcher Christian and the Mutineers of the Bounty*. William was a relation of Fletcher's mother and I found a handwritten copy (his I think) of his paper in the archives of Tullie House Library in Carlisle, together with some letters to him from Lady Belcher, who had Morrison's journal at the time; she was the stepdaughter of Peter Heywood and wrote a book about the mutiny and the mutineers. At first, she scrawled to William Fletcher saying she was not well and could not find Morrison's work but later advised she had sent it by rail.

William Fletcher does not note any sources so presumably the originator of rumours of Fletcher Christian's return to the area current in 1808 and 1809 is Sir John Barrow, based on Heywood but published decades later. I spent many days reading every newspaper I could find that exists from the period and from the area but there is no hint of Fletcher's return in them and I think this is just the type of gossipy story that would have been printed. William Fletcher says Fletcher is thought to have been visiting a favourite aunt, but he didn't know that all Fletcher's aunts were dead by then. Isabella Christian Curwen was alive but a cousin.

The thrust of William Fletcher's story is that Fletcher Christian avoided discovery by hiding in the thick forest that covered the hills around Lake Windermere and the grounds of Belle Isle. It is a melodramatic theory, in the best tradition of the Victorian novel. The repentant mutineer, bullied into abandoning his coloured consort and bastard children, journeys halfway around the world in disguise to live out a life of lonely misery within sight of the real Isabella, rich, beautiful but forever unattainable.

The descendants of John and Isabella no longer live on Belle Isle but Windermere still enthrals tourists with the suggestion that, as well as genuinely being here as a child and young man, Fletcher Christian might secretly have walked where they do after his mutiny, that he might even be buried on that romantic island. This is impossible, proven by a discovery of a print in a Cockermouth shop.

When I was there in late 1979, Noreham House on Main Street, which once belonged to Fletcher's grandparents, John XIV and Bridget Christian, had become an antique and junk shop. In a remote corner of the shop, I found an engraving of Belle Isle dated 1796. There are almost no trees on the island and most of those to be seen cluster close to the round house. Vitally, there are few trees on the hills that surround Windermere, nothing that would make secure hides for Fletcher. Later research showed it was John Christian Curwen who planted most of the millions of trees that coated Cumberland by 1864.

John started planting on the island in a small way in 1787 and seems continuously to have improved or changed the style of the gardens. The original formal gardens had been demolished in the early 1780s and a raised gravel walk was constructed right around the island at the water's edge. Dorothy Wordsworth gives in her journal for 8 June 1802 the final lie to the possibility of hiding in a dense screen of trees on the island. She writes:

> The shrubs have been cut away in some parts of the island. They have made no natural glades: it is merely a lawn with a few miserable young trees, standing as if they were half starved . . . And that great house! Mercy upon us! if it could be concealed . . . Even the tallest of our old oak trees would not reach to the top of it.

This pretty much clinches the impossibility of Belle Isle as a hiding place. It was not covered with bushes or trees in 1802, and seven years later when Fletcher was said to have hidden there, every traveller with the will could visit the island and it was also the main summer house of the social John and Isabella Christian Curwen, who introduced boating regattas and swans to the lake.

A fugitive on Belle Isle would have to have been as fey as a sprite to avoid detection by the *ton* of Cumberland or the house's servants. By 1809, Fletcher Christian would have been 45 and his upper body must have been crippled by his injuries, which would have made him something less than fleet. He could not have rowed himself to the lake shore or have swum there without great physical difficulty. As well, the supposed axe wounds about his head and neck would have left hideous scars and there is no chance that such an appearance would have been unnoticed and widely commented upon by someone.

Supposing Fletcher had the guile and luck to escape detection and the physical ability to get to and from Belle Isle, he would have little cover there or elsewhere because the shores of Lake Windemere were *not* thick were trees in 1809 or thereabouts. William Fletcher mistakenly thought what he saw in 1864 had always been like that, a common error.

It cannot be said that John and Isabella Christian Curwen bought silence from those who might have discovered the presence of Fletcher Christian in Cumberland; today's Cumbria refers to the combination of Cumberland, Westmoreland and other regions in 1974. As a rich crusader and a distinguished member of the Old Minority of Whig reformers, John Christian Curwen had many opponents who would have paid handsomely to report the harbouring of his criminal relative Fletcher Christian.

There was no hiding in Cumberland for Fletcher Christian and little reason so to do. His mother and brother Charles were on the Isle of Man. Edward was Professor of Law at the *East India Company College* at Hailey, Hertfordshire, 19 miles north of London. The one person who might be expected to tell us of Fletcher's return is his brother Charles. The cruel, forced anonymity of a younger brother whom he considered to have been driven to temporary madness by the intemperance of another was too meaty a subject for him to abjure. As a further and proximate example of man's inhumanity to man, his pen would have worried at the idea over many pages.

If Fletcher were back, he would have gone to Man to see Charles and his mother or had some sort of contact. If he did, Charles must have alluded to it, but he did not.

None of Fletcher Christian's supposed hiding places is verified by contemporary printed or written evidence and none of the stories that incorporate such suggestions has an identifiable ultimate source. There is no trace of belief or proof within the family, either in England or in the South Pacific, that he returned. Indeed, my great-aunts from Norfolk Island would redden and refuse to countenance even the suggestion, let alone the possibility and this was always so within the family.

The seed of Fletcher's escape was planted as early as 1796, with the publication of the fictional *Letters from Mr Fletcher Christian*.

Whoever wrote it certainly knew a lot about South America, and many readers must have believed it to be true because of that ancient need for romantic rebels not to be punished. Remember the stories that Elvis Presley wasn't dead, that James Dean and many other such popular heroes lived on? There have been triumphant stories like this in every civilisation from Ancient Egyptians to Incas and Aztecs and it is the basis of Christianity. The meme lost none of its magnetism when romantics and conspiracists attached it to Fletcher Christian.

Once Pitcairn's last mutineer Adams was dead on 5 March 1829, different versions of his stories emerged. In 1831 Sir John Barrow published the first really comprehensive book about the mutiny on *Bounty* and Pitcairn Island. In a footnote he first revealed Heywood's reported sighting of Fletcher Christian in 1808 or 1809.

Then, in 1834 Dr Bennet who was the surgeon aboard the whaler *Tuscan*, Captain Stavars, was shown a grave beside a pool said to be that of Fletcher Christian, something mentioned in a long *Narrative of a Whaling Voyage*, published in London in 1840. It has been ignored by, or unknown to, most authors or visitors to Pitcairn, possibly because the book is hard to find and because it is not consistent with other records.

There was one person who could have set the record right, Mauatua, the widow of Fletcher Christian. She had remained slim and relatively upright, true to her nickname Mainmast. She had a shock of white hair and was renowned for her stories, told only to her family. The awful truth, at least it is awful to a descendant, is that Europeans could probably not bear to question her. She seems to have been a perfect fright in her old age.

In March 1830, a young man aboard the vessel *Seringapatam* wrote in his journal:

> An old woman has a world of prejudice to surmount before she can become anything but an object of pity, and often of disgust ... we recall the stories of witchcraft malice and cruelty imputed

to the old and infirm of the female sex. She looked so old and corpse-like that I gladly escaped from her awkward expressions of pleasure at the appearance of my clothes, gun, etc.

Naturally, I always rather hoped I would never find proof that the young man was referring to my great-great-great-great-grandmother. But he was. In 1841 24-gun HMS *Curacao*, called at Pitcairn and stayed a couple of weeks to help with an epidemic of fever and flu. There are many important records of this visit, including the acerbic journal of the ship's doctor, Gunn. He could not help but note the sadness of a Ma'ohi community that insisted on dressing their children when they swam. I deciphered a previously ignored note in his book, which said that the Christian children were thought to be simple in the head, 'perhaps the influence of their Tahitian mother'.

That must be seen in early nineteenth-century context, when black skin was universally associated by Europeans with lower intellect. Only when I was left a privately owned and previously unknown journal of another of *Curacao's* complement that another reason for Gunn's remark became clear. The author of a beautifully illustrated record of this visit to Pitcairn was George Gardner, one of her officers. He noted that the females never ate with the males and called it a relic of the barbarianism, a custom of the uncivilised inhabitants of the South Seas, handed down from Tahitian parents:

> There are two of the Tahitian women still living. [One is] Isabella Christian . . . the wife of Fletcher Christian who headed the mutiny. Isabella Christian is the most perfect picture of an old hag I ever saw. She is still surprisingly active. Her age is supposed to be between 80 and 90. She remembers Captain Cook at Tahiti and from what she herself says must then have been a mother. In this tho' there is nothing very extraordinary since they marry even nowadays at the age of 13 or 14.

So, Mauatua looked like an old hag. No wonder visitors did not talk to her and thought her children might be mentally deficient. It's also proof she was known as Isabella, although she introduced herself to visitors as Mrs Christian. Mauatua was certainly over 80 in 1841 and this is the first indication that she might have left a child behind on Tahiti, something I used to dramatize her story in *Mrs Christian* – Bounty *Mutineer.*

What Gardner and other visitors fail to note is Pitcairn's more recent history, notably that the witch-like Mrs Christian and every other woman over 18 had been franchised since 1838. Whatever they looked like, they had a status no other women in the world shared. There were two reasons they wanted the vote, and both were to protect themselves from interfering men, first Anglican missionaries and then Joshua Hill, who all cloaked themselves in Christian self-righteousness.

There were more versions of Fletcher Christian's end to come. One of the least known and most fascinating appeared in a book published in 1898 called *The Mutineer: A Romance of Pitcairn Island.* Turgid with high passion and purple patches in the best manner of the Victorian novel, it purported to be the first true story of what had happened, written by two men, Becke and Jeffery. Becke was an extraordinary Australian adventurer about whom it was said he was 'one of the rare men who have led a wild life and have the culture and talent to give some account of it'. In Sydney's Mitchell Library and in the National Library in Canberra, I found a great deal of correspondence, both with his collaborator, who lived in England, and with various critics and associates including his agent in London.

The Mutineer said that Christian survived the gunshot wounds and being hacked at with an axe and then recovered in his cave. When he was well enough, he attempted to put to sea in *Bounty*'s boat to join a sailing ship sighted off Pitcairn, which might explain why he did not need the K2 chronometer. Adams tried to prevent him to protect the secrecy of the community and in the struggle, shot and killed Christian. Before he died, Christian asked to be buried in an unmarked grave as he did not wish people to point out the grave of 'the mutineer'. No wonder Adams lied, Becke said. He had killed Christian, albeit accidentally. No wonder everyone else had conflicting stories. They were protecting their patriarch and it was Fletcher's own wish that his grave be not known.

This was such a perfect solution to the mystery of Fletcher's death, even if found in a factional book, that I had to dig deeper. How had Becke come up with this version? The answer is astonishing; he said he got it from Pitcairners. Among his correspondence I found a letter to Egan Mew, QC, of 3 Gray's Inn Place, London. He was a writer for *The Critic*, which had just given *The Mutineer* a wishy-washy review. Becke wrote in his defence:

> I know the descendants of the Bounty Mutineers and the native story of Christian and his life better than any man living. This sounds very egotistical of me but it is true.

> And instead of Christian being . . . the 'full-blooded villain' he was the very reverse. I have been told over and over again by old natives that Christian was the very reverse of a sensual man; that he was intimate with only one Tahitian woman whom he afterward took away with him to Pitcairn; that this woman was seduced by Young; that the other Tahitian men and women would have killed Young, but that Christian, horror-stricken at the bloodshed that had already taken place, carefully protected the man who seduced his wife; and the story of his life in the cave as narrated by Jeffery and myself is true not embroidered fiction.

> Furthermore the story of Christian's death by gunshot accidentally received from John Adams/Alexander Smith whilst endeavouring to prevent Christian from putting to sea in the Bounty's boat, is I believe, strictly true.

Anyway, I prefer to believe the native account of the Bounty story to the vague surmises of the many authors who have written on the subject but who only obtained their data from the Court Martial of some of the mutineers or from John Adams' carefully considered statements to Naval Officers. Perhaps you can make an interesting par[agraph?] of this?

Becke's journals show he did stay on the island but the exact dates are not clear. Letters that passed between him and his collaborator show that neither was above twisting the story for the sake of drama but Becke passionately believed he had solved the question of Christian's fate.

Is it true, though? Somehow it is too true, and, of course, the 'old natives' were anything but witnesses to the events, for Becke's stay was probably in the 1850s or 1860s. Even so, my research into his background and his book showed me that I could not lightly ignore this version. Neither could I ignore stories that believed Fletcher Christian had escaped and was the inspiration for Samuel Taylor Coleridge's, *The Rime of the Ancient Mariner.*

That idea was first suggested by a Mr Porter, who claimed Coleridge's so-called fantasy poetry was based on events and places and people he knew of or had read about. The sufferings of the Mariner can certainly be related to those of Fletcher Christian and it is possible to make a case for the poem being about Fletcher's secret journey back to England. Coleridge had helped Mary Russell Mitford write her poem *Christina: The Maid of the South Seas,* supposedly based on Fletcher and Mauatua's daughter Mary, beautiful once but who died a crabby old spinster on Norfolk Island, where her gravestone mentions neither her mutineer father nor her Tahitian mother.

Coleridge once penned a note to himself about Christian's adventures, making the possibility of a link even stronger. Add to this the friendship of William Wordsworth with both the Christian family and Coleridge, and there is enough substance in the enigma for a book, as C. S. Wilkinson proved with his persuasive *The Wake of the Bounty* published in 1953.

Once I had read that, my confusion was complete. I had to do something to sort this out but had no idea what until it was clear that as a descendant my research had to include going to Pitcairn Island. The stories of this Royal Geographical Society expedition and my time on Pitcairn Island are woven into *Fletcher Christian* Bounty *Mutineer,* an extended version of that previously published as *Fragile Paradise – The Discovery of Fletcher Christian*, Bounty *Mutineer.*

In October 1793 the men killed on Massacre Day, now all headless skeletons, were buried in a communal grave. Only Fletcher was supposedly buried separately in his garden and I had found a solid clue about this grave in the journal of Dr Bennet, surgeon in the whaler *Tuscan*, Captain Stayers. While on Pitcairn 1834, Bennet tells us:

> Fletcher Christian and John Mills were shot on the same day, by
> the Tahitians: the grave of the former was pointed out to me: it
> is situated a short distance up a mountain and in the vicinity of
> a pond.

When Captain the Hon. William Waldegrave visited Pitcairn aboard HMS *Seringapatam* in March 1830 he was walked to the graves of Christian and Adams. He wrote: 'They are some distance from each other – the former near the spot where he fell, murdered, about one third from the summit of the island.' I hope that by summit he meant Lookout Point.

Once I was on Pitcairn in August 1980, I asked throughout the village about ponds, springs and wells, secretly hoping the mountain mentioned might be towering Lookout Point in which was Christian's Cave, because I now believed this to be part of Fletcher's original property.

In 1980, the site on which Fletcher Christian was supposedly shot was easily shown to those who enquire and had been agreed upon since Pitcairn's first nineteenth-century visitors. Fletcher Christian's grandson, known as Duddie, who in the early twentieth century remembered Mauatua, is just one who indicated that site. There were two questions I had to solve. Why is this supposed site of his death so far from Fletcher's house? Why should the site of Fletcher Christian's murder be remembered but not his grave site?

When I stood where Fletcher Christian was supposedly shot on Massacre Day, I rehearsed the version of Fletcher's death given many years later by Jenny, who was then off the island. The day for the murders had been chosen because the women were going up into the mountains to collect birds' eggs. Here was the first anomaly. If anything could be called 'up in the mountains', this supposed murder site could. It is only a few hundred yards below the island's long ridge, at the top of John Mills Valley, suggesting it was Mills's land not Fletcher Christian's. As then, it is protected by thick bush and totally insulated from the village, both out of sight and an arduous hilly trek away from it. I don't think this is where Fletcher Christian was gardening.

Fletcher Christian is said to have groaned loudly and said when he was shot, a sound heard in nearby plots and recognised by some as the sound of a dying man. Other men who heard it thought it was Mauatua calling her two children to eat or dismissed the shot as killing the pig that Tetahiti had promised. This all becomes transparently impossible when you are standing where 'tradition' says Fletcher was shot.

Jenny's story clearly implies that most men were gardening close to the village, while the women were as far away as possible up in the mountain. There was no reason in those days for the men to garden in the hills. There was plenty of ground close to home for so few to cultivate and any gardens they did have in other parts of the island were simply divisions of naturally occurring fruit trees. The supposed site is amid such steep and rugged terrain it is unlikely any of the mutineers walked over to discuss an unexpected sound or even that they could have shouted to one another.

The biggest clue to the site being a fraud is the impossibility of Mauatua's voice to have been heard as far away as this. If Fletcher's groan and his supposed last words 'Oh, dear' were heard by other men, it had to be closer to the settlement.

Jenny shows this is so by remembering something both intimate to Fletcher and Mauatua and important to a woman. She specifically remembered Fletcher was working close to home that day because Mauatua had not gone with the egg collectors as she was close to giving birth to their third child. That does make sense. On the flatter, more open land around the village it would have been easy for men to saunter over for a chat or to shout at one another. It would also be possible to mistake a sound from the direction of Fletcher's house and garden as coming from Mauatua calling from her door. There was no doubt in my mind that the site traditionally shown as that where Fletcher was shot was an ancient fiction, *ha'avere* with a very long life and perhaps this was done to hide where he was buried.

Young's lost diary said Fletcher was buried close to where he was shot, yet the supposed site of the shooting I was shown has never been pointed out as his grave. The plot continued to be used as a garden and I can't believe his family continued cultivating what was literally the soil of their forefather. It seemed likely that site was a successful red herring of Adams and/or the Ma'ohi women, that, like good stories everywhere, became accepted as fact.

These days, Pitcairn Islanders point to a different site for Fletcher's death, up Ah Flat, and that story, too, came from the 'old people' but they have only been told what other 'old people' thought was true. The different versions of where he was shot doesn't matter so much to me as where Fletcher Christian was buried and in 1980 this was my more important objective.

Ben Christian, Island Secretary for over 18 years, let me borrow the record of land deeds. Land is divided among a family's children and then subdivided and so on, thus it was possible broadly to piece together Fletcher Christian's original plot of land in the village. Within this swathe at the north-westerly end of the settlement stood Thursday October II's house, the oldest on the island, uninhabited and still showing the sliding shutters used instead of windows and doors. This extraordinary link with Pitcairn's past has inexplicably been pulled down just when better shipping means more visitors to Pitcairn and nothing would be more thrilling for them to see.

This site was directly below Tom and Betty Christian's house, which stands on the site called Fletcher's, undoubtedly the vicinity of Fletcher Christian's house, even if foundations have not been found. Further afield are gardens still owned by Christians and like some gigantic barrier, Lookout Point bounds the north-west extremity. This provides a simple reason for the naming of the cave. It would be Christian's Cave simply because it was on his land, rather than because he adopted it as a den. It would be unlikely to have been called this if it had been on someone else's property, just as Mills Valley was part of his.

Fletcher's original gardens are within shouting distance of his house and Mauatua really could have alerted him by a call at the start of childbirth. If he were shot somewhere in this vicinity, his groan might easily have been mistaken for Mauatua, for everyone else was in their domestic property south or south-east of this site and both sounds would seem to have come from the same direction.

Following tangents simply so I could return to my base with a clear head, I went with Tom Christian to his garden below Christian's Cave. Tom was going to point out working sites where stone tools had been shaped, and we hoped to find a partly worked or broken tool for me as a memento. I was thrilled to find the lower half of a broken stone chisel at least 600 years old and that was polished with use; I have donated my Pitcairn pre-*Bounty* stone relics to the outstanding *Bounty* Museum in Weinfelden, Switzerland.

A few minutes after we plunged into the bush, Tom stopped literally open-mouthed. I followed his gaze and quickly understood what had caught his attention. There was as plain a dried-up pool as one could imagine, once one knew.

Close to gardens still being used by Christians, it was right in the middle of Fletcher Christian's original plot, within shouting distance of his house, and it was a short distance up a mountain, Lookout Point. Not only did the pool fit Bennet's and Waldegrave's descriptions, it neatly tied a knot with the threads of my thoughts and Jenny's accounts.

On available evidence both the Pitcairners and the expedition agreed this was all a fair conclusion, although forty years later it seems to have been forgotten. Fletcher's supposed murder site is not the same as his burial site although I do think they must be on the same site.

Identifying the pool did not prove Fletcher Christian was buried nearby but discounting one possible murder site and establishing another was a major step forward in the search to find out what happened to Fletcher Christian.

By travelling so far and thinking about the reality with an eighteenth-century mind I have proven to my satisfaction that Fletcher Christian never left Pitcairn Island. He didn't sail single-handed (in what?) without K2 or a compass over thousands of miles of the empty South Pacific, then crossed South America or sailed around it, crossed the Atlantic and then kept his anonymity in England with an axe- scarred face and neck and a bullet-shattered shoulder and arm.

The ultimate wonder about Fletcher Christian's supposed escape from Pitcairn is not the contradictions but that there should be such a myth. The answer to that is precedent. It seems mankind has always needed heroes of protest to survive. Fletcher Christian was quickly and firmly put into the temporal pantheon because he struck a seminal chord in universal yearnings for adventure and freedom, goals few achieve in reality.

The hot pioneering courage and imagination of Fletcher Christian make him worthy of a far more dramatic end than that of perishing five days before his 29th birthday with his head axed into the red earth of Pitcairn, slowly blackening in his own blood and the scorching sun. In the absence of a tombstone or grave to prove his death, the world's romantics have given Fletcher the more enduring memorial of making him into a legend, with a distinct claim to a degree of immortality, from a literary point of view at least.

I still feel I should raise the funds to return to Pitcairn and finally mark the graves of Fletcher Christian and Mauatua. Surely the dominating founders of Pitcairn Island, whose exploits have fired the imagination of millions of men and women for over two centuries, deserve something better than unmarked pits?

Or is the great lonely rock of Pitcairn the most extraordinary mausoleum that one revolutionary young Englishman and his visionary Tahitian wife have ever shared?

My Pitcairn Descent

Fletcher Christian = Mauatua

Charles = Sully, daughter of **Teio** and unknown Tahitian male

Isaac = Miriam Young: granddaughter of **Edward Young** and **Toofaiti** and daughter of **Elizabeth Mills**, thus granddaughter of **John Mills** and **Vahineatua**

Godfrey = Frances Edwards (American)

William = Evelyn Smith (Irish–New Zealand)

Royce = Enid Pitman (English–New Zealand): Colin = Nola Rowlands: Keith = Patricia Barber

Glynn: Bruce: Faye: Ross

For information about Pitcairn Island today, and how to get there, see: www.visitpitcairn.pn

Sources and Bibliographical Notes

The bibliography of the *Bounty*/Pitcairn story is enormous but most works on the subject are variations of someone else's themes or the expansion of slim theories in the hope they will become fat facts. I used primary material in libraries and private collections, well before digitalisation and the internet. I had to go where they were.

The major source for information about the Christian family and the Isle of Man was the private collection of Ewan Christian, which had been used as reference for *The Yesterdays Behind the Door*, Susan Hicks Beach (University Press, Liverpool, 1956). These remarkable documents have now been generously donated by Ewan Christian to the Manx Museum in Douglas, Isle of Man. The MSS accession number is 9381 and the microfilm references are MIC69 and MIC70.

North Country Life in the eighteenth Century, Vol. 2 by Edward Hughes (Oxford University Press, 1965) is packed with important Christian family material and the sources for this are all in the Christian Curwen and the Senhouse MSS in the Cumberland Records Office in Carlisle Castle. The papers of William Fletcher MP are across the road, in Tullie House, Carlisle.

Details of Royal Navy life were mainly taken from *Sea Life in Nelson's Time* (Methuen & Co., London, 1905) by John Masefield. Several articles published in *The Mariner's Mirror* over the years give excellent insight into the fitting out of *Bounty*.

The background to classical Tahitian life was drawn from the three volumes of Professor Douglas Oliver's *Ancient Tahitian Society* (University Press of Hawaii, Honolulu, 1974) and cross-checked with several of his sources, which include the manuscripts and published works of Bligh and James Morrison, *Bounty*'s boatswain's mate.

What Happened on the Bounty (George Allen & Unwin, translated, London, 1962) by Bengt Danielsson and Rolf DuRietz, clearly presents the complicated story of what happened on Tahiti after *Bounty* left.

For the day of the mutiny, I used Bligh's works, Owen Rutter's edition of *The Court-Martial of the* Bounty *mutineers* (William Hodge & Co., Edinburgh, 1931), *The Voyage of the* Bounty*'s Launch John Fryer's Narrative* edited by Stephen Walter (Genesis Publication, Guilford, Surrey, 1979), *The Appendix* by Edward Christian (London, 1794). The latter must be regarded as primary material, not just for what it reports, but also because of the dramatic revelations and corroboration of Edward's subsequent pamphlet *A Short Reply to Captain Bligh's Answers* (J. Deighton, London, 1975). This second, exceptionally rare and rarely used pamphlet reveals the methodology of the first, explains the danger and disgrace risked by the eminent men who helped collect evidence if they were to be found liars, and even shows that Bligh's servant went independently to the Christian family to give a version of the mutiny different from that of Bligh. *A Short Reply* also reveals that McIntosh was threatened for talking to Edward Christian and demolishes the methods with which Bligh appeared to get some men (e.g. Lebogue) to retract earlier statements.

The travels of Fletcher Christian after the mutiny were not fully known until the brilliant detective work of Professor H.E. Maude, which was published as 'In Search of a Home' (*Journal of the Polynesian Society*, Vol. 67, No. 2, June 1958, Wellington). James Morrison gave excellent anthropological detail about Tubuai. The abstracts by Captain Edward Edwards of the journals of George Stewart and Peter Heywood are in his papers, which were recognised in the Admiralty Library, London, by Bengt Danielsson.

For events on Pitcairn Island, each of those mentioned has something to offer and F.W. Beechey's *Narrative of a Voyage to the Pacific and Beering's Strait in His Majesty's Ship* Blossom . . . *in the Years 1825 . . .* , 2 Vols.

(Henry Colburn & Richard Bentley, London, 1831) is by far the fullest. I decided to accept as authoritative the versions given by the Tahitian woman Jenny; my expedition to Pitcairn Island proved I was right to do so. See what she said in the *United Services Journal*, London, November 1829, Part 2, pp. 589-593.

The most masterly and thorough interpretative and critical works published about *Bounty* and her men are by the Swedish bibliographer Rolf DuRietz based in Uppsala. As well as a series of small articles and pamphlets he published *Studia* Bounty*ana* (Dahlia Books, Uppsala, Sweden, 1979, Vols 1 & 2) and had begun a new series titled *Banksia*. Banksia I (Dahlia Books, Uppsala, Sweden, 1979) is 'Thoughts on the Present State of Bligh Scholarship' and puts into focus the problems of writing about a figure who is so well known. An important work on Fryer was published in 1981.

William Bligh has had many enthusiastic biographers and apologists. None has been more honest or painstaking than George Mackaness, in *The Life of Vice-Admiral William Bligh* (Angus & Robertson, Sydney, 1931. New and revised edition 1951). He subsequently found and published the startling Bond material published in *Fragile Paradise* the originals are in the National Maritime Museum, Greenwich. As this material was not known to Gavin Kennedy, he did not discuss it in his rich biography *Bligh* (Gerald Duckworth & Co., London, 1978), so a reassessment of his subject could not be made. Gavin Kennedy's later book, *Captain Bligh: The Man and his Mutinies* (Gerald Duckworth & Co. Ltd, London, 1989) incorporates the material and is an important reference book.

Sir John Barrow's *The Mutiny of the* Bounty (John Murray [pub], London, 1831) is one of the best works on the subject overall and covers a wider spectrum than my book.

The Heritage of the Bounty by H.L. Shapiro (Simon & Shuster, New York, 1936) gives an excellent perspective on Pitcairn's development and David Silverman's *Pitcairn Island* (World Publishing Company, Cleveland, 1967) is a worthwhile collection of often overlooked sources.

The Pitcairnese Language by A. S. C. Ross and A. W. Moverley (Andre Deutsch, London, 1964) includes some excellent essays by Professor Maude and his son and is worth the trouble to track down. The simple style and genealogical charts of *The Pitcairners* by Robert Nicholson (Angus & Robertson, Sydney, 1965) make it important, but the marriage date he gives for Fletcher Christian is 'entirely his own work' and unsupported. The famous article by Luis Marden 'I Found the Bones of the *Bounty*' is in the *National Geographic Magazine* of December 1957.

The only other book I know written by a descendant of the mutineers is *Mutiny of the* Bounty *and Story of Pitcairn Island* by Rosalind Amelia Young (Pacific Press Publishing Assn, Mountain View, California, 1894), who was born and brought up on Pitcairn and who is buried there. It gives details and facts not otherwise collected and remains an excellent and entertaining book. Otherwise, I find books about Pitcairn Island fail accurately to represent the island and its people.

Naturally William Bligh has been a major source for this book and most of his important papers are in the Mitchell Library, Sydney. His letters and correspondence with Banks are most fruitful, and much work could still be done. These are collected on three reels of microfilm: MLMS C218 (Reel FM4/1756): MLMS Safe 1/35 (Reel CY 178) Bligh documents and correspondence: MLMS A78 4 (Reel FM4/1748) the Banks Brabourne papers.

There is Bligh material in the Dixson Library, Sydney, and in the National Library, Canberra, you will find the Rex Nan-Kivell Collection, which includes interesting secondary material and outstanding illustrative material.

The Dawson Transcripts of Banks letters, which are held in the Natural History Museum are little referred to in connection with *Bounty*. This is where you will discover the letter in which Banks says he expected to be blamed if anything went wrong with the breadfruit expedition. These transcripts also show that the letter of 7 September 1787 in the Banks Brabourne papers, thought to be from Sir Joseph

Banks to Sir George Yonge, is the reverse; it is a copy of Yonge's letter to Banks about the former's visit to *Bounty*. Banks had actually sent the original on to Evan Nepean. The complete correspondence (DTC 5:245-9 and DTC 5:259/60) seems to show Bligh was playing these two men off against one another, pretending, for instance, to Yonge that he didn't know where he was to go or to where he was to return.

Dorothy Wordsworth's quote is from *Wordsworth's Hawkshead* by T. W. Thompson (edited by Robert Woof, Oxford, 1970) a book that contains much detail of meetings between the Wordsworths and the Christian Curwens.

For illumination on Fletcher Christian's hyperhidrosis, I consulted Professor John Ludbrook, MD ChM DSc MMedSc FRCS FRACS, Professor Emeritus, University of Adelaide and a Professorial Fellow, University of Melbourne Department of Surgery, Royal Melbourne Hospital. Professor Ludbrook is a vascular surgeon and vascular physiologist with professional experience of hyperhidrosis.

Much material on Christian's mental condition came from professional psychologist Dr Sven Wahlroos PhD and his masterly *Mutiny and Romance in the South Seas: A Companion to the* Bounty *Adventure* (Salem House Publishers, Div. of HarperCollins, Topsfield, Massachusetts, 1989). He, in turn, quotes from the *Diagnostic and Statistical Manual of Mental Disorders* (third edition, revised, Washington DC, American Psychiatric Association, 1987). There is now a fourth edition. Dr Wahlroos' work is a vital reference book, both the only chronological account and a detailed encyclopaedia, and is well overdue for republication. Further insight came from clinical psychologist Paul Rodriguez, BA (Hons) MPsychol MAPS.

For greater clarity on Bligh's command after *Bounty* sailed from Tahiti, I am grateful to my loyal friend and full-time *Bounty* enthusiast Topher Russo, who gave me access to his unpublished Master's thesis, 'Mr Bligh's bad discipline: laxity and recklessness on the high seas' (University of Hawaii, Honolulu, 1994). Similarly, Tasmanian historian Ian Campbell is responsible for new perspectives on Bligh's health and his behaviour during the second breadfruit voyage on HMS *Providence* in his paper 'Mr Bligh's bad health', which is based on his BA Honours thesis (University of Tasmania, Hobart, November 1994)

First-hand accounts of Bligh as Governor of New South Wales are from *Distracted Settlement*, edited and introduced by Dr Ann-Maree Whittaker (The Miegunyah Press, Melbourne, 1998).

Undoubtedly there is still more information to be found, which may change my views. I look forward to seeing that material, which is probably amongst the whaling and sealing archives of the United States, as are further artefacts from HMAV *Bounty* taken from Pitcairn Island. Much more, I look forward to the day when there is no longer the urge to cast Bligh or Christian as black or white. They are men who are remembered. Few men who are remembered can have been wholly one or the other.

About the Author

Glynn Christian is the first biographer of Fletcher Christian and of Mauatua, his Tahitian consort, his great-great-great-great grandparents. As well as this major academic contribution to *Bounty* literature, he has written an historical-fiction account from Mauatua's view *Mrs Christian BOUNTY Mutineer.*

Well-known as a distinguished food writer and pioneering TV-chef, Glynn is honoured with a Lifetime Achievement Award from the Guild of Fine Foods and his book *REAL FLAVOURS – the handbook of gourmet & deli ingredients* was voted Best Food Guide at the Cordon Bleu World Food Media awards.

He continues to write and lives in Battersea, London.

Index

'ava (kava) mood changing drink on Tahiti 34, 129

Adams, John (Alexander Smith): Chronology ix, versions of FCs death 175, story of FC financial obligation 28, Tubuai 90-8, joins FC 93, 94, 126, Massacre Day 131, 137-9, 163, 170, 175, 183-7

Adventure Bay, Bligh invokes displeasure there 29

Age of Enlightenment 24, 78

Ahu, original Pitcairn name for tapa cloth 128

Alexander, Caroline, *The Bounty* 151

Ancient Mariner, theory 179, 187

Ancient Tahitian Society (3 volumes), Douglas Oliver 195

Appendix, The, 156, 161, 162, 196

Banks, Sir Joseph, advisor on breadfruit collection 1, Bligh tells of FC financial obligation 29, sends 2nd breadfruit expedition 108, dangers to him of counter charging 146, documents in Mitchell Library 152, Natural History Museum and Banks Brabourne papers 198

Barrow, Sir John, Capt. Edwards described 141, 1st mutiny/ Pitcairn book, reveals supposed Heywood's sighting of FC 178, 183

Beach, Susan Hicks (née Christian) 195

Becke, Louis, author *The Mutineer*, claims to have visited Pitcairn 185, story of Adams killing FC 185, claims special knowledge, defends FC 186

Beechey, Captain, sees Young's journal 134, his authorative *Narrative* 196

Belcher, Lady, 179

Belle Isle (Windermere) impossibility of being FC hideout 180

Bennet, Dr, shown FC's grave 183, 188, 192

Betham, Richard, 18, 20, 76

Bethia, see *Bounty*

Bligh, Elizabeth (Betsy, née Betham) 20, 152

Bligh, Francis, father of Wm Bligh 17

Bligh, Jane (née Pearce), mother of WB 17

Bligh, William Chronology ix, enhances diet 4, changes to *Bounty* 5, 6, introduced to FC 15, appearance 18, veneration of Cook 19, introduces three watches and compulsory dancing, humane 25, promotes FC 26, Cape Horn 26-8, money start of disagreements with FC? 28, criticism in Adventure Bay, does not punish Purcell 29, 30, chronic inconsistency 110, fails to solve problems with Huggan 31, in Tahiti 33-40, insults FC on Nomuka Island, contradictory orders 41, 42, boasts he could take ships with four men 43, coconut theft accusations and threats to officers but not mentioned in his published account 44, the mutiny 50-60, behaviour compared to Cook 60, views on officers, 61, no homosexual relationship with FC 62, his mental state and personality Wahlroos and Humble 69, open boat voyage 71-4, 75, 'odious' behaviour on 2nd breadfruit expedition 109-15, 151, court-martialled 115, writes defensively to Banks 152, 155, 172, Narrative omits lines that mitigate officers 146

Blossom HMS 126, 196

Bond, Lieutenant Francis Godolphin aboard *Providence*, 2nd breadfruit expedition, describes Bligh behaviour and illness 109-15

A Book of the Bounty, omits *A Short Reply* 162

Borderline Personality Disorder, explanation of FC on mutiny day 66, 67

Bounty, **HM Armed Vessel** (formerly *Bethia*) purchased 1, first RN ship to sail with no pressed men 2, alterations and conditions aboard 3/4, provisioning 5, too small for marines and officers 7, muster 8, voyage to Tahiti, including Cape Horn and Simonstown, from 24, arrives Tahiti 33, events on Tahiti 37, sails from Tahiti 39, crew after sailing from Tahiti 101, voyages with FC commanding 102-105, burnt/sunk off Pitcairn Island 121, by Quintal? 121, by women? 122

Breadfruit, nutritional value and uses, supply for West Indies planned 1, quickly collected 36

Breadfruit 2nd expedition 108
Brief Reactive Psychosis, FC's
    mental state 66
Briton HMS, 170
Brown, William *Bounty*,
    Chronology ix
Browne, Rita Christian, family
    historian 169

Calcutta, HMS 162
Cambridge HMS, FC not aboard,
    Bligh 6th lieutenant 13
Campbell, Duncan, employs
    Bligh, 20, 21, 53, 158
Cape Town, see Simon's Town
Carteret, Captain Philip 105
Childhood in Tahiti, disfigurement
    of boys and girls 12,
Chinese bowl, FC's, given to
    Folger 170
Christian, Ann (née Dixon,
    FC's mother) family, loses
    Moorland Close, takes FC to
    IOM 12, see Chronology
Christian, Ben 190
Christian, Betty 191
Christian, Bridget, (née
    Senhouse, FC's grandmother)
    royal descent 12, 180
Christian, Bridget, (FC's
    cousin) 24
Christian, Charles (FC's
    brother, surgeon)
    Joins militia 12, meets Fletcher
    after *Middlesex* mutiny

22, 23, descriptions of FC,
    extracts from unpublished
    biography 23, reaction to
    mutiny 45, questions mutiny
    reason 62, conversation
    Bligh/Taubman 65, writes
    to Bligh's father in law 76,
    quotes *Providence* marine
    captain 151, not visited by
    FC 182
Christian, Charles (FC's father)
    life and death 11, 12, 124
Christian, Charles ('Hoppa',
    FC's second son) resonance
    of being allowed to live with
    club foot, sign of women's
    determination for change 124,
    GC descent from 194
Christian, Edward (FC's brother)
    academic achievements 76, 150,
    re coconut incident 44, 1794
    publishes vindication of FC, The
    Appendix 156-61, 1795 publishes
    A Short Reply 161, insulted by
    Bligh 172
Christian, Ewan (head of English
    family) 168
Christian family papers and
    history of, discovery of 168
    see also *Milntown* by Derek
    Winterbottom
Christian, Fletcher, birth,
    background, schooling 11,
    12, living siblings 1768 12,
    to India as midshipman on

Eurydice 13, promoted to acting lieutenant on *Eurydice* aged 19 14, appearance 15, described by Bligh 92, writes to Bligh 15, on *Britannia* with Bligh 15, comments about by Lebogue 15, by Lamb 16, learns of breadfruit expedition 16, signs on *Bounty* 5, *16*, meets brother Charles before sailing, learns of brother's mutiny, comments about by Charles 23, no peer group on *Bounty 24*, represents Bligh in Tenerife 25, charge of third watch 25, promoted to acting first lieutenant 26, Cape Town and evidence of financial obligation to Bligh 28, demonstrates strength/teaches Heywood 29, in charge of Point Venus breadfruit camp 33, life on Tahiti including tattoos-leaves Tahiti 138, extra duties given 41, insulted by Bligh on Nomuka Island 41, 42, accused of stealing coconuts 44, weeps before Purcell 46, plans to leave the ship 47, humoured by Stewart 49, never blamed for mutiny 50, decides Bligh should go 50, events of mutiny 51, homosexuality dismissed 62, drug addiction impossible, 64 violent perspiration' and hyperhidrosis 64, no syphilis of other VD 65, mental state on mutiny day 66, introduces voting 78 and uniforms on *Bounty* 80, mutiny not piracy 79, chooses Tubuai 81, compliments by Bligh loyalists 191, defended by Edward 192-6, choses Tubuai Island, first contact 82, 213-6, returns to Tahiti 86, return to Tubuai 86, chooses site 88, Fort George built 89, events on Tubuai 90-8, asks for *Bounty*, others volunteer 92, cuts cable and leaves Tahiti 99, not a kidnapper of women 99, long search for a home 101-105, discovers Pitcairn is mischarted 105, lands on Pitcairn Island 106, *Bounty* burns 265, land divided unevenly , shot on Massacre Day 134 bogus letters from 171, Chinese bowl given to Folger 170, children described 173, versions of his death 175. rumour of sighting in Devonport 178, gravesite mentioned by Bennet 183, pool site identified

Christian Family, volumes of family history discovered, donated to Manx Museum 302

Christian, Glynn, discoveries and new material include Christian Family History 168,

bio of Charles Christian,
mutiny of Charles Christian 22,
Gray's Inn success of Edward
Christian 76, first use of Bond
papers 109, significance of no
Bounty pregnancies and birth
of Thursday October 122,
significance of Charles (FC and
Mauatua son) being allowed
to live 124, identification
of Mauatua burial site 166,
discovery of possible FC burial
site 183

Christian, Humphrey (FC's
brother, soldier), dies on
Barbary Coast after news of
mutiny 76

Christian, Isabella, see,
Mauatua/ Mainmast

Christian, Jane (later Blamire,
FC's cousin) 24,

Christian, John (FC's brother,
attorney) 12, second wife and
death 168

Christian, Lt-Col John Monsell 302

Christian, John XVII, later
Christian Curwen. New
family 12, elopes with Isabella
Curwen 13, changes name 76,
see Christian Curwen, John

Christian, Joseph (of Strand,
London) 149

Christian, Mary Ann (FC's
daughter) 134, 174, 187

Christian, Mary (FC's sister) 12

Christian, Mrs, see Mauatua

Christian, Sully (FC's
daughter-in-law) 120, 129, 166

Christian, Susannah (FC's
daughter-in-law) see Teraura

Christian, Thursday October
(later Friday, FC's son) born
and significance 122.123, turns
three days after Massacre 135,
139, boards *Topaz*, 169, says
Mauatua is dead 170, dies in
Tahiti 164, descendants 166

Christian, Tom 191

Christian, Vio 169

Christian Curwen, Isabella
(second wife of John XVII)
elopes 13, 180, 181, 182

Christian Curwen, John
(**John XVII,** FC's 1st cousin)
saves Anne Christian and
family 12, elopes with Isabella
Curwen 13, changes name 76,
180, 181, 182

*Christina, The Maid of the South
Seas* 175

Chronology, *ix*

Churchill, Charles 9, 38, arrests
Bligh 52, 55, 59, 81, 87, 95

Cockermouth 11, 158, 180

Cockermouth Free Grammar
School 12

Coconut incident on *Bounty* 44

Cole, William, 40, 47, 59, 73

Coleman, Joseph, 38, 51, 56, 89,
141, 147, 159

Coleridge, Samuel Taylor 175,
179, 187
Cook, Captain James 4, 5,
Resolution 18, 19, 35, contrasted
with Bligh 60
Courtenay, Captain George,
commander *Eurydice*, youngest
RN post captain 13
Curacao HMS 184
Curwen, Henry 26, 27, 36
Curwen, Isabella, 2nd wife of John
XVII, see Christian Curwen

Danielsson, Bengt 196
Darby, Madge 62, 63
Deemsters, IOM, generations of
Christians, 11
Dillon, Captain Peter 126
Douglas, Isle of Man 51
Downs, a merchant service shelter
off Deal 16
DuRietz, Rolf, Bligh cause of
mutiny, 56, recognises Bond
papers 197
Duke, HMS, *Pandora* survivors
tried aboard 146

Edward 1st, FC's descent
from 12
Edwards, Captain Edward (HMS
Pandora), 80, appointed to find
Bounty and mutineers 141,
arrives Tahiti, arrests all *Bounty*
men, constructs infamous
Pandora's box 142, abandons

prisoners when *Pandora*
founders 142, 145
Elliott, Captain Russell, accepts
Pitcairn as Crown Colony
confirms votes for women 165
Ellison, Thomas, 50, on Mutiny
Day 53, 59, 89, hanged 147
Elphinstone, William 16, 75
Eurydice, HMS, FC aboard, 13,
14, 23, 24
Ewanrigg/Unerigg family seat in
Cumberland 11

Faahotu, 118
Fasto – see Faahotu
Fletcher, William MP, tells of
Heywood sighting FC 179, 180,
mistaken 182
Flinders, Matthew 109
Folger, Captain Mayhew, 1st to
find FC's hideout 125, 169,
given K2 chronometer and FC's
porcelain bowl 170, 174, 175
Fort George, FC chooses site 89,
construction and size 89, events
on Tubuai and abandonment
90-8
Fryer, John, Master's duties 26,
unlikely to expect promotion
at sea 26, refuses to sign
accounts 31, 38, describes
Bligh/Christian relationship 42,
Nomuka 42, coconut incident
44, does not have arms chest
keys 51, on mutiny day 53,

open-boat voyage 73, Coupang 73, visits Joseph Christian to tell different version 149

Gardner, George describes Isabella Christian 184
Glottal stop, indicated by 'in Ma'ohi/Polynesian words
Gorgon, HMS 144
Gunn, Dr comments on Pitcairn 184
Guthrie, Lieutenant 115

Ha'avere, Tahitian custom of lying for amusement 125, 126, 139, 170, 175, 190
Hall, Thomas 75
Hallet, John on mutiny day 50
Hayward, Thomas 37, 47, 49, on day of mutiny 50, behaviour aboard *Pandora* 142, 144
Heywood, Peter, writes about Cape Horn 26, 27, taught by Christian 29, in breadfruit camp 33, meets FC Matavai Bay? 98, prisoner on *Pandora* 142, tried and pardoned 146, writes to Edward Christian with defence of FC 146, sighting FC in Devonport? 176
Hill, Joshua 165, 185
Hiti au revareva, Ma'ohi name for Pitcairn
Hitihiti 86, 95
Hough, Richard 63

Huggan, John, surgeon, health, drunkenness, Bligh's failure to deal with 32 dies 37
Humble, Richard, comments on Bligh's personality 69
Hunter, HMS 17
Hyperhidrosis, effects and FC a sufferer 64

Insanity, FC on day of mutiny, comment by Bligh 65, 134 - see Borderline Personality Disorder and Brief Reactive Psychosis
In Search of a Home, H E Maude 196
Isabella, name given to Mauatua by FC 13
Itia, 33, 86

Jeffery, Walter, see Becke 185
Jenny, goes to Tubuai with Adams 87, Tubuai conspiracy 91, encouraged FC 100, Maude reference 101, misunderstands FC's methods 103, talks to Captain Dillon 126, Massacre Day and afterwards 131–136, more on Massacre Day 189, acceptance of version 197
Joan of Acre, Princess, daughter of Edward 1st, FC ancestor 21

Kava, see 'ava
Kendall, Larcum/K2 chronometer, supplied to *Bounty* and value 5,

with Bligh on Cook expedition
19, given to Folger 126, not taken
by FC 178, 185, 192

Kennedy, Gavin re Bligh
punishment 39, 162, 172, 197

Kidnap of women from Tahiti,
denied, 36, 99, 100

Kingston, Jamaica 79

Lamb, Edward, FC aboard
Britannia 68

Lebogue, Lawrence, on FC 15, 21

Ledward, Thomas 37, 75

Letters from Mr Fletcher Christian
(bogus) 171, rebutted in The
True Briton 172
*The Life of Vice-Admiral
William Bligh* 13

Linkletter, Peter 75

Ludbrook, John Professor 199

McDonald, Sir Archibald 149

McIntosh, Thomas 78, 86, 147,
150 threatened 159, 161

Mackaness, George, Bligh
biographer 13

McCoy, William 43, 51, 89, 93,
Massacre Day 132, distills
alcohol, goes mad 137

Mahu, Tahitian men brought up
as females

Ma'ohi – more common name at
the time for Polynesians

Maimiti, invented 20th century
name for Mauatua qv

Mainmast, see Christian,
Mauatua 118

Manahune, lowest class, Tahiti

Manarii 111, 117, Massacre Day
131, 133, 134

Mareva 118

Martin, Isaac *Bounty* AB,
mutiny day 50, 93, Massacre
Day, 131, 132

Massacre Day Pitcairn Island,
participants and deaths, 131

Mauatua, Mrs Christian, bio,
other names 118, not mentioned
during *Bounty* stay 34, goes to
Tubuai 86, encouraged Fletcher
to leave Tahiti? 100, significance
overlooked of birth Thursday
October, first Pitcairn baby 122,
birth of second son Charles
shows further revolution in
women's thinking 124, protects
FC's reputation 126, Massacre
Day and birth of daughter Mary
131-4, no records of how Fletcher
treated her 139, possibility of
women responsible for massacres
139, importance of whereabouts
on Massacre Day 189-91, gives
Folger K2 chronometer, azimuth
compass and FC's Chinese
bowl 170, present when Captain
Elliott to make Pitcairn Crown
Colony, confirming women's
voting rights 165, descriptions of
in old age 183, dies of influenza

166, burial site now uncovered
166 , possible child left on Tahiti
184, 185
Maude, H.E., 1st to discover
Bounty's route to Pitcairn
Island, *In Search of a Home* 101
Middlesex, East Indiaman, FC's
brother Charles aboard 22,
reveals participation in mutiny
aboard 23
Mills, John 9, Mutiny Day 50,
93, 123 Massacre Day 131, 188,
189, 194
Millward, John 38, Mutiny Day
50, tried and hanged 147
Milntown, Christian seat IOM,
bought 11, family records
discovered 168
*Minutes of the Proceedings of
the Court-Martial, Barney*,
published 1793 154
Mitchell Library (Sydney) 152,
155, 185, 198
Mitford, Mary Russell 175, 187
Montrose, HMS 17
Moorland Close (FC's birthplace)
18, description 20, lost through
debt 46
Morrison, James, describes
events in Adventure Bay 30,
observation about uniforms 80,
on Tubuai 87–97, acquitted of
mutiny, pardoned 146, effect
of his *Memorandum* 109,
Memorandum published 1935 185

MRS CHRISTIAN *BOUNTY
MUTINEER*, fact-based novel
by GC
Muspratt, William on Tahiti 38,
supervises uniforms 81, escapes
Pandora's box 143, convicted
but discharged 147
Mutineers Trials, 145
*The Mutineer: a Romance of
Pitcairn Island* 185
Mutiny on HMAV *Bounty* 50
onwards
*Mutiny and Romance in the South
Seas, A Companion to the
Bounty Adventure* 66, 69, 199

Nancy, see Toofaiti
Nantucket Whaling Museum,
displays FC's Chinese bowl 170
Narcissus, HMS 142
Narrative of a Whaling Voyage,
describes FC's grave 183
National Archives, UK, source of
values in today's money 12
National Geographic Society 198
Navy, see Royal Navy
Nelson, David botanist 34, 74
Netherhall, home of FC's
paternal grandmother, Bridget
Senhouse, 22
Niau, youngest Tahitian on
Pitcairn 117
Nicholson, Robert (The
Pitcairners) 198, invents
marriage of FC

Nomuka Island, Bligh's conflicting orders to FC 42

Norfolk, Duke and Duchess/ Norfolk House 90

Norfolk Island 120, 129, 166, 182, 187

Norman, Charles 50, 54, acquitted 147

Norton, John 71

Oha 262

Oliver, Douglas (*Ancient Tahitian Society*) 195

Open-boat voyage, Bligh and others 71-5

Otaheite, see Tahiti

Pandora, HMS, arrives Tahiti, arrests all *Bounty's* men 141 infamous box built 142, wrecked 143

Pandora's Box disgrace of, 142

Papeete 164

Peckover, William 33, 49, 73, 159

Penis acrobats, Tahiti, 36

Pipon, Captain 171, 175

Pirates/piracy claim dismissed 79, 146, 174

Pitcairn Island first permanent British settlement in South Pacific vii, history is about women vii, route to discovered 1958 101, FC chooses 104, sights 105, Forefathers and Foremothers 117-9, early days 120, importance of no pregnant women realised 122, epiphany of Charles' birth 124, Massacre Day 125-40, discovered 125, land ownership 127, differences for women 128, alcohol 129, history by men about men 137, true role of foremothers 138, Establishment pawn 163, moved to Tahiti 163, influenza deaths and return 164, Crown Colony with votes for women and education for girls 165, population moved to Norfolk Island 166, some return: see MRS CHRISTIAN – *BOUNTY* MUTINEER

Pitcairn, mistakes in play about 94

Pitcairn Island Council 357

The Pitcairners Robert Nicholson 118

Polynesians, known as Ma'ohi at the time

Providence, HMS, 2nd breadfruit expedition 108

Prudence see Vahineatua

Puarai 118

Purcell, William, disagreements Adventure Bay disruptive 29, FC weeps before 46, 56, confrontations FC/Bligh 57, open-boat voyage temper 72, arrested 74, 159

Quintal, Matthew Mutiny Day
50 agrees to sail with FC 92,
blamed for *Bounty* fire 121, 131,
Massacre Day and after 131-7,
murdered 137

Ra'atira, middle class Tahitians,
Ranger, HMS Bligh aboard 63
Rarotonga *Bounty* is 1st European
encounter, FC introduces
oranges 102
Resolution, HMS Bligh sails with
Cook 18
Resource 74
Rodriguez, Paul J, psychologist
on FC's mental state on mutiny
day 66-8, 199
Romilly, Samuel 149, 157, 158
Royal Geographical Society 188
Rumbold, Sir Thomas 35

St Bees School (Fletcher not a
pupil) 43
St Mungo's church, Brigham,
FC's father buried there 24
Sarah, see Teatuahitea
Samuel, John, Mutiny Day 50, 75
Senhouse, Bridget, see Christian
Seringapatam 183
Shillibeer, Lieutenant 176
Simonstown, 28
*Short Reply to Capt. William
Bligh's Answer* published 161,
162, 196

Smith, Alexander, see Adams
Smith, John 45, 48, 55 tells
different story of mutiny 149, 159
Spikerman, Captain 73, 74
Staines, Captain Sir Thomas
171, 175
State Library of NSW 29, see
Mitchell
Stewart, George replaces FC
26, tries to dissuade FC 48,
49, Mutiny Day 50, 78, 80,
on Tubuai 82, 91, prisoner on
Pandora 142, drowned 144,
journal abstracts 196
Studia *Bounty*ana 56, 197
Sully 118
Sultan 126, 171
Susannah, see Teraura

Tagus HMS 171, 174, 175
Tahiti: Social classes, girls' and
boys' upbringing, food and
motherhood restrictions and ill
treatment of women including
forced infanticide, girls and
boys both physically deformed
99/100, European-style games
played, cross-gender *mahu*,
penis acrobats, tattooing, class
system and *arioi* society 36, 37
Taio, a Tahitian blood-brother
Talaloo see Tararo
Tapa, cloth made from treated
and felted bark 37, 106,

original patterns demonstrate foremothers' break with tradition 128, collection at British Museum unseen 129, 170

Tararo 117

Tattoos/tattooing *ta'tau* 36, 37

Taubman, Captain/ Major 15, 65

Taubman, Dorothy (née Christian, FC's 1st cousin) 15

Teatuahitea 118

Teehuteatuaonoa (Jenny) 118

Teimua 117

Teina 33, 86

Teio, 118, arrived Pitcairn with baby Sully, who married Charles FC's son

Teraura, 118, youngest Ma'ohi woman on Pitcairn, married Thursday October, present when voting for women became law

Te Tupuna Vahine, Ma'ohi foremothers of Pitcairn Island 118, 128

Tevarua 118

Thompson, Matthew 87, 95

Tinafanea 118

Titahiti, brother of chief Taaroa of Tubuai, 117

Titreano, Tahitian pronunciation of Christian,

Toaroah 37, 38

Tobin, Lieutenant 109

Tofua 44, 71, 104

Tongatabu 103

Toofaiti (Nancy) 118

Topaz, American sealer, finds Pitcairn 125, 169, 177

Tubuai: first arrival 82, return from Tahiti 86, site for Fort George 88, conditions there 87, events leading to abandonment 90-8

Tu 33

Tuscan 183

Unerigg, see Ewanrigg

Vahineatua 118

Valentine, James, death 31

van Este, Governor 74

Venus, Point 33, 36

Vlydte 75

Voting rights for women, Pitcairn 165

A Voyage to the South Seas, Bligh 69

Wahlroos, Dr Sven, first explores FC insanity theory 66, diagnosis of Bligh 69

The Wake of the Bounty 158, 179, 187

Wallis, Captain Samuel 85

West India Planters and Merchants 1

West Indies 16, 20, 67, 73, no pirates in 18th century 79

Wilberforce, William friend of Edward Christian 24, 158

Wilkinson, C.S. 158, 179, 187
Williams, John 79, 94, 106, 129,
    Massacre Day 131
William, Thomas 23
Wordsworths, Edward Christian
    recovers debt 76, 150, 158
Wordsworth, Dorothy 181, 199
Wordsworth, William 158,
    173, 187
Workington Hall 13, 76

The Yesterdays Behind the Doors,
    history of branch of Christian
    family 195
Yonge, correspondence with
    Bligh 199
Young, Edward 13, signs on
    and 'bad' appearance 88,101,
    Mutiny Day 50, joins FC 94,
    101, Massacre Day 131-4, 135-7,
    dies 137, 139, 190

Previous *BOUNTY* Books

Fragile Paradise – *The Discovery of Fletcher Christian,* BOUNTY *Mutineer*

Hamish Hamilton, London: 1982

Atlantic, Little Brown, Boston: 1982

Book Club Associates, London: 1983

Doubleday, Sydney (revised): 1999

Long Riders Guild Press: 2005

Fletcher Christian *Bounty* Mutineer

Hendon Books, London: 2019 - colour, b&w and e-book

Mrs Christian *Bounty* Mutineer

Long Riders Guild Press: 2011

Hendon Books, London: 2019